THE LIBRARY OF HOLOCAUST TESTIMONIES

The Single Light

With best wishes

Ernest Levy

The Library of Holocaust Testimonies

The Single Light

From Boyhood to Manhood and from Nazism and Communism to Freedom

Bratislava–Budapest–Auschwitz–Belsen–Glasgow

ERNEST LEVY

Compiled and adapted by David Spear

VALLENTINE MITCHELL
LONDON • PORTLAND, OR

First published in 2007 in Great Britain by
VALLENTINE MITCHELL
Suite 314, Premier House
112-114 Station Road
Edgware, Middlesex HA8 7BJ

and in the United States of America by
VALLENTINE MITCHELL
c/o ISBS, 5824 NE 58th
Avenue, Suite 300
Portland, Oregon 97213-3786

Website: www.vmbooks.com

British Library Cataloguing in Publication Data

A catalogue record for this book has been applied for

ISBN 978-0-85303-747-7 (cloth)
ISBN 978-0-85303-748-4 (paper)
ISSN 1363-3759

Library of Congress Cataloging-in-Publication Data

A catalog record for this book has been applied for

Printed and bound in Great Britain by
MPG Books Ltd, Bodmin, Cornwall

Contents

List of Plates

The Library of Holocaust Testimonies

Ten years have passed since Frank Cass launched his Library of Holocaust Testimonies. It was greatly to his credit that this was done, and even more remarkable that it has continued and flourished. The memoirs of each survivor throw new light and cast new perspectives on the fate of the Jews of Europe during the Holocaust. No voice is too small or humble to be heard, no story so familiar that it fails to tell the reader something new, something hitherto unnoticed, something previously unknown.

Each new memoir adds to our knowledge not only of the Holocaust, but also of many aspects of the human condition that are universal and timeless: the power of evil and the courage of the oppressed; the cruelty of the bystanders and the heroism of those who sought to help, despite the risks; the part played by family and community; the question of who knew what and when; the responsibility of the wider world for the destructive behaviour of tyrants and their henchmen.

Fifty memoirs are already in print in the Library of Holocaust Testimonies, and several more are being published each year. In this way anyone interested in the Holocaust will be able to draw upon a rich seam of eyewitness accounts. They can also use another Vallentine Mitchell publication, the multi-volume *Holocaust Memoir Digest*, edited by Esther Goldberg, to explore the contents of survivor memoirs in a way that makes them particularly accessible to teachers and students alike.

Sir Martin Gilbert
London, April 2005

*I dedicate this book to my
four wonderful grandchildren, who give my life
constant and abiding pleasure*

This publication was made possible through sponsorship and donations from many sources, some of the main sponsors being Glasgow Jewish Community Trust, Morris and Joseph Bloch Trust, The Giffnock Synagogue and Mr Nasim Khan.

I would like to thank them and all the other contributors for their kindness and generosity.

After publication costs, the author's proceeds from the sale of the book will go to Jewish Care Scotland and the Holocaust Educational Trust.

Foreword

Have you met someone in your life, so inspiring, that you have felt honoured just to meet them? Ernest Levy is such a person.

I first met Ernest more than fifteen years ago and we have become very good friends. Indeed I was privileged when he asked me to write the foreword to this, his second book.

The Single Light is the remarkable story of this inspirational man's horrific journey through the darkest period in human history. It is the story of a young Jewish boy in Bratislava growing up in a loving family, enjoying the music that inspired him and with the strong faith which helped guide him. We read about the teenager playing football in the street with friends using a ball made of papier-mâché held together by string, and of a family hounded out by rising anti-Semitism and being welcomed in Budapest by a frenzied fascist mob.

Within a year Ernest was forced to travel in one of the infamous airless and cramped cattle trucks to Auschwitz. Tragically this was to prove a one-way journey for almost a million people who were murdered there. But for Ernest Auschwitz was only one of seven concentration camps he survived.

The Single Light entertains, inspires and at times makes you want to scream at the top of your voice in anger. It is an intensely personal story and at times it is unsettlingly graphic. Ernest shares his emotions, reflects on a faith jolted which he later rediscovered and also recalls how he was saved from a pit of exhausted bodies in Belsen concentration camp upon its liberation. He also talks of an amazing chance meeting in Belsen with a young lady whom sixteen years later, in Glasgow, was to become his wife, Mrs Kathy Levy. Kathy is a friend to so many and like other survivors has chosen to reflect privately about her own experiences of the Holocaust.

In the midst of the anti-Semitic madness of the many, Ernest also reminds us of the courage of the few who stood against the system. We learn about Max the German farmer, Anton the factory manager and Helmut the Wehrmacht soldier, each of whose individual acts of courage are rightly recorded. It is sad that their families may never have known about their kindness. But perhaps it is these individual acts of real courage that even to this day help Ernest always to see the best in people.

I have walked along the snow-covered train track in Auschwitz's eerie darkness. I thought of Ernest and the many thousands, whose names are unknown, who perished. I thought of the grotesque suffering, the sheer destruction of human life and of the children whom had they survived would today be grandparents, but on their arrival were separated from their own parents and sent to the gas chambers. But in this the bleakest place on our planet something still lives on. It is the innocence of those who perished and the unbroken spirit of the survivors. I know that for Ernest part of him still lives on in Auschwitz.

For more than forty years Glasgow has been Ernest's journey's end. He is loved and revered by generations who have listened and been inspired. In a world of all too frequent darkness the Reverend Ernest Levy OBE is a Single Light.

**Jim Murphy MP
November 2006**

Acknowledgements

When setting out on this writing adventure, I felt that the road would be an easy one; after all I had done it once before. The reality was to prove the exact opposite. Advancing years made the recalling of my early life more difficult, not because the memories weren't there, but because they had become so intertwined with each other.

Writing them down in a logical order was a long hard struggle and it was only when I was introduced to David Spear that the book took form. With his help and his flair for words we began to assemble my notes and writings in a proper sequence and found a style and language that suited us both.

David constantly questioned details and made great efforts to validate facts, ensuring that what I remembered to be true almost always was. This gave me a lot of comfort, as trying to recall details from sixty years and more ago in my past could all too easily have resulted in inaccuracies. To him I owe my heartfelt gratitude for all the work and effort he put into making my stories come to life on the written page.

It was at this point that my stepdaughter Judy, who had introduced me to David in the first place, took an active role in ensuring that my resolve to achieve publication did not falter. She kept pushing me to use all my personal contacts, when publishers were reluctant to take on our manuscript.

Eventually, with the help of my dear friends Jim Murphy MP and Liz McGettigan of East Renfrewshire Council, my dream of publishing this second book was realised. They and their colleagues came together helping with raising funds, finding a publisher, creating a website and much, much more.

Finally, I would like to put on record my sincere thanks to all my friends, family and supporters who contributed, each in their own way, to the fulfilment of this project.

Glossary

Aliyah – going to Israel as a new immigrant, with a view to settling and becoming a citizen

Anschluss – the annexation of Austria by Germany in 1938 (in German it means to connect)

Barmitzvah – the coming of age of a young Jewish boy, turning from boy to man at the age of thirteen

Chassid – a righteous Jew

Haupstadt der Bewogung – the Capital of the National Socialist Movement (Fascists)

Kike – a derogatory term for a Jew

Konditorei – a bakery (also Conditorei)

Kosher – food cooked and approved in accordance with Jewish dietary laws

Lagerführer – the camp commandant

Macher – a fixer, a negotiator

Mazeltov – congratulations, good luck

Mensch – a real human being, kind, considerate and thoughtful

Meshugener – a nutcase, a bit crazy

Mizrachi Shul – a synagogue that would be attended by religious Zionists

Sabbat Chaggim – the Sabbath, when the Sabbath coincides with a Jewish Festival

Shoah – another word meaning the Holocaust, taken from the Hebrew

Shul – a synagogue, a place for worship and a house of Jewish learning

Sochet Cantor – a Sochet is a ritual slaughterer, a Cantor the person who leads the congregation in prayer, the one in charge of the vocal and musical part of the service; sometimes these

two activities are carried out by the same person, particu-
larly in small rural communities
Tish B'Av – the seventh day of the Jewish month of Av
Yeshiva – a rabbinical school or college

PART I
THE END OF FREEDOM

1 Childhood in the Shadows

BRATISLAVA, 1936

She is about 7 years old, blonde hair in plaits and pretty in a pale blue dress, the very image of the Nazi ideal German child. In our way on a canal towpath, challenging us. I'm 11. My brother Alex – nickname 'Munky' to the family and the kids around – the serious one, the scholar, a bit older than me, is by my side. He and I are muddy from a game of football and close to home. We'd been through this bit of theatre before. The 'bait' challenges, you react, then out of the bushes comes a gang of older boys to beat you senseless. We looked around. There were some behind, some atop a wall, legs dangling, looking, silent.

Her challenges were a parroting of the street insults we had become used to hearing from older people in the city. Deeply insulting and full of spite, to say those things in the way of attack distorted the face. The little girl's prettiness had vanished into a variety of contortions as she hurled the kind of abuse that ran its words together, leaving us in no doubt who we were what we were by the way why were we here and not there in the ghetto we made the place untidy and our music stank!

The script wasn't hers, but she delivered it with feeling. We felt. Our situation on the towpath was an impasse. We knew from previous challenges that hers was a ritual opener to a series of actions we were meant to prompt by retaliation, giving the gang the pretext for doing what they had planned to do all along. The essence of the pogrom in the hands of the young. The pity of it was that these were neighbourhood children. We knew this girl and some of the boys by name.

Back in 1933, a change had come over the people of Bratislava. The Germans of the city saw a bright light on the horizon of their future in the assumption of Adolf Hitler as Chancellor in Germany. They had not been at ease with the new state of Czechoslovakia, and had never stopped hankering for the grandeur of the Austro-Hungarian period. From 1933, the dull-witted populism of the Nazi self-perception squashed flat any objections to its desire to advance itself, choking protest, moral choice and conscience, like a mad weed unchecked in a flower garden. By 1936, we had ceased to be neighbours, friends and working colleagues, becoming figures of hate and derision, dangerous to know, let alone like. Pariahs and targets; Jews.

The stand-off between these children and ourselves looked to have one bloody resolution. We had nowhere to turn, short of jumping into the canal or scaling the ivy-covered wall and then down into an unpromising wood yard. A shout. Mother was approaching fast from behind the girl. Not seeing the adult, the girl had continued her barrage of taunts, her face red with excitement at the prospect of imminent violence. A second later, she was airborne, hoisted aloft by Therezia Lowy, mother to eight including Munky and me, nor was she let down until her bottom was given its due at the hand of my parent. The tanning was as profound to me as it had been surprising. Mother had never lifted a finger to either of us. As the other children rapidly dispersed, deserting their live bait, they cat-called: 'Not long now Kikes. Hitler's on his way.'

'He's going to boil you in oil.'

'Munky can't play football to save his life.'

They were gone. My mother released the tearful girl, who, when out of reach, started running. Over her shoulder: 'You'll be sorry you old witch. You'll burn.'

Therezia Lowy was well able to look after her family. In our world, her pedigree was enviable, a blending of rabbinical families hailing from Austria and Holland. As with many Bratislavan Jews, her links with Austria were as close as Bratislava is to Vienna. Austrians of all sorts had found their way

4

to what had become a cosmopolitan city; Hungarians too, and many, many others. Native Czechs often found themselves second-classed on their home ground, pushed into low-pay jobs, living outside the well-heeled neighbourhoods, sometimes excluded, but always one-up on the ghetto Jews. Always that. In such a climate, Mother had so far seen us grow strong.

I have no recollection of ghetto life. My birth in 1925 coincided with a change in the family's fortunes and I woke to this existence in a large shared family house in a polite quarter of Bratislava where Jews lived, but were not packed tight into an exclusive bundle. With Christian neighbours, we were just a little less ordinary, as our improved social exposure took in fresh fields of acquaintance and friendship, not influenced by our beliefs so much as by our location. Bratislava had a cosmopolitan air and we were able to breathe it deeply in my early years. My older siblings had experienced old and new conditions, were multi-lingual and open to change. Max, Karl, Fritz and Hedwig had all been born around the time of the First World War; Else, Lillie, Alex and latterly me, in the 1920s. Very much the afterthought, there were worries about the pregnancy, but I was fine and Mother was fine, for a woman giving birth in her forties. The local rabbi was right in his forecast, I was a boy. I was the indulged, funny, cheeky, inquisitive one. With adults for siblings covering such a wide age range, the children were group-divided by time. My days of growing cemented a closeness with Alex, nicknamed 'Munky'. We shared a room, the bed and household chores. Munky was the straight man to my clown. Lillie and Else, being of our decade, shared our growing, a little unit within the family team.

Schanzstrasse was in the Czech quarter. Our move there from the ghetto was of immense significance to Leopold Lowy, our father, whose franchisers had given him a leg-up. He was their golden boy in sales of woollen goods. He felt he had arrived. A large detached house – admittedly shared with other families – was the crowning glory. He was a country boy, born the eldest of five in the tiny village of Kapuvar, and when his father, Eliezer, became cantor to its synagogue, the family moved to the town of Papa in north-west Hungary. Eliezer was very proud of his golden boy.

A stone's throw from open countryside, the inhabitants of Schanzstrasse were neighbourhood proud. There was even a by-law that required you to keep the street outside your house clean and clear. If you didn't wash your bit of the pavement, you could be fined fifty krona. Munky and I loved the job. A watering can and a brush? Two small boys could get a lot of fun from such a task.

I grew up not knowing or caring about the rigours of an outside toilet, but to my older brothers, and particularly my sisters, it was just heavenly to have the toilet indoors. For my mother, the most enjoyable change was the kitchen, unshared and sizeable, a place to create. Father's younger brother, Charles, had moved away from Papa with his family and lived up the street, adding to our happiness with the place. We had good neighbours, neighbours who seemed not to find us forbiddingly exotic, with whom sharing life and laughter came easily. I liked our life.

The building housed two more families: the Friedmans, and a Christian Hungarian family, the Fehrers. Later these families moved on and Father acquired the whole building. We all got on, and life was trouble-free except for the time when the janitor, Mr Hoffman, a man obsessed with things mechanical, tried in the basement to unpick a grenade he had found, created smoke, panic and lost an eye. His daughter, Eva, was the first girl I ever kissed. The first in a line. I was a terrible flirt, much to the disapproval of Munky who was very po-faced about my continual falling in and out of love with the neighbour girls. For him, it was going to be only the once.

'Probably sorted by a matchmaker,' I would tease.

He would then give chase and we would end up wrestling on the back lawn, giggling and laughing, finally laying back to enjoy sunshine and the sweet scents of the flowers that surrounded the summer grass. So I care to remember it.

The local kids came and went. One, a young German lad,

Helmut Palme, was forever under Mother's feet in the kitchen. They even came on outings. Our little gang, Munky, Lillie, Else and I, used, with permission, to take off into the country, sometimes for day trips with father's friend Uncle Ore, sometimes overnight by ourselves at youth hostels when Kalman Hilvert, an older boy, joined us and kept us in order.

Father was a generous host. His liberation from the ghetto led to an outpouring of generosity which put a strain on household finances, impairing my mother's ability to cope with the family's daily demands. The open-house nature of the lifestyle Father had adopted was fun, but hard work and expensive, as he was also generous with the odd handout. All this led to debt and non-payment of taxes.

As the pre-war years matured, things at home became precarious. My older brothers, Max and Karl, spent a lot of their time away from home. Fritz, by general consent, had become a parental surrogate, taking some of the weight from Mother. Father, when not working or entertaining, was engrossed in cabbalistic study, his religious orthodoxy being the single most important feature of his day-to day existence. He had, for a while, played host – as did others in the Jewish community – to penniless religious students, known as *Bachurs*. Mother went along with his orthodoxy in spite of her more liberal background. She had, in her own words, not wanted to marry a 'yeshiva boy', but she did. The blending of their backgrounds gave rise to interesting collisions of cultures. We developed a love of nature from Mother's pantheistic leanings, her God to be found out there in the hills, yet we respected and followed, in varying degrees of intensity, Father's orthodoxy; indeed, his ambition was that his sons be religious philosophers, one and all. It left us ill-prepared for the changes after 1933.

Karl, a brilliant Talmudic scholar, a *dux* at the Galanta Yeshiva, finally left home in 1936 to become a cantor. Though my initial religious schooling had been strict, maybe Karl's establishment as cantor took the pressure off me, so I went to the local Yeshiva K'Tana, a bit less glamorous. Not only did our upbringing leave us unprepared for the years to come, the same years left Father high and dry. His earnings decreased, but the lifestyle remained the same. The agency he ran selling woollen goods was in decline as social tensions increased. With Karl away, Father installed Max and Fritz in the agency, and with reduced capital, he had to let go a long-time employee, Mr Weiss, who happened to be the accountant. Max and Fritz were maturing slowly. Their hearts were not in the business, and neither could manage or account. Consequently, coinciding with growing social unrest, the business went into free fall as the two young men chased girls or argued over points of religion with their feet up on the office desks.

There was the day when Mother stuffed all her jewellery in Munky's and my pockets and told us to go take a walk for a few hours, not to return until after lunch. Confused, we did. As we passed down the hall to the front door, we glanced into the dining room. Father was standing in there with a very serious-looking man. On the table were sheets of paper laid out. They were studying them in close detail. Neither man saw us go, and Mother shut the door, very quietly, behind us. We decided to head for the country lanes up the road. We felt incongruous in our overcoats on such a warm day, but nothing would have removed them from our backs, carrying, as we were, the family wealth reserve. With what turned out to be the tax inspector gone, we finally returned to a late lunch and a kiss from Mother. Later that day, I heard her arguing quietly with Father over the events of the morning, and all he kept saying, defensively was, 'Don't worry Therezia, God will provide.'

He believed this, just as he believed implicitly in the coming of the Messiah. In fact, the worse things became in the world, the more likely it would be that the Messiah would put in an appearance. Hitler, therefore, and the growth of organized fascism on the streets of Bratislava, could be seen by him and his co-religionists as just another passing phase in the European experience of Jews, or, delight of delights, the coming of the Messiah. Either way, stick around, grit your teeth and ride out the storm.

Uncle Charles was also a businessman. A believer, but not strictly orthodox, he did not require his wife to wear wig or scarf. Being a political animal, he was aware of social and governmental change, how the Hitler influence had cast a very long shadow over our region, infiltrating every corner of daily life. He had become friendly with those who attended the Mizrachi, a religious Zionist organisation, and was rapidly becoming convinced that wisdom lay in uprooting from Europe, emigrating to Palestine and contributing to the formation of a new Jewish state. In the orthodoxy to which my father adhered, this was a heresy, one which, in an angry exchange, he had told Charles never to mention again under his roof. To emigrate to the Holy Land ahead of the Messiah's coming meant bypassing God's promise to lead the Jews there. So they waited. I thought that my mother sympathized with Charles, though in her loyalty to her husband, she held her tongue for the moment.

Being intensely musical, all of us, the house echoed to the rafters with the home-made variety. Else had a great mezzo voice which, due to Father's orthodoxy, could only be heard in the house. The girls were frustrated by him in other ways. Hedwig was already engaged to an eye specialist from the community, with tacit approval from our parents. Lillie and Else, however, were not following their big sister's example. Of the new breed, they were creatures of fashion, loved light music and, along with Munky and me, adored film, being addicted to Hollywood. Else at 16 was a stunner who wore the kind of clothes that accentuated her beauty, and according to Leopold, increased his heartache. A rabbi, too old to be considered, asked for her hand, but got short shrift from a shocked family. Lillie just broke every rule, was into Bratislava nightlife, taking up with the 'wrong' men, returning home in the early hours. Her attitude was generally rebellious, and nose-to-nose confrontations with father were commonplace.

But music soothed our souls. The day we bought the gramophone, a little revolution took place. Records, anything from Schubert *Lieder* to Benny Goodman, it was all embraced, played loudly to the rest of the neighbourhood through open

9

windows, May to October, and just to ourselves the rest of the year. Great.

One morning in 1937, our house was awakened to sounds of relentless hammering. Mother and Hedwig were trying to light the kitchen stove. Max came in with an armful of wood.

'What a racket. What's going on?'

Father sat at the table reading a book. He tried to ignore the noise, but eventually gave up and, opening the window, looked out.

'It's coming from Charles' house. Ernest, go and see what he's up to. Go!'

At the front door, a couple of men were nailing up crates. Cousin Jacob jumped across from the stairs into the yard.

'Yankel. What's happening?'

'We're off to Palestine, Ernesti. Isn't it great?'

'You're joking.'

'Nope,' he practically sang it, 'we're on our way.'

Uncle Charles' tall frame filled his doorway.

'Morning. Beautiful day for a journey. Leopold wouldn't believe me when I told him.

Tell him again Ernest … and when you can, come visit.'

I flashed my uncle a smile and returned to the house with the news.

'What?'

My father's voice was loud with shock and temper. Made us all jump. He banged his book down, which made us jump a second time.

'I'll soon sort this out.'

Mother's face was a picture. In a quiet voice:

'I knew it … and you know what? I've a strong feeling that he's doing the right thing.'

Ignoring her comments, Leopold was out the door and thundering down the stairs, tearing across the street, ignoring the traffic. Mother met my glance. Shrugging, she said to the room, 'Come, let's eat. Your father's going to be some time.'

Needless to say, Charles did not heed my father's warnings, and set off for Palestine.

A year later, my thirteenth, Charles came back to Bratislava for a brief visit. He was tanned, happy, a man enjoying an improved life. We young ones were full of questions, but too shy to ask beyond the information he volunteered. We know that he and Father fell out again. Years later, in a place called Batyam near Tel Aviv, Charles let on about their quarrel.

'Ernest, you know how he was, God rest him. He saw us pioneers as breakers of a sacred trust. When God wanted us in the Holy Land, he would lead us there. Until then, life could throw us whatever obscenity it chose, the faithful would wait, just as the Book says. Pardon me, but a human hand wrote the Book. Time was when sacred truths were not written, but handed on verbally. Was I to stake the lives of my kids, let alone your aunt's and mine, on the Hebrew equivalent of chinese whispers?'

I took the point, and at the time, it fuelled the flame of my agnosticism, lending credence to the socialism that was having a wrestling match with my orthodox bias, post-war.

Back to 1938. The argument hinged on whether Hitler was going to swallow Czechoslovakia, or whether the coming Munich conference with the French and the British would prevent the realization of the dictator's desire to unite all Germans.

'"*Ein Volk, ein Reich, ein Führer.*" He's said it, and, they'll need more land. He's got Austria. Sudetenland that's next. *Lebensraum.* That's the industrial north making space, you bet. He'll get the north, the rest of the country will collapse with the economy … Leo, can't you see that?'

'I can see Czechoslovakia resisting him. I can see the League compelling him to hold.'

'Oh, they're going to do that. The only people that might worry him, apart from Russia, are the Americans, and they're keeping out of the picture. This is Europe and he knows he can nail the place up. Look at the size of his army.'

Leopold drew on his pipe.

'Defence against Stalin.'

Charles stretched and looked at his older brother. Was he really that complacent?

'And the rest. Leo, the man has a kink in the brain about us. He wants all Jews double-dead. He is unhinged. You realize that?'

Leopold nodded. Charles went on.

'He'll make agreements wherever and whenever. Then, like any criminal, he'll renege. In the Torah, Leo. History is full of liars and cheats who gain crowns, tyrants who mass murder. It's happening now. This is a new Egypt, there is a need to move on, to escape.'

'Look, if he invades, we could cross the border.'

'And you think Hungary will be safe? Cut your losses Leo. Look, it's not as if your business is booming. Sell up. I know for Palestine to be acceptable to you, the least you need would be Moses himself telling you to go, but there's America, or Britain. Get out while the going's good. Once Germany controls government here, Jewry is a sitting duck. At least get the kids out.'

Leopold was angered by this. Knocked his pipe out, stood: 'Charles, you are my brother. I love you, but don't presume to tell me what to do with my family.'

'Leo, I'm not telling. I'm begging. The very stones are crying out.'

Leopold shook his head slowly. 'Revelation is for God, not rocks on the floor.'

'That's petty.'

Leopold looked at his watch. 'It's late. Charles, you are a guest under my roof, please do not involve any of the family with your thoughts while you are here.'

Charles left the comfort of the leather armchair in which he had been reclining and stood with Leopold in the centre of the room. His hand rested on his brother's shoulder for a moment of togetherness. They left the room. Only the smell of pipe smoke and good brandy remained.

Leopold's request was honoured by Charles. Later in the year, the international meeting in Munich saw the Sudetenland

12

made over to Germany, and the Czechs told no help would be forthcoming in any future conflict over the matter. A little earlier that year, Mussolini made a meal of Abyssinia.

Charles returned to Palestine while we felt the heat of Czechoslovakia's inner turmoil in every corner of our lives. As things developed around us, after Uncle Charles' visit, we boys became intrigued to know more about the Zionist cause. Munky had been stunned one morning, when his best friend, Helmut Palme, turned up at the front door, resplendent in the uniform of the Hitler Youth, and very formally announced to Alex and the rest of us within hearing distance, that he could no longer be his friend. Not a flicker of remorse or regret, just goodbye. It severed one of the last connections we as a family had with the neighbourhood. With the rise of the Nazi doctrine, relationships had become more and more tenuous. The Jewish community in Bratislava had largely kept to itself, but had forged links and friendships; assimilation didn't happen much. But it had all been relatively harmonious. Now, hostility shadowed our every waking moment beyond the security of hearth and home.

As boys, Munky and I had become accustomed to catcalls and the odd rock thrown in that last year. Since losing Helmut, Munky had become a bit withdrawn. One day, heading for *shul*, he suddenly turned to me.

'There's another family in our street off to Palestine. Siggy's family.'

'Siggy who?'

'Siggy-in-my-class Siggy. Blond boy. They're off next week.'

We walked on. I broke the silence.

'Must be nice to live in a country where there are just us, just Jews.'

Munky looked across the street where a group of youths were idling. Eyes met, but they were more into their cigarettes and a couple of girls chatting with them. The girls turned to look at us, turned back to a comment. The group laughed loudly. We walked on. Munky replied:

'Jews are not alone in Palestine. Arabs live there. Lots of them. They get on okay with the Jews who have been there since long before the Roman Empire. There have been a few fights with incoming Europeans.'

'How do you know this?'

'Cousin Yankel told me. He used to go to the Mizrachi *shul*. Interesting that it's in the same building, that they use the same front door ...'

I smiled at the idea.

'And we could so easily mistake *shul* for *shul*, and nobody would be much the wiser.'

Munky looked at me with his long, serious, two-years-older look.

'We tell no one. Imagine what would happen if Father found out.'

'Better a beating from him for wanting to know about an alternative homeland than hanging around waiting for a Bratislava mob to get the wink from Hitler.'

The Mizrachi *shul* was full when we arrived, but we were found space and made to feel very welcome. The young were much in evidence, their involvement more than just being there. One, Emil Zimet, who spoke with passion about the cause, argued that attempts to assimilate or indeed segregate had not made our situation any better in European history; that removal to Palestine where a homeland could be forged from potentially fertile ground was the only desirable solution.

We went a few times after that first enlightening session, but Father got in the way of a future there when he learned from a tattle-tale what we were doing in our *shul* time. Munky was enthusiastic about going away on a learning weekend with a group from the *shul*, but before he could broach the subject with him, Father was summoned to be told by our teacher what had been going on. The teacher had been upset, Father more so:

'Palestine is for God to give. Become a Zionist and you break the faith.'

Leopold was angry and concerned about his family and their increasingly disparate leanings, and his business

14

bothered him. It was as though fate was dealing him a series of bad hands. The political and social upheaval of the late 1930s was affecting his trade, yet he had to deny that the evidence at home and abroad was of any significance when set against biblical revelation. People like Uncle Fritz had fled Austria, and in spite of his accounts and the accounts of others, Father had to shut his ears. His social progress, his escape from the ghetto, his business, his pride in his beautiful wife and children, and most of all, his impregnable faith, should be enough, were enough in the best of all possible worlds. Nazism had to be, simply had to be, a passing storm. You had to batten down the hatches, but it would pass. Losing what he had by running seemed like defeat and the end of a cherished realization.

Though 1938 was the year of my bar mitzvah, the mood in the family and the Jewish community at large was not conducive to celebrations. For me, then, no plans, no family party, just a ceremonial progression into 13-year-old adulthood. Just football, our beautiful game, was our fun and our solace. Sport brought disparate groups together for hard competition on the field of play. There were often quite noticeable differences in the affluence, if not the ability of all the teams. Our team, for example, was a rough-and-ready agglomeration of available Jewish lads who had – by and large – to play in their street clothes and shoes. Our practice balls were made of papier mâché plus string; no bounce and of variable weight. When we met up with better-equipped teams, encounters with studs proved painful. However, 'love conquers all'. Most districts and streets had their own teams and we were no exception. So despite being Jewish, we were part of the league, where we were also known to win a few. Which is why a team we had played before accepted a game with us that fateful year, in spite of their being German, well-funded, strong; and our being us. We were neighbours. Schanzstrasse was a mix, but a couple of streets on, and the neighbourhood became entirely ethnic German. As children we had strict instructions to stay away. We strayed, they strayed, there were some bruises. Now, nobody strayed. However, Kalman Hilvert and Egon Reisman, our fixers, had managed to negotiate, beyond hostility and within the fixture list, a game with our neighbourhood rivals that autumn. A game with a 'for-real' ball, and goalposts. A treat. The only drawback was that the game was due to be played in the German quarter. Weeks before, they had hovered on the edge of our area shouting, taunting our practice games and our lack of gear. Brother Max warned us:

'You realize you are crazy, don't you. Don't let Fritz find out you're going ahead with the game. He'll lock you both in the attic and throw away the key.'

In spite of all the warnings – and Fritz – on the day we strode boldly into the German quarter to meet our fate on the field.

As a team we looked pathetically amateur, not having a strip to compare with the black-and-white kit of the German lads; only some of us had boots. Standing on the pitch as they came on, I turned to Munky:

'We're going to get hammered.'

Munky smiled grimly.

'Better give them a reason then, eh?'

Within thirty minutes of the first half, Munky had scored. Nearing half-time we had made it to 2–0, incurring the wrath of players and spectators alike. The calls from the touchline were anti-Semitic and physically hostile. The tackling by the Germans was foul and yet went unpunished. Offsides were not given. We knew the rest of the game would be impossible. If we left, it would be a league walkover, but we could see this was shaping up for public violence, and injuries were inevitable.

Kalman called us together and briefed us that at his signal, we take off. There were four exits we could use, plus a wall, scalable, that would land us back in the Czech quarter. The game continued, the tackling getting harder. Then Munky scored again just before the half-time whistle. The goal was reluctantly allowed by a scared ref, and we knew it was time to go when he blew the last blast. Kalman gave the signal as the touchline supporters, along with the opposition team, made their angry way towards our end of the pitch.

We ran. Munky and I made it to one of the exits, the rest of the team scattered with us. I was just ahead of him when I swung on to a tram at the corner of the Schondorferstrasse. I was on, but Munky missed as the tram accelerated. He came home later that evening covered in cuts and bruises. He had been caught and beaten. My parents said nothing. Fritz could not find it in himself to be angry. Munky volunteered that our taking part in the football game was a matter of honour, not to mention local pride.

Father gave us one of his stares. He puffed at his pipe, looked across to Mother and looked back to us:

'Ernest you were lucky. Alexander, you are getting too old to get caught up with petty rivalry, even in the name of football. Live down the taunts. They come from a source you can afford to ignore.'

We nodded and sat down to the evening meal. I noticed what I imagined to be a proud gleam in my mother's eyes, not to mention the slightest hint of a smile from my father.

A sunny Saturday. My brothers and I had returned from synagogue, leaving Father talking to one of his friends. Fritz was an ambler, so Munky and I were home first. Time wore on. Fritz was back, lunch was nearly ready, but no sign of Father. Mother sighed and fiddled with the table setting.

'Probably yattering with the yeshiva students again.'

A noise in the hall. We left the kitchen in time to see the front door slowly swing open and Father shuffle in. His Shabbat clothes were ripped and torn, across his forehead, a deep and bloody gash. His right arm dangled helplessly to his side. A small man, he looked even smaller, reduced in his shock. He had a stern, almost thoughtful look when he came through the door, but on seeing the look of horror on our faces, he simply burst into tears. I had never seen him break down, and the moment brought on my own tears, and the tears of the whole family.

At the synagogue he had talked on for a while and finally made his way homeward. There was an alley shortcut he had taken which led out on to the Schanzstrasse. About midway along the alley, he was confronted by a small group of youths, who after a period of insults and shouldering, went the whole hog when Father protested at their behaviour. The beating was followed by some well-aimed kicking. This left him on the floor badly bruised, with a broken shoulder blade, facial cuts and a stricken realization that fascism had touched his soul. Nothing material had been taken.

'I can hear the alarm bells ringing,' this to Mother as he choked back the tears.

'We must go. We must leave Czechoslovakia at once. There is no future here.'

Among the rest of us standing in the hallway, surrounding him, comforting him, the perturbation at his emotional response to the attack was palpable. Mother, however, remained unchanged. Her concern and fright were upper-most, but she and I exchanged glances in the middle of this hiatus, and I was certain she had her doubts over his sudden conversion. Sure enough, later, after hospital treatment, arm in a sling, he joined us at table for a very late Shabbat meal, refusing to discuss the attack or the remarkable turnaround he had made midday.

'We are not going to let these things spoil our Shabbat.'

Mother glanced my way and gave a little smile.

Songs were sung across the table, grace was beautifully said after the meal. The subject was shelved. We resumed our life of averted gazes and catcalling kids on the outside, and forced jollity around the house. For Father, God's provision and God's saving grace would outrun the Nazi threat which would return to its cave when it realized its own futility. A long view indeed.

The international agreement to annex the Sudetenland was signed in September 1938. On 4 November, we received word via the congregation at the synagogue that Hungary was busy annexing parts of the Slovakian highlands. The Hungarian dictator, Horthy, had made a deal with Hitler. We were in trouble as my father had not relinquished his

Hungarian citizenship. The annoyed Czechs would certainly be knocking on the door at some point soon, demanding explanation. The prospect was daunting. He didn't relish the embarrassment and the inevitable bureaucratic entanglement that could lead to deportation.

It had started to rain that night as we left the synagogue. It was that fine rain that penetrates. Heavy with the news about the Hungarian invasion, the walk home seemed longer than usual. The slight wind was northern cold, and our collars were up. Through the door, we relished the cosy warmth of the family home, and a deal of hand rubbing went on in front of the living-room fire. Therezia and her daughters had cooked us a wonderful meal, but we men were muted and not very hungry. Father was being uncommunicative, and it was left to Fritz to break the news which put the dampener on the whole family. No one sang that evening, silence entombed the house, food seemed to be forgotten, except by my stomach. I know my father felt embarrassment, as well as present fear, at his failure to apply for Czech citizenship. He sat staring at the tablecloth, probably mulling over how imminent might be the Czech reprisal on resident Hungarians. I tugged his sleeve. He roused himself.

'Alright, let's eat.'

The household came alive again as Father clapped his hands, and talk blossomed. We didn't hear the small fleet of buses pull up outside in the Schanzstrasse.

Father was standing, about to recite the kiddush, had placed the goblet of wine back on the table, when a loud knock broke into our happy–sad occasion.

We froze.

Mother straightened up and drew Lillie, her youngest girl, to her. Father stood where he was, dazed and confused.

A second, louder knock. Fritz volunteered: 'I'll get it.'

He opened the door, and without invitation, two men pushed their way into the house. The first, a small man in civilian clothing, stood in the hall removing his raincoat which he

19

shook, sending droplets of water in all directions. Behind him, a Slovakian policeman, reluctant to be there at all.

'Are you Leopold Lowy?' The question came in Czech with a strong German accent. The little man give Fritz a menacing stare. Father came into the hallway. He addressed the official in German: 'I am Leopold Lowy. What do you want here?'

The small man eyed him coldly. 'According to our records, you are a Hungarian national. Unless you have evidence to the contrary, you and your family must leave Czechoslovakia tonight. You have ten minutes to pack. Limit yourselves to essentials. We have transport waiting. Hurry.'

We offered no resistance. We had stepped across into a zone of unreality, familiar by group memory and tradition, a fatalism that at some time, somewhere, we would have to go through this experience of moving on, of being moved on. Our history. We were just plain scared. There was only now. We didn't know what to do with now. We looked from one to another. Mother stirred us into action. She helped the girls pack under the eyes of the Nazi and his big minder. The Nazi even supervised my sister Else when she had to use the toilet. My thoughts ran to Mother's jewellery, now our only realizable wealth. The Nazi would probably be on to any attempts to stow such valuables. On balance my bet was with Therezia having the foresight to cover this eventuality, since our crossing the path of the tax inspector. I couldn't ask. I packed some clothes. The Slovak policeman was embarrassed and apologetic, within the limits of his uniform.

'Make sure you pack some food, and wear something warm.'

He kept his voice low. The official bothered him, the situation bothered his policeman's mind. At one point he even offered to help us carry things out.

Mother made little bundles of bread and cheese before she took the younger ones, including me, out through the rain to one of the line of red buses waiting. The rain was falling hard, and the wind had picked up, gusting icy blasts at our faces and legs as we hurried on to the bus. On board were families we knew, as well as familiar faces from street or synagogue. They looked as terrified as we felt.

I looked across. The house lights were still on. There was still food on the table, there had been no time to clear, and now, no family there, no prayers, no music. The rain obscured the view from the bus, and the warmth from our bodies met the cold of the interior, fogging the windows. I wiped my window in time to see my brothers hurrying across the street to the bus. Where was Father?

Leopold Lowy, father, householder, businessman, stood alone outside his front door, parcel and case in hand, about to be hurried down the steps to the waiting buses opposite. One by one the house lights were being turned off. Police and workmen were crowding round him, ready to board the place up. He stood, reduced, ignored and desolate as his property was seized. The small Nazi had his raincoat back on, and coming through the door, held out his hand. Leopold responded by surrendering the house keys, after which the little bureaucrat gave him a light push. Like a sleepwalker, my father started his long journey away from his realized ambition. We watched his progress to the bus tearfully. Midway, he paused, staring hard as if waking for a moment and realizing something crucial. From my seat in the darkened bus, I couldn't work out what had caught his attention.

A few people were ahead of him as he joined the bus. Finally he appeared, edging his way up the aisle, tears and rain mingled on his face. He sat beside Mother, drawing out a handkerchief to wipe away the wet. In a low voice, trembling with emotion:

'You won't believe this, but Kraijchirovich is standing there in the doorway of his shop, watching all this with a smile on his face.'

Kraijchirovich, the German who had cut my hair since I needed a plank across the armrests of his barber's chair, who had watched us all grow, cutting our hair, commiserating with us about school, teachers, losses on the pitch, cheering our

21

little gains in life. He who inquired solicitously about the family each time one of us was in for a trim, knew our nicknames, laughed at our jokes, was smiling? Had he secretly hated us all along? Was he jealous of us? He had a family, a business; he earned from us. What then? Maybe the music and laughter coming through the open windows of summer. Whatever, our neighbour from the shop opposite was pleased to see us go.

From Max: 'He's losing five regulars from one family, and however many in these buses, and he's smiling? He's a *meshugener.*'

From Father: 'Hate makes you mad, even crazier if you have to hide it and appear the opposite.'

From Munky: 'Still, we've escaped his open razor.'

From Mother: 'His wife never used to speak. Strange eyes.'

My sisters joined in with recollections of Kraijchirovich and his family. Lillie left her seat to give Father a consoling kiss on the cheek, which brought on more tears from a man desperately holding on to the last shreds of his dignity.

A child started crying loudly, which killed conversation. The crying had a chain effect as other youngsters started wailing and complaining. Across the way, our house had been silenced, darkened, bound and gagged, kidnapped. A policeman entered the coach and shone a torch into the darkness, along the seats, into our scared faces. Satisfied it was full, he slid the door shut and okayed the driver. The engine was started and revved. A minute or so passed before the buses moved away slowly in convoy. I wiped the window again with my arm and watched our still-warm house and the Schanzstrasse slide into memory. I was full of a mix of excited fright and wonder, the child in me overwhelming the coming man.

2 The Shadows Lengthen

The bus moved through the night, the driving rain slashing against the windows. The lights of Bratislava soon dwindled, giving way to an outer darkness. Our silence was finally broken by Max, who, with Fritz, began to discuss with Father something Munky and I had heard at the Mizrachi *shul*: that local bureaucratic planning was not only abreast of Hitler's actions, but to an extent was slightly ahead, anticipating the Führer's next step. Officially, Czechoslovakia was against annexation in the north, but the Germans within the bureaucracy seemed to be something of an advanced guard, placing down the welcome mat for the mad Chancellor. There seemed to be agreement about this among those close to us in the bus. Hungarian invasion, and the same day, all Hungarian Jews out the door. That took planning, documents drawn up and transport arranged, well before the fateful day. No pause for all of us to consider taking action. The buses had been ready, all scheduled to a given signal. And we should have known.

The rain had turned to sleet and hail, which cracked against the coach windows. The vehicle began to rock as we left the tarmac surfaces for rougher terrain. We were in deep country. After a punishing period of suspension bounce, the line of buses came to a stop in what seemed to be impenetrable blackness. The policeman slid the door open and ordered us off. One by one along the lane, we stepped out into the wind and sleet, off the steps of the buses and down on to a rutted track, a mess of mud and puddles. Shoes and boots sank into the cold wetness, soaking the feet instantly. In the dark, our family clung together as a crowd of around 200 stood in profound shock, while the police with their hand torches waved us up the lane as if they were gruff usherettes. All done, they boarded one of the red Bratislava buses which then accelerated past us, the small convoy providing temporary light to our darkness that very quickly enveloped us in its chill embrace.

To one side of where we stood there seemed to be woodland where there would be a little shelter; to the other, fields which were beginning to whiten in the sleet.

'Where are we?' Max shielded his eyes against the weather and looked around.

'Got to be the border area, but which way?'

The voice of a stranger next to us in the dark:

'The policeman pointed that way.'

Max, in the dark: 'Which way?'

The stranger: 'Across the fields. Hungarians go back to Hungary,' he said.

'Good God, where? How?'

We slowly became aware of all the other moving shapes. Some lit pipes or cigarettes. One or two had oil lamps. The murmuring of a couple of hundred people had its own measure of inner strength in spite of the pressures from climate, along with the shock of a sudden end to normality. The young were looking after the old, young parents were busy attending to their children. Backs were turned to the wind. Huddling helped. Mother and Else were cuddling Hedwig, who hadn't been well since the death, from cancer, of her fiancé, the eye surgeon. She had just recovered from a bout of pneumonia, and the weather surrounding us all would be doing her no good. Max had seen a small light flickering across the fields.

'What d'you think?'

Munky: 'A farm?'

Fritz: 'Whoever, whatever, they can at least tell us where we are, and how to get to a town. Who's coming?'

We were in luck. After crossing the fields in front of us, battling against waves of wind-blown sleet, we reached the source of the light, a house at the outer edge of the Hungarian

24

village of Kisabony, exactly on the border. Fritz explained to the startled householders that behind us, across the fields, were some 200 refugees from Bratislava hunkered down and suffering the foul weather. The village quickly came alive as word spread, and help was immediately there. There was the example of Kraijchirovich, and now God be praised, this. The sleeping had been raised, doors opened and food prepared. Fires had been relit, milk warmed for the little ones. Villagers headed out into the night to the no-man's land where the Slovaks had left us, to collect the exposed, bringing them back to warmth and human beings who cared. Most of us spent the night sheltering in the village's tiny synagogue. After the provision of warming food, we slept.

I woke to the smell of extinguished candles and the leather mustiness of old books, mingled with the sweet wood smoke from a log fire. First light filtered in through the synagogue windows. As I came to, I noticed Fritz was missing. Together with my sleeping brothers, those around me were people of all ages and classes, some of whom I knew. Many were already awake – maybe they hadn't slept – some were shivering, due as much to reduced morale as low temperature. A lethargy was creeping over the group, one or two men were weeping as they prayed. Fritz appeared through the doorway, smiling. He had learnt from the villagers that a few kilometres down the road was a larger village, complete with railway station and a sizeable Jewish community. Morale rose, we all felt a little warmer. Fritz enlisted around twenty willing souls, including Munky and myself, to make the journey down the road to ask for help from the Jews of Dunajszka Streda.

In clothes damp from the night before, we set off to walk what turned out to be a ten-kilometre hike. It was bitterly cold, though thankfully no longer raining. Father, Mother and the girls were billeted a few metres down the village street from the synagogue. After informing them of our plan, we set off. Max and Fritz strode ahead, their trousers rolled up to prevent mud from forever ruining good fabric. Munky and I followed on, speculating animatedly as to what the future

25

held. Already the family unit was in trouble. Where could we find a place quickly to be together?

From time to time, Fritz or Max would turn to see if we were keeping up. Ten kilometres was in itself not a problem, but the terrain was. Muddy and uneven, cold, and in damp clothing, even colder. The conditions and the promise of some kind of rescue put resolve in our step, in spite of the shivers.

Twenty men in a bedraggled state was the sight that met the eyes of a group of men and boys on their way to their synagogue for the Saturday service. They stopped on our approach and greeted us in wide-eyed surprise. Bold Fritz as usual stepped out from our group and, introducing himself, went on to explain the circumstances surrounding our expulsion from Czechoslovakia, how we came to be standing before them. In the attentive group was an older man, tall, with an air of authority. After listening to Fritz and the various pleas for help coming from the rest of our little delegation, he spoke:

'Come with me. Come. Come.'

We followed, a little meekly, behind this striding figure. We were joined by the smartly dressed men who moved alongside and engaged us in conversation about our experience. At the synagogue, our shepherd pushed open a large, heavy oak door and strode in. The men inside were in mid-prayer, which hushed to silence as we entered. All looked up startled. Our patron, we quickly realized, was the senior warden of the community. After a brief explanation of the situation, the sympathetic worshippers, like those in Kisabony, were galvanized into action. The rabbi gave dispensation to all, so that the normal Sabbath prohibition on work and travel could be bypassed and the good people of Dunajszka Streda could use their horses and carts to transport the remainder of our group from Kisabony to this place and its railway station.

Two rather well-heeled young men, about the same age as Max and Fritz, with similar dress sense and slicked-back hairstyles, left the synagogue together, one throwing a set of keys to his companion saying, 'Take the other one.' A little while later I noticed through the synagogue window the two young men go past in separate cars, one a very luxurious Tatra, while the other was large and looked American.

So it was in Dunajszka Streda, in the middle of our turmoil and tragedy, that love was to blossom. Not once, but twice. The handsome owner of two cars returned from Kisabony with my mother and sisters. Beside him, up front, sat Else. Bernat Rujder took the women straight to his family home where they were made welcome. Bernat and Else displayed a mutual attraction that quickly blossomed into love, later to marriage. Bernat, it turned out, was not only charming but he was that rare creature, someone who was naturally inclined to put others ahead of himself. And so the girls stayed with Bernat's family. I was billeted, along with Mother, with the family Weiss. My brothers and Father were guests of people related to the warden. The family was separated, but safe.

The Weiss family seemed central to Jewish social life in this little town. A well-to-do couple with three children; two girls, Lici, then 11, Medy, 13, and a boy Erno, 16. Once inside the door we were made very welcome, which helped dull the pain of the last twenty-four hours. We were to stay with the Weiss family for seven days, but for me time had stood still. I was in Love. In spite of the fear and the worry for the future, love, like a starburst, popped my brain. Medy. What could I do? Big blue eyes, soft brown hair falling down about her shoulders. Instantly beguiling. The man began to assert himself over the boy. From the moment I met her, she would not be out of my mind. Whenever we encountered one another around the house, my knees went weak. I watched, fascinated as she moved. She had a natural grace that compelled attention even from those fools not entranced by her. That first Saturday as we played cards across a small table, our legs happened to touch; the sensation passed through me like an electric shock. She alone occupied the centre of my existence, became for me, something divine. I was overtaken by the need to be in her company, continually.

Hardly 14, living in the presence of my secret love was

comforting after what we had just been through. It was the week of the Hungarian annexation of the Slovakian highlands. In the street, Medy and I stood, a couple of kids, watching what seemed to be an endless procession of troops sitting triumphantly on their shaky horse-drawn wagons. Stiff with outdated weaponry, the rag-tag army was being jolted from side to side along the cobbled carriageway. I confess to paying more attention to Medy than the passing parade. She must have sensed my feelings for her, but our strict religious upbringing dictated that she could never acknowledge this. Nor could I openly express my feelings for her. Love, however, found a way. Mrs Weiss discovered I could sing, and, after an embarrassing audition over cups of tea with my proud mother egging me on, I became a voice to be shown off to visitors. It gave me a chance to express my feelings for Medy in song. Though nobody else guessed the target of my songs' affections, I'm certain she did.

A week later, we moved on. The family had to be split up, that was clear. It was time to call in a few favours from those who had been beneficiaries of Father's generosity at Schanzstrasse or from his wallet, mainly relatives from the large extended family. We were to go our separate ways. It was decided that I should go stay with Grandfather Eliezer in the little town of Papa.

It was early Sunday. My mother was saying whispered goodbyes to our hosts. On my way downstairs, I noticed the girls' bedroom door ajar. I sneaked in and, much to the amazement of her little sister, I went over to Medy's bedside. She was still asleep when I touched her hand. As she awoke, I pressed her fingers to my lips. She said not a word, but gave me a long blue-eyed look, and just the hint of a smile. Hearing my mother's whispered shout from downstairs, I quickly made for the bedroom door. Glancing back at her one more time, I wondered what the chances were of maybe meeting again.

Munky and Else stayed on in Dunajszka Streda while Mother, Father and the others were about to leave for

Komarom, which was about a hundred kilometres from the home town of Papa. While Father put me on my train, my mother and sisters put on a brave face watching us from the opposite platform, waiting on their train. Therezia wiped her eyes as my train rolled out. Father, from the platform gave me a curt, friendly nod and a little wave and I was on my way; the first of many rail journeys that punctuated my life over the next thirty years.

Exhilaration gave way to fatigue soon enough on this first solo adventure. The train had wood slats that were painful to the bony bottom of a skinny lad. The ride seemed endless and standing up for relief landed me in a passenger's lap when the train lurched. This caused a ripple of laughter in the carriage. I did a little Chaplin imitation to cover my embarrassment, which brought on a few more chuckles. I returned to my seat to look out the window and wiggle about to ease my bones. Arriving at Papa station found me standing by my case, scratching my head. I thought I would know the way from earlier visits, but on my own I was not so sure. Everything beyond the station looked unfamiliar. Which way? A station official, quick to spot a passenger in trouble, approached.

In response to his question, I replied in German (as yet I had little Hungarian): 'I need to find my grandfather. He lives here.'

He was able to reply: 'You've still a bit of walking to do before you reach town. The place is full of grandfathers. Nobody with you?'

I shrugged: 'I came on my own.'

He lit a cigarette. 'Where from?'

I told him the Bratislava-to-Hungary saga. How we'd been helped, how we had to split up. He listened thoughtfully, then asked: 'What is your grandfather's name?'

'Elieizer. Elieizer Lowy.'

The official smiled broadly.

'So you are one of Eliezer's many grandsons. Congratulations, he's a much-respected man around here. Listen carefully.'

Following the man's elaborate directions, I made my way, case in hand, into the town, easily locating Eliezer's cottage. At the door, I knocked. A tall elderly man with a warm, friendly face and a goatee beard opened the door. His deep, black eyes widened when he looked down and recognized his visitor. Little Ernest standing there alone. His bushy eyebrows rose in smiling surprise. He used his nickname for me:

'Moishe. What on earth are you doing here? Where are Leopold and Therezia?'

He looked out past me up and down the street.

'Just me Grandfather.'

He ushered me into the cottage.

'Alone? Moishe, what has happened? Is everyone alright?'

I told him the story. He turned from me to face the cottage's bay window. His shoulders gently shook as he wept for his family and the golden son who had lost his house and his fortune. Penniless as a peasant. All those years of hard work, swept away in a single tragic night. Wiping away his tears, he turned to me with a gentle smile.

'You must be hungry, my son.'

I smiled back at him. I was always hungry. My impressive grandfather beckoned me ahead of him and ushered me towards the kitchen.

At that time, the Jewish population of Papa numbered around three thousand souls. Eliezer was their *oberkantor*. Just walking by his side along the street made me feel proud and privileged. He had a natural dignity which had the effect on passers by, Jew and non-Jew, not only to greet him, but also often to accompany the greeting with a discreet bow. He still remains clear in my memory, one of the most wonderful human beings I have ever met, the embodiment of tolerance and understanding, and with a strong sense of humour to ease the stress of all that goodness.

Just at the beginning of my stay, the news of the German orgy of violence against Jewry, *Kristallnacht*, filtered through. Eliezer took me through the details and we discussed it, and how, for him, prayer still held good. So we prayed together, and sang together. His one-storey cottage was in the grounds of the synagogue where he held his position. The synagogue's acoustics were extraordinary. When Eliezer sang there, it felt like a hundred bells, a deep rich tenor voice, not unlike Caruso. He had an operatic strength. I imagined him singing in *The Meistersingers*. It didn't take him long to find out that my voice had improved since last hearing, and he immediately wanted to help develop it.

'You have a nice voice, a good voice. Talent. In our little time together let me introduce you to some of the secrets of good singing.'

Taking me under his wing, he began to coach me. My delight at this attention brought on a great desire to learn, and learn I did.

'Never open your mouth too wide and keep everything around your mouth soft and relaxed.'

He imbued me with technique for voice projection, gave me advice on its protection. Taught me many of his liturgical songs, or what he called his 'party pieces'. One that he had composed himself was *Achenu Beith Ysrael*, a song based on a spoken prayer for all Jewish people who suffer persecution. This I still sing today. The few days spent under his tuition were without price.

While with him, I had my first 'professional' engagement. I had been under his roof ten short days, when my father turned up, together with a couple of relatives. Not, as I thought, merely to collect me, but to attend a large wedding for which he had received an invitation, not to be passed up. Simply the most important social event in Papa's recent history, I wanted desperately to go to the evening celebrations, but Leopold said that would be impossible.

'Tomorrow we're on the train to Budapest. I've found an apartment for us. It's a long ride. You'll need your sleep before the journey.'

'I could sleep on the train.'

'On those wooden benches? Don't be silly.'

'But ...'

31

'No buts, early bed.'

So, despite my appeals, I was left alone in the cottage that evening to sulk under the covers, where I eventually dropped off. At midnight I was awakened brusquely by my father pulling back the bedclothes.

'Ernest, get up. Your grandfather wants you at the wedding. Why didn't he say so before? Too busy officiating. I'm not a mind-reader.'

He cast my clothes in my direction, in his haste tried to dress me but got in my way. I was in a sleepy sulk.

'I don't want to go any more.'

'Don't argue. If Grandfather says you're to come, that's it, you're to come. Now hurry.'

Along the darkened streets of Papa, I was half-dragged, half-carried by my father, overly anxious for me to get to the wedding earlier refused me. Eliezer had spoken, and his word was sacrosanct. It is true that my father was right that I should get a night's sleep, but equally true that a patriarch should be obeyed; so it was with us. As we stumbled through the door into the reception hall, we were greeted with a barrage of laughter, conversation, music, tobacco smoke and the smell of alcohol; truly a celebration. Lots of guests. The bride and groom were clapping along with others as half a dozen young men danced in a ring. I woke properly to this sight and sound.

Eliezer spotted us. He strode over to us, grabbed me and hauled me to a table in the centre of the hall where he swept crockery and glasses to one side, placed me atop the table, my muddy shoes leaving their mark on the pure white cloth. He seized a glass of Bull's Blood and thrust it into my hands:

'Drink!' he commanded.

I downed the rich, thick red wine as little 'grown-up' boys will do when they have adult sanction. He pulled me to him, and in a rasping, wine-heavy voice:

'Moishe. Moishe. Listen to me. Remember what you've learned about singing from your grandfather. That piece I taught you yesterday. Sing it now.'

I looked away from his excited stare and into a sea of

people, some facing me, others milling around since the dancing ended. I eyed up a passing tray of gateaux, sweet-meats and fudge cake. He caught my gaze.

'Sing for me, and the whole tray is yours.'

I sang. And sang. And sang. Liturgical pieces, I sang Grandfather's own compositions, putting my whole heart into a vocalizing that startled me, delighted him and reduced a noisy crowd to long silences and cheering the *boychick* up there on a trestle table, having brought them to tears. Eliezer stood in front of me, keeping time like a music master, thumping the table, telling me what next to sing. The guests called for more, so I gave them more. My first public performance with my proud, beaming grandfather standing in front of me, acknowledging the applause on my behalf. I did manage my own bow and blew everyone a kiss before my father took me from my stage, and ushered me back to the cottage, my hands full of cake.

No sooner had my head hit the pillow than I was off to dreamland, only to be re-awakened by my father seemingly minutes later. It was dawn and Leopold threw me my clothes which, yawning, I carried to the bathroom.

After the wine, the cake, the lack of sleep and all that singing, and the reek from the cheap Hungarian cigarettes everyone at Papa station seemed to be smoking, I felt pretty wretched. My stomach was churning and I felt nauseous. My father and I were ready to board the morning train to Budapest.

Eliezer had come to see us off. He and a couple of pals, still high from the night before, but staying very dignified in front of the peasants who thronged the platform. He gave me a bear hug.

'Ernest. Become a professional, maybe even cantor. Don't bury your talent. Now where is my golden boy?'

He released me and grabbed my father. The embrace was silent. They shared a tearful moment, and as if magicked on board, we were waving our goodbyes from the moving train.

Father and I had managed to squeeze some space for ourselves on the heavily crowded train and, though the slatted seats were uncomfortable, my tiredness overwhelmed the discomfort. With eyes closed, then slowly, heavily opened, my memories of the night before mingled with the sight of frost on sunlit farmland and hedgerows as the train moved through the countryside. I was pleased Grandfather had insisted on my singing, and though there were some small hints my soprano was about to vanish, it was still able to stir hearts, even though at this time we were all on an emotional knife-edge as we began to feel the heat from the fascist 'blast furnace'. The stamping of feet and the calls for more following that short silence at the end of a song had me hooked. I loved the lift such appreciation gave me. And I could still feel the kiss of the rabbi's daughter, the bride. The memory of the night before sat like warm sunshine on my soul, not to mention the good red wine and the gateau that followed the kiss. My stomach rumbled, prompted by the recollection. I was hungry. We had had no breakfast, and in the haste to leave, no food was prepared. I would have to grit my teeth, fasting being good for the soul. Mercifully, sleep took over.

I woke to the curious stare of a small two-year-old girl, who, greasy-mouthed, was holding with difficulty a pig's trotter which was part-chewed. I smiled. She smiled, and proffered the trotter. I shook my head politely, my orthodoxy my shield, my hunger my torment. I looked down the carriage and the space was very full. Her parents called her back and admonished her for looking at strangers. Apart from us in our formal black, separate in our demeanour and dress, everybody else in the carriage seemed to know each other. Jokes and conversation bounced around in the smoky atmosphere perfumed by the smell of vodka, wine, tobacco and body odour. As if on a pre-arranged signal, bundles had been opened one after another to reveal the usual peasant fare of blood pudding, palm-sized lumps of fat bacon and chunks of bread cut with clasp knives from huge loaves. Dominating all the smells because of its sharpness, paprika. Eating had spread down the train like a wave of gossip. The only ones not joining in were the two Jewish *oddniks* in the corner, looking in on a non-kosher 'promised land'. I was not a little envious. Father seemed unperturbed, though I thought that maybe I heard his stomach grumble.

I had to move. I had been sitting squashed up against one of two fat sisters who, side by side, seemed to be spreading. They also smelled bad. That bit of discomfort didn't change, I was close now to their feet, sitting on the floor in front of Father; but I was free to move about. Father had given me his coat as the train had no heating. I was beginning to have visions of the child's piece of pig as the train began to slow, pulling into Tatabanya, a mining town. There was a lot of action in the train with people getting up and off, people getting on. Father got up to get some food from the platform vendors. He needed his coat. I knew he would be short, so I slipped my treasured, months-hoarded *pengo* coin into his coat pocket before handing the garment back to him. By the time he had his coat on, the aisle had become jammed with people getting off. He had to shuffle slowly to the doors. I grabbed his seat and relaxed, spreading out as much as the bulk of the nearer fat sister would allow. She smiled indulgently my way, but offered me nothing from her huge supply of bread and cake. I shut my eyes and eased into quiet reverie.

A jolt from the train woke me. It was moving slowly out of Tatabanya. Where was Leopold? Shocked, I leapt to the window, slid it down and leaned out. I looked down the platform to waving people. No Leopold, no Father. The train gave a long whistle and gained pace. I must go on to Budapest with the Ugly Sisters. What a fate!

At the far end of the carriage I caught sight of him waving. Breathless, he reached me, I moved to allow him to sit.

'Just as I found a vendor with acceptable food, the train started to move. Just about managed to get on the last carriage.'

'No food then?'

'No food. Is this yours?'

He handed me back my *pengo*, smiled, leaned over and kissed my forehead.

The train seemed to take forever to reach Budapest. At long last we stepped out of the station, eating some apples purchased on the concourse. My first look at Budapest, and I loved it; the size and vitality of the place, and its appearance. A grand architectural achievement. I would come to love the bridges that crossed the Danube and linked Buda to Pest. My time as a tourist on this particular day was short-lived and confined to the tram ride from the station to Karoly ring road. As we stepped down from the tram to the pavement, round the corner came a parade. We stopped to watch. A crowd of screaming people, hundreds, five hundred maybe, who knew? Plenty anyway, crushing their way forward, at us, past us, round us, jostling us, hollering their hatred of Jews, therefore me, Ernest Lowy from Bratislava, not quite 14, and in the city fifteen minutes. Who were they? What were they? As if I didn't know.

'Who is Imredy, Daddy?'

The mob liked him. They were using his name as a mantra, waving banners with his name emblazoned, along with crossed arrow banners and the swastika.

'A fascist who loves Hitler and all things Nazi.'

My father met my horrified eyes. We had walked into a pond full of alligators? First Bratislava, then not even a month along, we were experiencing more of the same? I was sure he was finding all of what was happening around us hard to credit. Yet here it all was, naked hate on the street, so self-engrossed it swept past us as if we were invisible. Except for that woman. Middle-aged, in a flower print dress part-covered by a flapping overcoat, carrying an Arrowcross banner. Just off the tram, there we were, standing agape, obviously Jewish in our formal clothing, neat, tidy and very obviously orthodox. The woman separated herself from her companions and came round to one side of my father. With her banner, she swiped him about the head, her teeth bared, swearing street-dirty. His hands went up to his face to defend himself, his hat fell to the pavement, and rolled.

Without a thought, I kicked the woman's left shin, hard.

36

Her howl of pain turned heads. She hopped and clutched her way to a bench, somehow maintaining her hold of the banner, her symbol, her status. I had had a day of it and this woman, this harpy, had become the sum total of my frustrations. The kick felt good and felt even better when the parade turned the corner into Museum Street. The harpy had been left behind to nurse her injury and seethe in her hate, alone. My father retrieved his hat, dusted it down and placed it back on his head. Ever the gentleman, as we left in the opposite direction to the crowd, Leopold doffed his hat to the woman and bade her 'good day'.

Father had managed to rent a one-room flat in the Jewish quarter, close to the Dohany synagogue which edged on to the ghetto. Though the landlady at first thought that she was letting the room to one man and his son, she made no fuss when more of us arrived. She turned out to be sympathetic to our plight. The room had no toilet facilities or anywhere to cook, and when the rest of the family turned up, we slept sideways on the double bed, made use of the sparse furnishing and the floor. Makeshift to be sure, but under a roof, in the dry.

So, fresh from Papa, just we two Lowys settled into our space. Then a happy accident. On the second Friday, an old business acquaintance came up to my father after worship in the Kazinczy synagogue, doffed his hat, and smiling, gave my father a pleasing shock:

'Good to see that Karl has made it here safely. You must be delighted Herr Lowy.'

'What?'

The acquaintance smiled:

'That was Karl I saw outside just now, surely. You must be delighted to have him safe and well ...'

Leopold looked at the man long and hard, the unspoken question hanging there. The acquaintance broadened his smile and nodded. Leopold grabbed him by the hand, shook it fiercely, turned on his heel and sped from the synagogue, leaving me to make small talk with the man who, realizing the situation, encouraged me to follow my father. I thanked him and left. I reached the steps to find Leopold rushing up and down outside from group to group of men doing what they love best after worship, gossiping. Finally, over the way, he found his big son. The reunion was an emotional one, the hugs and the kisses there on the street brought smiles to the faces of those who had watched Leopold chase around outside the Kazinczy. Arms round each other, we made our way back to the tiny new apartment.

Karl hadn't known about our expulsion from Bratislava. He had come to Budapest after *Kristallnacht*, his Hungarian passport saving him from immediate detention when he had gone to see his mentor rabbi to tell him of his decision to leave a Germany now so utterly dangerous that breathing had become an insult to the Reich. Before he could reach the poor man's apartment, the rabbi was being rough-handled down the stairs, under arrest. Their eyes met, and, so obviously were they connected, that the SS demanded papers of Karl. Hungarian passport, temporary salvation. He stood on the stair watching his friend and teacher taken.

I listened to my brother giving his sad account of leaving Germany, but that wasn't just sadness on his face; Leopold noticed it too. Pain. Karl was hurting. He didn't look well. He moved in with us that day, happily leaving a grimy sub-let. The following morning found him doubled-up on the bed. A journey to the hospital revealed a perforated ulcer which had been bleeding away to a dangerous level. Karl, deeply sensitive and a quiet soul, had been taken down by what had been happening to and around him, as life for Germany's Jews descended into chaotic fear. Max, who had turned up that very morning, proved to be Karl's lifeline, being a blood match for his brother. For once, our extremity seemed divinely aided at the hospital. My father led us in prayers of thankfulness.

A few days later Father announced to me that a cousin of his in Fulek could use a bit of help in his hardware business.

It meant a measure of payment; mother and the others wouldn't be arriving for a few weeks, maybe I should make the journey, stay with my uncle and his family. It made sense. As yet I hadn't enrolled in any school, and it looked as though there would be a fascist block on Jewish *kinder* learning in the state schools. Anyway, we needed to earn more than learn. With Max and Karl in the apartment, the place was filling. Munky wasn't due to arrive just yet, so the fare was scraped together, and off I went. It freed Father up to look for work. He had also undertaken to find me something in Budapest, as he didn't want his family split up for longer than was necessary. Karl remained in hospital, recovering steadily. I made a last visit before Max saw me on to the train to Fulek.

The journey was cold, but I had been supplied with food, a bottle of soda pop, a book (religious) plus a newspaper full of politics and news from several fronts where conflict was developing. My clothing shouted my orthodoxy, and though a couple of Jewish men were in my carriage, our eyes never met. The men talked incessantly in Yiddish, until a couple of feather-hatted gendarmes joined the train. They sat near me talking loudly about Admiral Horthy, Hungary's present leader, who feigned friendship with Hitler. Though he was a professed anti-Semite, still somehow the Jews exercised undue influence in Hungary's affairs. When their man, Szalasi, was recognised by the Hungarians as the true patriot leader, worthy to be standing shoulder-to-shoulder with the great German example, Chancellor Hitler, the Jews would be straw on a bonfire. With their backs to me, their target audience was the pair of Yiddish speakers, men in their fifties who were deeply intimidated by the swaggering presence of these two armed militia men. Working-class patriots to a fascist cause, their beliefs grounded in a 'back-to-roots', 'foreigners-out' policy wedded to Hitler's pursuit of racial supremacy; something they knew meant them ... sure of it.

The non-Jewish passengers on the train appeared bored by the loudness of the two gendarmes who were performing for the benefit of anyone nearby interested. Their uniform, made ridiculous by the absurd feathered bowlers that brought Laurel and Hardy to mind, would over time develop as the Arrowcross militia emerged from their ranks. They were with the train all the way and, at various stops, were joined by others, until by the time the train reached Fulek, the carriage was full. Leaving the train, the platform seemed packed. I stood in the midst of tomorrow's mass-murderers, case in hand.

'Ernest?'

I turned to face a couple in their mid-thirties.

'Yes.'

'I'm your father's cousin Hugo. My wife Illonka.'

I was to come to love this uncle and aunt who in spite of their modest circumstances, proved warm, outgoing, generous to a fault. And they were funny, not to mention modern.

'We've come to take you to my brother's place. They're sorry not to meet you, but they are very busy ...'

'... and we are at a loose end.' Illonka butted in.

Both laughed as if at some private joke.

'Let's get you off the platform before these hens start pecking.'

Hugo glanced warily at the clusters of gendarmes assembling. As we walked together through the small town, Hugo explained that the gendarmes shared a barrack at the edge of town with the regular Hungarian army.

'The regulars can't abide them. There is a lack of mutual respect which boils over into fights. It won't be long before there's a death.'

Illonka: 'Better each other than us. The threat is always there, Ernest. Watch your step. You are very exposed in a town this size.'

Hugo: 'Just a little further through the town and we'll be at your uncle Leopold's. Once you are settled in, come visit. We're just down the road.'

Illonka: 'That's assuming you get time off of course.'

Hugo nudged his wife, stifling a laugh. 'Your aunt is only joking.'

Illonka: 'Is that so?'

I prayed she was.

Uncle Leopold's house reflected his success and wealth. A nineteenth-century house, detached, in its own grounds, proclaiming to one and all that those within would be well-heeled and comfortably bourgeois. We stood in the porch, waiting for a response to the bell pull, which came in the very formal shape of Aunt Sari, who greeted me with a polite handshake, which I was left comparing to Aunt Illonka's hug. Aunt Sari seemed remote and Uncle Leopold was still out on business. She invited us through the doorway. Hugo and Illonka went through into the lounge while I was ushered upstairs, following Aunt Sari to my attic eyrie. Once unpacked, I came down to find my seniors in the lounge, talking quietly and drinking coffee. I stood in the doorway. Aunt Sari looked up: 'Ernest, come sit, and tell us all about your adventures.'

I did, for half an hour, and they listened intently as I added examples to their list of outrages against us. The late afternoon sunlight shafted in low through the French windows, casting a dappled effect into the room, shading it here and there in charcoal grey and causing my relatives to glow in a deep orange half-light, as I watched the shadows lengthen.

3 From Fulek to Budapest

Uncle Leopold ran a hardware business, both wholesale and retail. The proceeds from this well-run affair kept him and his family in very good order. The trading was conducted from a shop and a warehouse in the town. The family consisted of Leopold, Sari, their four children, two of each, one of whom, Kato, the youngest, closest to me in age, had my whole entranced attention. Barely 14, my growing awareness of the changes in me was challenged by her beautifully rounded figure, bronze, shining shoulder-length hair and low, husky voice. Unlike me, for her age, she gave off an air of maturity and responsibility. The whole household was redolent of the day-to-day formality of the provincial bourgeoisie. That Kato helped with the running of the business came as no surprise to me. Around the house, I did my best to impress, to appear witty and sophisticated, just as Kato and her older siblings would do at table. Being on the edge of manhood and a little bit lost, I fell back on joke telling, bad impressions and copious quotes from the Marx brothers' movies. I prided myself on doing a good Mussolini; my Hitler, a gem. I tried with Neville Chamberlain, but it required a deadpan approach, no less circus than the other two, but I wound up creased with laughter; always a 'no no' for aspiring comics. It was all met with indulgent laughter, later, smiles, then tolerant smiles, then not much of anything. I began to lose my audience. My mission to brighten up their dull lives with my sharp contemporary comedy was coming unstuck. Which, of course, made me try harder. For me, the weak link was Aunt Sari who found me unfunny and irritating, though to my face she was formally polite, greeting my antics with a small, tight, frozen smile.

The final straw came one afternoon when, unknown to me, she was entertaining. I had followed Kato into the house pretending to be Harpo 'after the girls', the way I'd seen him do it in the movies. Kato was laughing merrily at my antics and ran upstairs calling out how silly I was. I decided to serenade the whole house, so I went into the music room and did some single-finger Chico on the piano, followed by a bad Groucho singing, 'I really must be going'. It turned out to be prophetic. One evening when Illonka was visiting, I chanced to hear Sari complain about me in the sourest terms.

'... simply doesn't know how to behave. No control. What on earth goes on among the Lowys ...? I know they have been through a bad time, but there's little evidence in the boy of a proper upbringing. Rough at the edges, loose. I know he doesn't mean to, but he's driving me mad, my teeth are permanently on edge ... mine are past that silly stage ... Illonka, I'm asking as a personal favour, please, could you see your way to putting him up until cousin Leopold calls for him to join them in Budapest ... my nerves are in tatters.'

I made it to my little room at the top of the house and wept the last of my childhood tears in realizing that, though I stood at the threshold of adulthood, no one had asked me to cross it, nor did I have the know-how or courage so to do. The child-man wept into his pillow. And I was angry at Aunt Sari for being an unmitigated snob, belittling my beloved family. Face it, I didn't want to stay under that roof any longer, anyway.

Sweet revenge came my way when, in 1943, the beautiful Kato married my brother Karl, or Charles as he came later to be called. They had met in the provincial town of Szolnok where she had come to stay, and where Charles had a post as cantor. I knew the whole family rejoiced, certainly Uncle Leopold was pleased. As for Aunt Sari, I hope she was resigned. It made me giggle at the time. And only for a time: in 1944 Charles was hauled off to a labour camp. At their farewell, Kato was pregnant. Left alone in Szolnok, she decided to return to Fulek to give birth in the bosom of her family and friends. The child was a boy. Ten days later, the entire remaining Jewish community of Fulek was deported to Auschwitz. All, all gone.

It was fairly cramped with Hugo and Illonka. In the company of their four children, who were closer to me in age than Leopold's family, my life took on a sunny aspect. Little Frank was 9, Edith, 11. Yanko, he was 13, Sannye, older than me at 15. Fulek suddenly seemed a jolly place. I saw Kato in passing, which would gladden my day, but best of all was the laughter around the house. I found I had rivals in the telling of bad jokes and poor impersonations; sometimes after a bout of fooling, my ribs would hurt. Between them all, colourful modern people, I found fondness and easy laughter. The remainder of my stay in Fulek was as smooth as honey on bread.

Then there was Moses, the *sochet-cantor* at the synagogue. He had been taken by my singing there, and wanted to learn at the feet of the young 'master'. I had been given a pay-my-way job at the hardware store as general 'tidy' and messenger boy, which continued after I had left the first household. One morning Moses strode purposefully into the shop. A big guy, black suit, white tieless shirt, black hat, ringlets, beard, big mitts, Moses clumped along the bare wood floor, took me by the hand. With a big naïve smile:

'Ernest. I've decided. I need to learn some of your lovely cantorial chants. Will you teach me? Come to the synagogue after work. We'll discuss.'

Moses stomped out of the shop, singing to himself. Uncle Leopold was on hand: 'Don't do it, if you don't feel like it, *boychick*. It's your time. You're coming cheap, you'll be doing him a favour to learn one of your songs. Where did you get them? A certain cantor in Papa?'

I smiled, nodding. Uncle Leopold shared more than a name and family likeness. He shared Father's warmth and gentle humour.

Needless to say, later that day I made my way to the synagogue. The familiar smell of old books and extinguished

candles greeted me at the door. I sat down in a pew, waiting
for Moses. My pupil had a good, strong voice, but little control
over where it went, having an unhappy knack of singing just
under the tone, not getting the notes spot on. I liked the man
for his unabashed readiness to learn from me, such a young
and inexperienced tutor. In spite of my dislike of his odour, a
combination of tobacco, red meat and garlic, he was pleasing
company, and in a reasonable vocal state by the time I left
Fulek. Already a popular figure in the community, Moses
would soon run through a service without assaulting the
congregation's eardrums. And he learned some new songs as
he had wished. The big man found it hard to suppress a
delighted smile when he stood to sing, and so did I when I
listened to the result with some pride. Already popular in the
community, his new-found range and quality of singing
added to the air of charming innocence that surrounded him.
I loved his sincerity. It was worth the forty-five minute wait
that evening, a small figure among the pews.

The happy months in Fulek were cut short for me by the
news that my father had found me a job in Budapest, and the
family was back together. He had also found himself a job and
was now looking for a bigger apartment for us all. I was sent
instructions on where to rendezvous in the city, but how I was
to get to there was glossed over. I think Father Leopold was
leaving it up to Uncle Leopold, who just happened to have a
truck due to make a delivery of kitchen hardware to a new
restaurant in Budapest. What was also glossed over was that
it had become illegal to give transportation to Jews under new
fascist legislation. So it was going to be risky. Uncle Leopold
used a couple of Slovak drivers who were willing, for a
shilling, to take a little lad to the capital.

There were fond farewells at Uncle Leopold's house. Even
Aunty Sari held me close for a moment, telling me to keep my
head down in the truck, also to be polite to Imre and Bela, the
drivers. Kato gave me a big hug as did the others. Earlier I had
a tearful time with Hugo and Illonka, who had provided me
with a couple of giant jam sandwiches wrapped in grease-

proof paper. I popped into the synagogue to say goodbye to Moses. The big guy was very upset and, with tear-filled eyes, bade his farewell to his young teacher. This task complete, I rejoined Uncle Leopold in his comfortable saloon car. He had ferried me from Hugo and Illonka's to his own place, then to the synagogue, and onward. I felt very privileged as we splashed our way through the pouring rain for an early rendezvous with Imre, Bela and the truck outside Leopold's lock-up across town. Uncle put me down, then after a brief farewell handshake and a quick hug, drove off. The truck wasn't there, but my uncle had assured me it would turn up. I sheltered from the rain in an alcove with a locked door at the side of the small warehouse. The day was very grey, very wet, with low cloud, ragged and slow-moving, obscuring the hills surrounding the town. Alone again. I sang to myself and sent my mind forward to Budapest and seeing the family; all of us under one roof.

A large truck rumbled round a corner, headlights blazing in the dark grey of the morning. A woman crossing the road made a dash for the kerb and I had to dodge the water splashed up from the truck's tyres as its squeaking brakes brought it to a stop beside me.

'You Ernest Lowy?'

Imre, as I later learned, leaned out from the cab. Bela was half-hidden beside him. All I could see of him was a cap and pipe smoke.

'Where's your gear?'

'My what?'

'Gear. Stuff. Bags and baggage.'

I gave him a wide smile and held up my small travelling bag along with my pack of sandwiches.

'Right here.'

'That's it?'

'That's it.'

Imre left the cab to unlock the warehouse, Bela joined him from the other side. They had that slightly puzzled-cum-pitying look. Something didn't quite add up. Boss's relative

46

hitching a ride, understandable; no luggage? A puzzle. Maybe 'poor relation' would occur to them down the line.

Bela: 'Want to make yourself useful?'

Me: 'Sure.'

He gestured to the truck.

'There's a rumble seat behind ours. Put your stuff there, then come and give us a hand.'

No sooner said than done. Imre had raised the warehouse shutter, a stack of packing cases stood ready for loading. When the truck was backed up, we started. Loading took twenty damp minutes. Warehouse locked, me safely lodged behind them, with Imre back at the wheel, he and Bela checked the road for traffic, and we were off, Budapest-bound. I had been up early for this, and with the heavy lifting, I was tired enough to fall asleep to the rhythm of the windscreen wipers battling against the torrential rain, to the fragrance of Bela's pipe smoke, reminding me of my father and Uncle Ore, and to the low murmur of the conversation of my hosts for the day.

I woke alone in the cab. We had stopped. The two drivers had gone for coffee and food. According to the clock on the church tower opposite the filling station where we had stopped, it had only just gone nine a.m. Spontaneously responding to my hunger, I ate both sandwiches. This left me nothing for the day, but it took care of now. The rain was streaking down the steamy truck windows. Imre had left one window open a few centimetres and through the space, with a heart's leap, I saw a police car had been driven into the filling station. It had been parked a short way off, but still in view. The drive-side door opened and a bulky frame eased itself out and upright. The uniform was tight to the policemen's frame. His shock of red hair spiked out from under his cap. His large, pink face had the puffy appearance which goes with drink or allergy. His eyes were on the truck, and, as he headed towards it, I hit the floor. From the crunch of gravel I knew he had arrived up close to the window. I heard the squeak as his hand tried to wipe water away to look in. I looked up to see the side of his face pressed hard to the glass, trying to get some kind of a glimpse. His breathing was hoarse and he coughed a couple of times. The third cough sounded more distant and I couldn't hear him breathing, so I dared raise up and appeared at the window, just as he turned round for a second look. The policeman's voice was high-pitched, almost feminine:

'You, boy. Out! Get out of the vehicle now!'

I obeyed. As I opened the truck door, a short fat arm reached in and hauled me down. I missed my footing and fell at his feet. I struggled up. He pitched his voice higher. It was shrill:

'What are you doing in there? Where is the driver?'

He grabbed my arm. Behind him, Imre and Bela were making their way casually back to the truck.

'You, Baky. Leave the kid alone, he's with us.'

It was Bela's voice. He turned to face Bela and Imre. They knew this man?

The policeman gave a mean little smile.

'You two, again. Jew smuggling now is it?'

Bela: 'The kid's getting a lift. You'd leave him in the pissing rain? That's you. Kid's alone. He tells us he's got relatives in Budapest. We're going to Budapest.'

Baky: 'You buggers work for a Jew. Nothing to do with him of course.'

Bela: 'You're right, nothing to do with him. Picked the boy up soaking wet. Come on Baky, where's the harm?'

Baky seemed to soften. He gave me a wink, an attempted smile, and let go of my arm.

'What's happening here's illegal. I'll have to file a report. Could take a while. For now you're free to go.'

Baky walked off back to his car. Imre resumed the driver's seat in the truck. 'Bastard.'

Bela: 'Can't trust him even if you pay him. We're going to have to watch our step. Ernest. At the next stop make yourself invisible.'

I nodded vigorously.

As we came from the hills into lower undulating farmland, the sun replaced the rain, and the green of the maturing spring was that brilliant, fresh, light green colour yet to darken with the seasons ahead. In the hedgerows, patches of yellows and blues vied for attention against reds and purples; wild flowers set against the rich long grass, hawthorn and beech. My eyes were full of this beauty as the truck was driven hard through the countryside. Small hamlets and villages swept by as my companions talked about their chances in the card game which was the cause of all their haste. Toward midday, we arrived at a large lay-by where a number of trucks were already parked next to a large field of early growing wheat. A couple of tables had been laid out, and the obsessional Hungarian game of *Ulti* was already in progress. Their fellow truckers looked up and greeted them loudly, with raucous comments and gruff card-playing laughter. It wasn't long before Imre and Bela placed their substantial backsides on packing cases and had picked up a hand each.

Under strict instructions to stay out of sight, this I did, and in the bright heat of midday, snoozed. Then it came to wanting to pee. Looking out on the game, it had reached an intense stage with all heads turned toward the tables. I went to leave the truck when one of the lorries started up and pulled out. I ducked back in the cab. As it went by it sounded its horn; the players looked up and waved, then returned to their game. I tried again, leaving the truck through the door out-of-sight of the players. I slipped through the hedge and into the field further down for my pee. Finished, I started back through the hedge just as a police car pulled into the lay-by.

The two officers stepped out of their car and walked up to the card game.

The senior spoke: 'Okay, which of you lot is giving a lift to a jewboy.'

There was general protestation that anybody present would be that stupid. From the hedge hideaway, I saw Bela give Imre a concerned look as the police worked their way down the trucks, checking the cabs and interiors. They reached our truck, gave it the once-over, and moved on. Bela caught sight of me and gestured me back into the hedge. When the police were out of sight, I nipped into the back of the truck with the packing cases and ducked down out of the way. In the interior dimness, I heard the sound of conversation slightly out of range. It was tantalizing to take a peek, but I held back. I heard the police car take its leave. Everyone returned to their card game as though nothing had happened. When I could, I returned to the cab and hunkered down waiting for my chauffeurs. It was exciting to be wanted and on the run.

Eventually they returned to the cab, Imre taking the passenger seat, Bela the driver's.

Imre: 'Well, this is turning into quite a day.'

Bela crashed the gears, and the truck lurched into action.

'With a bit of luck and fair weather, we should make Budapest back of five. Alright by you Mr Lowy?'

'Yes. Thank you.'

Imre strained round to look at me: 'That's what I like about Jewish kids. Well brought up. You've been a bit of a good luck charm, sunshine. First there was the little bonus from your good uncle, now this.'

He held up a wad of notes from the game. The two men chuckled to themselves.

'Congratulations.' I smiled.

Imre opened a lunchbox, cut off a large slice of sausage, and offered it to me: 'Have some grub, you must be ravenous.'

I was, but I had to refuse his offer.

'Why not? It's obvious you're hungry, your mouth's watering'

'I cannot, under Jewish law. The sausage is not kosher, not fit for eating.'

'Are you insulting my wife, that she is giving me poison, maybe the butcher who sells suspect meat?'

Bela: 'The kid's maybe got a point there.'

Me: 'No, please, no offence. The meat is pork. We are not allowed pork. It also contains blood. We are forbidden any blood.'

Imre: 'You know these things, eh? Right then. How is it

50

that you Jews are supposed to use the blood of good Christian children in the baking of Passover matzos? You're a bright lad, how about that then?'

Bela: 'Stop winding the kid up.'

Me: 'Do you believe it?'

Imre: 'Me, I don't know. The people in my village say so, they seem to be certain. Knowing you, and your uncle's family, I don't want to believe it. You're a smart little Israelite, I was hoping you'd enlighten me.'

Me: 'The Torah, the Bible, tells us, it is Mosaic Law, the law of Moses, not to eat blood, any blood. Even chickens, the last drop of blood has to be removed before they are prepared for eating. Eggs, even if there is a tiny speck of blood in one, it has to be thrown away.'

Imre: 'Waste of good food.'

Bela: 'I like mine boiled, you wouldn't know.'

Me: 'So, if this is our belief, only an idiot would think we drank the blood of children, even Christians.'

They both turned round at this. A moment's silence, then as they turned back to face the road, they burst into fits of laughter.

'You're a cheeky little bugger,' Imre managed between chuckles.

The truck rumbled on through the countryside, with traffic increasing and more road signs pointing their way to Budapest. The cab of the truck had become hot in spite of open windows. The smell of hot leather and fuel are forever fixed in my memory, along with the thick necks and shaved heads of my two peasant chauffeurs, who, I learned from our journey, were cousins. They had pooled their resources to buy the truck, had contracted themselves out to people like my uncle. Their swarthy faces, wind-tanned, well-fed and jolly, dispelled the menace of our conversations about Jews. I felt no danger with them. Bela was whistling. Imre turned round again.

'What about circumcision?'

I looked up.

'What about it?'

Imre: 'If you're as smart as we think you might be, explain it. Why cut your dick?'

Me: 'According to our rabbi in Bratislava, it was like the final touch of creation. From the moment of circumcision, we are in a covenant with God, in partnership with his total creation.'

More laughter.

Imre: 'Crazy Jews, no wonder everyone hates you. In partnership with God, eh, and you people look after the cash. Is that the deal?'

Bela: 'It's a good thing women don't have dicks; they'd have God in knots and the world would turn pink and pale blue.'

At this we all laughed.

Bela then asked: 'Ernest, lad, you're pleasant enough, but why do you think everyone hates Jews?'

Me: 'I'm not sure everyone does, but those who do are probably envious because we claim to be a people chosen by God for a specific destiny, and according to my mother, favouritism always creates hostility.'

Imre: 'You're a smart kid. Mind your step in Budapest. Watch your mouth. Savvy? By the way. Who won the Jewish Beauty contest?'

Me: 'Okay, I give up; who did?'

Imre: 'No one.'

Imre and Bela roared with laughter. Me, I thought of Kato and Medy, and smiled to myself at how wrong they were.

By the time we entered Budapest, we were singing at the tops of our voices, songs we mutually knew. I was to be picked up. The rendezvous, the pick-up point for me, was a large hospital building on the outskirts. Our little world had ended; my farewells to Imre and Bela were abrupt and formal. We all became aware again that I was not a pal, but illegal cargo.

I had barely touched the pavement before the truck was off into the heavy traffic. As I took in my surroundings, home-bound people milled round me like a human river. The city was about to claim me back.

4 Greta

As I mounted the hospital steps, I caught sight of the truck as it headed into the city, and thought back on an eventful day. Fulek seemed a long way off and in a different dimension, as if the journey, along with the present moment, had expunged months of daily experience. This was Budapest. I breathed it in, a love affair had resumed. I waited an hour, no relative appeared. Evening was drawing in and the eyes of a passing policeman were on me. I felt uneasy about staying. I had no idea how to reach the family, but knew the whereabouts of the Jewish quarter, if I could only figure out how to get there. I stopped a female passer-by who rather impatiently gave me directions; she didn't seem that certain of her lefts and rights. I was grateful and gave her a winning smile which was returned, sort of, with a tight little grimace.

I set off through the crowds heading home. A boy alone and anonymous in the big city. It felt vast with its terraces of houses, shop fronts, noisy traffic, motor cars versus horse-drawn carts versus trams and bicycles. No matter how wide the cobbled thoroughfare, there was traffic to fill it. People crossed over, round it and through it. It was fascinating. What is more, they were all dressed as if going to a wedding, except the Hungarian soldiers and the gendarmes, who were much more in evidence than before, particularly the gendarmes in their feathered hats and show-it-off strut. I walked along the Fiumei road, which led into the busy Baros Place where stood the main station for the city, with its beautiful front facade dominating the area surrounding it. All those taxis fighting for space.

It was at this point, I later learned, that I should have gone left to walk along the famous Rakoczi road, an arterial route into the city centre, instead of which I went right. As I progressed, the quality of the structures surrounding me began to deteriorate, became tired-looking, peeling, neglected. There were little groups of men standing on corners, or leaning listlessly near drinking parlours which seemed very active as the daylight declined. What is more, the street needed a sweep and wash down; I was going the wrong way, but my curiosity took me further along it. The evening crowds were suddenly gone and I was virtually alone. In front of me on either side of the street were, standing or parading, brightly dressed young women and girls, each in their bit of road space, eyeing passers-by for trade. I had blundered into the red-light area. I could hear music from a bar. There were more women calling to each other from opened windows. I blushed deeply when I realized one or two of the street girls were calling me out. I passed a couple of youngsters who couldn't have been much older than me:

'Well now, what have we here?' grinned one of them.

The other girl laughed. I had paused to answer, and she ran her fingers through my hair.

'Very fanciable. Nice bit of cradle-snatching.'

I was hungry, they were friendly. In hope I rubbed my stomach and said 'food' in my best Hungarian.

'No food here, love, sorry.'

A tall blonde woman strode over.

'Problem?'

'Just another hungry kid. This one's Jewish by the looks of him.'

'Well, don't tease him. You hungry then, laddo?'

'I haven't eaten all day.'

'Wrong time for fasting. Come with me.'

I was being a chancer. Maybe she liked my cheek, who knew? She took my hand, led me from the girls and down a lane away from the street lights, in through a large shabby yellow door, up some stairs into an apartment – spare, neatly kept, ready for custom with its red lamps aglow – winding up in the kitchen, warm and gas-lit, where a mixture of cooked apples, baked potatoes and coffee sent my senses reeling.

'Sit you down. What's your name?'

'Ernest.'

'Greta. How do you do?'

We shook hands, and my bottom found a kitchen chair. In seconds my hand was holding a huge chunk of bread with a dollop of butter and apricot jam, soon to be wolfed down. A large mug of coffee appeared on the long bare wood table in front of me.

'Eat, little man. I'll be back in a minute.'

She disappeared into a nearby room from which stepped a girl who, without her make-up would be very young indeed, a child. The heels were high, the legs bare. The skirt, short, silk, split-sided, betraying no underwear. The blouse; low-cut, no brassiere, tiny breasts. She ambled over to the stove, a black-and-white cat purring around her ankles. She acknowledged me on her way across the kitchen, the cat diverting to my legs, quickly losing interest when my hand did not reach down to stroke it. The young girl attended to the stove. Over her shoulder:

'Haven't seen you around here before.'

'I'm just here from the country, today.'

'Where from?'

'Fulek. In the north.'

She brought a bowl of soup to the table and sat beside me. She smelled wonderful, like lime and candyfloss. I couldn't help it, my eyes travelled around her body which, amused, she encouraged by moving it to reveal more of herself, to pleasure me. Even the gold cross delicately placed about her long neck proved no deterrent.

'Heard of it. What are the girls like there?'

'Same as anywhere, I guess?'

'I take it you haven't tried any yet.'

I blushed to the roots which made her chuckle. She persisted.

'Any like me?'

She was now very close, the soup momentarily forgotten by her, the remains of the bread by me. Our eyes burned into each other. I felt the rush forward of the adulthood denied me in Fulek, brought on by an experienced child in Budapest. She whispered sweetly into my ear: 'Want to try me?'

She sat back, shook her straw-coloured curls and laughed a light, husky, streetwise response to my desire and my discomfort. Her power would be her meal ticket and her survival in the years ahead, disease permitting. I tried to cover my embarrassment with the coffee mug, quickly emptied.

Blonde Greta returned to the kitchen, heavy with perfume.

'Put him down Angel, there's no money in his pockets, pretty as he is.'

Angel pouted and laughed to the room.

'Come by when you've earned some wages. I could be good for you.'

Oh, I believed her. Those bare legs made my entire being tingle. Greta grabbed my free hand and led me from the kitchen. Angel returned to her soup, looked up and waved 'bye'. Greta led me down the stairs to the doorway.

'Sorry to give you the "bum's rush", Ernest, but we've got customers coming soon.'

As we parted company, she slipped five coins into my hand. I was so grateful, I went to kiss her hand. She withdrew it.

'Don't be silly, consider it a loan. Now, listen up, young man. Find your way back to the railway station and catch a 44 tram which will take you to the museum ring road. Get off there and ask. The Jewish quarter is a ten-minute walk.'

She gave me a little push and I was back out in the lane, now dark, with the girls nearby a little more occupied; night-time action felt as though it was about to make a start. I looked around, the yellow door had shut, locking me out of the little seductive world of Greta and Angel. I retraced my steps, smiling at the girls as they called me out. I didn't know it then, but for two years, as an apprentice, I would run a daily message for my boss that would take me through the red-light district, and I would become friendly with the ladies, on first name terms with a few. I would come to feel adopted by them.

Illes, my manager, was a bit of a mother's boy whose doting parent would make lunch for him, which, being the junior, I would collect. She was okay, Illes's mother, not that generous with her handouts, but when one was given, it was very tasty, tending to take away the drudgery of the walk, as did catching sight of Greta or Angel, or backchatting the other girls.

With the family pretty much reunited in Budapest and moved to a larger apartment, our circumstances affected a settled air. Of course, the mounting troubles between European states and kingdoms, with the swelling of the poison bag that Germany had become under a bunch of criminals, made for a permanent sense of impending doom, just out of reach but within range of one's heart and one's nostrils, as the armies they commanded set their jaws and crossed borders. We, the Jews, would always be high on their hit list. Some of us wisely took off for America, Palestine, Britain, anywhere where the 'little corporal' was unlikely to stamp his tiny foot. We boys were in thrall to our father, whose otherworldly orthodoxy kept us in prayer for a decent outcome to the troubles, and kept us in Budapest, hoping somehow it would pass by on the other side of our lives. Brother Karl saw it coming, and this had a galvanizing effect on family table discussions. Father had taken on an agency dealing in ladies' handbags, and a bit later on, a second agency selling sheets and towels. At the synagogue he became a part-time cantor, something he had loved to do in Bratislava. When I asked him for a small shoulder bag that took my eye, he gave me a quizzical look but never did ask why I wanted it, who it was for; just wrapped it up, and handed it to me.

It was for Greta. For nearly two years we had formed a friendship of passing conversations and happy waves. As yet I hadn't returned the favour of our first encounter, and here it was, Christmas, 1941. Sixteen and less embarrassed, I carried that bag daily for a week or two, never catching sight of her, not daring to knock on the yellow door in case she or Angel were occupied. Then one day, I passed down the lane in time to see an ambulance outside the yellow door and Greta, looking very pale and drawn, was being assisted by a couple of nurses back into her hallway. Still beautiful, something had gone wrong. The usually carefully prepared hair hung loosely about her shoulders. She glanced my way and I tactfully pretended not to see her. That winter, circumstances took me away from that quarter of Budapest. When next I made my way through the area, the yellow door had been repainted. All change, I guessed. The shoulder bag went to a cousin.

I encountered her again, by chance, one Sunday morning as I was going in to the Abbazia coffee house, a Budapest haunt; she was coming out. I knew her straight away. In two years, I had changed; still in my teens, but no longer the fresh-faced child she had so sweetly helped.

'Greta?'

She looked at me smiling her question.

'Ernest? Dear God. Quite the young man, and taller. I was on my way, but a girl can change her mind for a handsome young man, eh?'

She hooked her arm in mine and we found a table for two on the pavement where we could sip our coffee and have a quiet chat. The tranquillity of that spring morning in Budapest, with the freshly watered streets glistening in the sunshine, the air filled with the scent of acacia trees, would make the most miserable person smile and be glad to be alive; but it was 1943. I had the downcast air of a bothered 18-year-old. She was concerned. The pleasantries over, she broke into my little cloud of gloom.

'Trouble?'

There was an elegant authority about her that brooked no refusal. I wasn't about to lie.

'The worst.'

'Can I help?'

I received the very look that greeted me that hungry evening in the red-light district years before.

'My brothers Max and Karl have been taken to labour camps, along with most of the men in our neighbourhood.'

Her face darkened.

'Since 1933 they have hacked away at Jews. I heard many of you were being transported away for 'special treatment'. I feel so helpless. There's no organization to lend a hand, and I watch my countrymen primp and parade in Ruritanian uniforms, sounding off about the Jews. Gendarmes indeed. Stuffed shirts with a problem down below.'

I laughed momentarily, then quickly looked round in case we were overheard.

'Don't fret darling, you're among friends.'

The irony was overwhelming. The other tables on the pavement were unoccupied. It was early, after all.

'You know what gets me, Ernest, is how, no matter whether these clods are German, Hungarian or whatever, they all have this air of something wrong with them. Wearing a uniform only makes it worse. Makes it more obvious. Look at Hitler. He's inadequate. Genius, my fanny. Tell you what. Any whore worth her trick could spot a freak like him a mile off. Then she'd take him for a packet, better yet tell him to piss off back to his mummy.'

By this time, my smile was a mile wide. How she brightened my day by allowing the truth about the weak underbelly of fascism to be exposed to the morning air and my receptive heart. It didn't relieve the damage or the hurt we were all experiencing, but her remarks stripped away the fearsome mask to reveal the hopeless little clown that resided in the soul of each Nazi; just a moment of calm amusement before the reality that Nazism had imposed on the world re-asserted itself.

'It makes me so mad. Jews are industrious and talented. By and large, they produce, they don't waste. I've met bad, but bad is no-one's monopoly. Fascists get rid of the good example, then they don't have to go through the hard work of making changes in themselves. Which brings things round to me. Ask me what's new in my life … go on.'

I was apologetic and asked.

'… well, I'm married.'

I must have looked shocked. She laughed, a musical sound with a vulgar undertow.

'Don't worry, Ernest, I've shut up shop. He knows about the past and it doesn't matter. We are in love.'

She kissed the air. I was pleased for her, more than that, but I didn't have a word. So I gave her a silly smile and said, '*Mozeltov*. May your life together be long and happy.'

'We've got plans in that direction.'

'What's his name?'

'Kalman. He's centuries older than me, but he looks good on what he drinks.'

'What does he do?'

'Retired postman. He has a pension and is in great demand as a gardener around the big houses. We make out, Ernest. We make out just fine.'

'How did you meet?'

'Two years ago, I was hospitalized with abdominal problems. Do you know, when I came home in an ambulance, I could swear I saw you in the lane. It was you wasn't it?'

I blushed and nodded. She smiled and went on with her story.

'His sister was in the bed next to mine in the hospital. Occasionally we'd talk across at visiting time, that is when Angel, Marie and the others weren't causing mayhem round my bed. They would make me laugh deliberately, to hurt my stitches ... cows.'

'How is Angel?'

'Fine. Proud mother of a year-old boy. Living with the young father. Three children in one household. One small problem, he's joined the gendarmes. I've told him not to be so stupid, but he wants to belong and she likes the uniform. I've told them they must leave all that at home if they come by to our place. He will for her.'

She lit a cigarette and waved for more coffee.

'After a number of visits over a few weeks, and him sitting with his sister, I can feel a tension developing in Kalman about me. You can tell, know what I mean? Anyway, One day, she's snoozing and he's sitting like a spare whatsit and he turns to me, his eyes filled with tears as he takes hold of my hand and kisses it. Ernest, his voice was quivering with passion, or terror, then he says that he's had nothing but me on his mind since the day he first laid eyes on me. Imagine, a wreck in a hospital bed, and he fancies me. More, he tells me he wants to spend the rest of his days with me. He's a sweet man, a widower. Cut a long story short, in four weeks we were married. There, what do you think about that then?'

The coffees came, the morning began to warm, a few people had taken pavement tables. Intermittent Sunday traffic provided movement. Across the city, church bells rang out. I looked across at my friend, the elegant beauty with such unpretentious desires in life and holding an open door to Truth, and I realized a whole number of religious truths at once, none of which I could communicate without seeming pompous or simply 'out of order'. I let it rest with a little silent clap of the hands and a kiss blown to her across the table. She continued her story.

'That's nearly two years ago. Now, we have a nice little home in Upjest. I'm not exaggerating when I tell you that every day I share with him is sheer happiness. I want you to meet the best man in the world, Ernest. He's such a good, kind man, and he's mine. He treats me with untiring tenderness and love.'

I looked across at Greta and realized that I had been looking at her through the old red light. This was another being entirely, one liberated from the shadows of that world to bask in the rays of discovered human affection, away from use and abuse. We later parted in bright sunlight, with an embrace and a promise to get together so I could meet her paragon. Thanks to Hitler, it was not to be. Until 1946.

1946, a year of recovery. Back in Budapest, I went into partnership with a man older than myself, a skilled toolmaker, Frank Matushka. We had set up a workshop to produce fountain pens and propelling pencils. One day, in a break, I was talking with his wife, Libby, a corpulent woman with small features, a very quiet voice and a sweet demeanour; she was good company. Our talk strayed back to the war, as talk did so much in those early days, and we got to those people we knew who had risked their safety and their lives to help Jewish people to either escape or hide. Resistance in any shape or form was brave, but we both agreed there was a singular courage in helping fugitives.

'There was a couple, neighbours of ours, who did just that. I admired them so much. They sheltered a couple of Jewish boys back in '44. Kalman, retired postman and his wife Greta, tall blonde woman. She was younger than ...'

My heart leapt. I interrupted Libby.

'You and Frank lived in Upjest?'

'For a while. You know Kalman and Greta?'

'Greta, from way back. She once bailed me out when I was a boy. So she's still at it. Are they still there?'

'No they have a place in Tororkbalint. I have the address somewhere. You want it?'

I nodded vigorously.

'Tell me about the two boys.'

'A touch melodramatic, but then wasn't all of it? A cold December night, according to Greta. A knock on the door and the old girl from opposite was standing in the porch holding the hands of these two little boys, tearful for their mum and very frightened. The old lady had seen what had happened. Their mother had been beaten up by Nazis as she and the boys were leaving the Jewish quarter. The mother was dragged away, leaving the two boys standing, staring. Greta and Kalman took them in and sheltered them through the worst of the Arrowcross outrages, right up until their mother – who like you survived Auschwitz and Belsen – was re-united with them after the war. That was such a moment ...'

Libby Matushka had tears in her eyes recollecting. Me too, thinking on how Greta's loving spirit continued to raise my sights. The next weekend, before setting off on my motorbike for Tororkbalint, I went downtown and bought a good-quality leather shoulder-bag for someone special.

Tororkbalint and the countryside around is famous in Hungary for its fruit orchards and beautiful surroundings, so the ride there was in itself a treat for city eyes. I found their cottage nestling down a lane surrounded by fruit trees. Neighbouring them a little way up a hill covered with raspberry canes was a small city of greenhouses, a thriving horticultural concern.

There was a moment of uncertainty when she opened the door to my knock. She, because time had matured me; me because the blonde had gone and silver was taking over from her real colour which, though light, was never the Harlow shade she used to celebrate. The 'hello hug' went on long enough to bring Kalman to the door also.

'Kalman. This is Ernest. Budapest Ernest.'

A head of pure silver, a big frame, a large, even-toothed, handsome smile and a hand that smothered my paw, but chose not to crush it out of existence. Here was trust and safety invested in one human body.

'You are very welcome to our house. Come, come.'

Hand-in-hand, they led me into the heart of their home. I handed Greta her gift, reminding her I'd never repaid my debt. She was entranced, and I was duly hugged. We chatted away an hour or so, before sitting with drinks and light food in their heavily scented flower garden. The low drone of bees, the lack of wind and the gentle wine made my mind and body easier than it had been for a while. For a good while the conversation centred around me. How did I survive the camps? What was it like? Who in my family lived on? Angel was now a young widow. They spoke of anything but themselves, their reticence was charming, but frustrating. Eventually:

'What about you?'

'Oh very little really. Kalman continues to garden; has an interest in the market garden up the hill there. We're tucked up nicely for … ever. It's wonderful.'

Kalman laughed: 'She never stops. She has a finger in every local pie. Virtually runs the village. We were supposed to be out of it for a quiet life. Fat chance.'

Me: 'I hear you left Upjest with an heroic reputation.'

63

They both looked at me, a synchronized, almost wide-eyed, and questioning look.

Greta: 'What did Libby tell you?'

'Everything. The two small boys. Everything.'

There was a silence that seemed to hang in the air. They were embarrassed.

Kalman: 'It wasn't easy. A lot of the time we weren't sure whether someone would betray us. When Angel and Peter came by, we had to hide the boys, or lock them in their room with strict orders to stay quiet. Neighbours by and large were in sympathy. For the rest, it was ducking the attentions of the Arrowcross. Bastards.'

As we walked around their beautiful garden, they walked hand-in-hand. Greta took my arm.

'The hardest part was saying goodbye to them. Their mother had called them Franz and Joseph, can you imagine? That made us crack up for a start and the boys were puzzled by the giggles. Of course we couldn't tell them, but they would laugh along anyway. They were our little sons, Ernest, we loved them so much. It was so sweet the day their mother came to take them back. For us …'

She broke off in tears. Kalman's arm went round her.

'I'm so sorry Ernest, I'm being so stupid.'

The afternoon sun shone on the three of us in that gorgeous garden, on the pair who had each other in an eternal embrace of deepest affection and love, and the young man still learning about living.

Though I had promised to call on them sooner, it wasn't until 1958 that I visited the cottage again. Time, tide, love affairs, political orthodoxy versus religious orthodoxy in my brain and in day-to-day life, the Hungarian rejection of the Russians and the ensuing blood letting, all conspired to keep me away. I had acquired a place in a neighbourhood just outside Budapest, Szentendre, Leanyfalu. I needed fruit trees for the garden. Where else but the little market garden at Tororkbalint?

It was early in the year, and though blossom was showing,

there was a cold edge to the wind, so I had to wear leathers on the motorbike. There were intermittent showers and bright sun, but the day hadn't warmed yet. With the blossom in full bloom, the roads and lanes were a riot of ravishing pastels. Before going up to the market garden, I called at the cottage. Greta was there. She opened the door, saw me and drew me to her. The embrace was not one of excitement or pleasure, more a hold against a gale or a flood.

'He's gone, Ernest.'

'How?'

'Russian sniper in Budapest, in '56.'

'Why didn't you write or call?'

'To say what? I knew at some point you'd be round to see me. You wouldn't have wanted to see the mess I was for a solid year. How are you anyway? You look good. Except for those leathers; you look like Brando gone wrong. Much better in a suit, my lad.'

'Not much good on a motor bike.'

'Buy a car. You're in your thirties for God's sake.'

Five minutes and she was taking me over. I watched her as she moved around, getting me coffee and a bite. Still holding herself erect, her loss had aged her. The hair, now short, was pure silver, and her hands, like her neck, were showing the tell-tale signs of encroaching age, which on her would merely add to the grace she could not hide. She called loudly: 'Coffee up. Make sure you're decent, we've got company.'

A teenager tumbled down the stairs.

'Eva. Meet Ernest, the original Wandering Jew. Treats me outrageously. Comes to see me once in a blue moon, but I love him just the same.'

I held out my hand to shake hers, but she raised her hand in a half-wave and said 'Hi' in English.

'Kalman's granddaughter by his first marriage. Here to keep her step-relative from cutting her own throat, oh, and to give me something to do at three in the morning, chucking out spotty youths.'

65

'I'm studying horticulture. Got a job at the market garden. Granddad's fault.'

So my Greta was not alone. This young girl, with her fresh face and modern airs would mend her broken wings. Though Greta's eyes showed the measure of earlier suffering, there was plenty of the old sparkle to brighten a day.

The three of us sat and talked animatedly about everything at once. Kalman came into the conversation here and there, and one could feel the man's influence in the very air. I must have let something slip along the way. Maybe it was my desire to renew my faith, become a cantor, maybe talking about Israel and Britain, whatever; when it was time to leave Greta became quite emotional.

I said my goodbyes to Eva, who this time kissed me on both cheeks. As Greta walked me to the front gate, she quipped:

'Eva likes you. She wouldn't do that to just anybody. You made an impression.'

She took my arm and slowly we ambled to the gate and my waiting motorbike. Far from matronly, Greta would certainly enjoy her autumn years. Reaching the gate, I went to give her a parting kiss only to have her take my face in her hands, her eyes full of tears, yet smiling, as he said:

'I'm so glad we met Ernest.'

'And we'll keep on doing so.'

'I hope so. I hope so. Whatever you do with your life, I'm sure you'll shine. God bless.'

It seemed so final. As I revved the bike and moved off up the hill to the market garden, I gave her a final wave, which was returned with a kiss blown to the wind. Turning back to the road ahead, I found myself riding up a gently inclined avenue of pastel pink cherry blossom, capped above by a pale blue sky. I thought back to Bela's comment about women as he and Imre joked with me on the road to Budapest, and I smiled to imagine God in knots.

5 Work

By 1939, the family had at last gathered together again under one roof, in a large single room on the fifth floor of a Budapest apartment block. Though we were somewhat cramped, and in spite of being under increasing political and social siege, a measure of our personal concerns and worry had evaporated. Karl had healed, and I had Munky back. Else had sent him on, but she was happy to stay with the love of her life, Bernat, in Dunajszka Streda and prepare for married life.

With almost everything left and lost in Bratislava, we had to begin again. We had our various talents, more, we had each other, with the family bond holding firm. A Budapest winter can be hard. We needed warm clothing along with essentials, but our money just didn't seem to stretch. The war was under way. Propaganda against Jews, in its brutal untruth, had risen beyond its earlier absurdities. Good opinion in Hungary was being whittled away by the constant stream of German-influenced invective that filled newspaper pages and many radio broadcasts from home and abroad. Father's shoulder played up; it had never been right since the bruising attack by the youth of Bratislava. This didn't stop his work drive and because the agency he had taken up that traded in ladies' handbags wasn't by itself making ends meet, he took on another selling sheets and towels, to retail outlets across the city, thankfully many of them Jewish.

He had kept his promise to find me work so I started my working life proper at a light engineering workshop in another of Budapest's red-light districts, where we produced brass pipes which were then stored at the city's gasworks for ongoing use. The workshop was in a basement, and from my workbench, I had a grandstand view through a street-level window, of legs, high-heeled shoes and silk stockings. I played the game of trying to match the legs seen with faces known. If a liaison took place outside the window, I tried to guess the wealth or otherwise of the customer from the trouser cuffs and footwear. It broke the monotony. As the apprentice, I had to open the place each morning, and after the day's work, sweep the floor. It was essential to gather up every filing or chip of brass so that it could be recycled for future use. The work proved too much for a slightly built 14-year-old, whose winter clothing wasn't equal to much, and whose strength really wasn't up to the demands of the excessively long day. Inevitably, all this and the rigours of a wartime diet caused my health to suffer.

After eight months of it, and the family recognizing my condition, Father found me a different apprenticeship in a fountain-pen workshop run by a man from the local synagogue, Mr Scher. This job I liked and I took to it, showed skill and gained recognition for design. There was an element of good taste involved, which could not be said for brass pipes. Our task was to develop the whole pen, cellular tubes, gold inlays, everything except the nib. It was a small outfit with only three employees, so I had room to breathe and develop. The pay was three *pengo*, which was good, very good, making my contribution to the household a major one. For one *pengo* we found we could feed the whole family with take-outs from the local kosher restaurant; with no kitchen, cooked food simply had to come from there.

Munky had long hours too, considering his age. He had to work hard, labouring from early morning to quite late in the day, standing by dusty machines in a large knitwear factory on the outskirts of Budapest. All day breathing in fibres, then a long walk home; sometimes a tram in the rain. When he wasn't at the yeshiva, he would teach English and French around the town. Max too made a living teaching English, while Fritz gained work in a bank. Karl pursued his cantorial aspirations. Money was saved from all this effort, consequently stage by stage we found our feet and our dignity, making a move (the second in a progression) to a new, larger and better-appointed apartment on the ring road. These places were rented and barely adequate to our needs. The final move was in 1943, and the space allowed Max, Munky and I to share a room with a view – the Danube.

During 1941 I fell ill. The prolonged period of poor eating and the tensions involved in just existing and surviving day to day in a hostile environment had begun to tell. This wasn't helped by one of the tasks I had in the working week, which was to collect money for Mr Scher owed by his customers. A German speaker from childhood, my Hungarian was far from brilliant. Often the customers were Gentile and didn't hold back on the kind of abuse, presently fashionable, that Jews would come to expect the moment a request or demand was made. A repetitive series of foul clichés lifted from poster or page, or pure street bile. Such moments were unavoidable and made my body as tense as taut wire. Returning without the customer's payment would mean further abuse from Mr Scher. Though never happy, his never held the deep threat that hatred can conjure. Bad enough though for a lad of fifteen going on sixteen.

My immediate superior in the workshop was one Ilyes Lajos who, in spite of having a Jewish boss, showed his fascist credentials by feeding me a daily dose of anti-Semitic invective, along with libidinous tales of conquest that had the clang of exaggeration, and which often involved him leaning over me at my desk making his boasts on how the night before had gone for him with the latest conquest. Truth to tell, his 'conquests' must all have been impervious to halitosis; my ability to prevent myself retching improved dramatically as a result of our loathsome intimacy. Strangely enough, he grew to like me. As time passed, he trusted me with little odd jobs, one of which was to bring his lunch for him daily from his mother who lived close by the main railway station. To reach her, I had to go through the red-light area where Greta and Angel worked. Sometimes I saw them to speak to. I also became on good calling terms with the other street girls. For a period each day I was in the open, which was pleasing. Ilyes' mother made beautiful sandwiches. The first day that I collected them, I checked, though not once did I steal any; I was too scared of him.

Mrs Scher had noticed that for periods in the day I had to 'down tools' while my stomach cramped up. Kindly, she insisted that I see her doctor, who diagnosed stomach ulcers which, though treatable, would need careful dieting and more rest than I was getting. I would try. Ilyes was at his bragging worst on Mondays, leaving in his wake a trail of deflowered virgins. It aroused in me held-back desires, repressed and lost to view, now prompted by his vulgar mouthings. They were surfacing like a school of dolphins to dance and play on the surface of my imaginings. Somehow, my thoughts always turned to Medy who had, in her absence, assumed the role of goddess. Ilyes' intention was to make me blush, which often he did, but unknowingly, he had pushed open the door to my maturity. I knew his lie from my truth. Would I ever see her again?

With careful treatment, the ulcers were held at bay, though their principal cause, the daily intake of Nazi sulphur and general wartime worries, led them a merry dance. Ilyes had not softened in his invective, but for me he was making an exception. I assumed that, come the day of reckoning, Mr and Mrs Scher – maybe myself too – would be given a special dispensation, courtesy of Ilyes and his pal Adolf. Who knew? The thought made Munky laugh quietly when I made the observation in our darkened room, just before sleep.

Medy. My wishes nearly became reality. Nearly. One Saturday morning in the spring of 1942, Father, Munky and I were standing in the square outside the Dohany synagogue, enjoying the usual post-service chat with other members of the congregation. As we emerged from the doorway the bright sunlight was dazzling. It took a moment or two to adjust, by which time I had noticed a group of young girls standing in a group talking and laughing. I kept looking over while our group chatted away. I was sure it was her, standing among them. Taller, wearing a hat, looking even more beautiful than in my memories. She glanced across and our eyes met. Her body gave a slight jolt as she realized I was standing there.

Her smile was for me, and I was responding when Leopold caught the moment, and, being strictly formal inside his orthodoxy – especially on the Shabbat – grabbed me and with conversations abruptly at an end, we parted company from the group from which I swear I heard indulgent laughter. I had no time to explain as I was herded by my parent along the street. What did he know of the free adult within? He knew the kid. Munky wasn't much help either, with his usual straight-faced tease about my wandering eyes, how this was an offence, why wasn't I ashamed? With my father concurring, I had to wait a few dozen metres before I let loose the lie that I had left my gloves in the synagogue. Before question or argument, I was haring back to the square, where the groups were still enjoying the spring sunshine. The girls had gone. I stood alone and bereft for a moment, before chasing around in several directions to maybe catch sight of my lost love. For weeks I just attended Dohany, but not once did she return. My anger at losing her became sorrow, became a moodiness; then she settled back in my memory, a phantom of pleasure.

But for others, love was truly in the air. Else, Hedwig and Lillie. Else's wedding found us back at Dunajszka Streda, and though the day found Hedwig in tears, still mourning the death of her fiancé, her smiles a little later, along with our rejoicing, were heartfelt. We all agreed Bernat was just the man for our beloved Else. A short while later, Hedwig met Tibor at the public swimming pool. Love at first sight, she was enthusiastically welcomed into his family, and in the first year of marriage, a child. Leopold loved his daughters, was ecstatic that Else and Hedwig had found happiness, but Lillie remained a thorn in his side.

She had not been mellowed by our recent experiences, and, if anything, showed even more rebellion. When she met and became engaged to her Andre, Father was incandescent.

71

Andre's work was in the shadows of commerce; an 'importer-exporter' was the euphemistic term used when discussing what he did around Budapest. A *Macher*, a fixer, he was obviously a survivor, an attractive smoothie, perfect fodder for Leopold's disapproval. He had more time for Tibor who was, in Leopold's view, a worthy being, a family man who, in spite of his limp, showed strength. A real *Mensch*, a good man for Hedwig. Lillie's Andre would, however, in the days ahead, prove his worth. My sister was anything but stupid; she knew her man, even if Father couldn't see it.

My mother, as with my sisters, had on her arrival in the city set about forging links with relatives and contacts, cementing a network of social connections within the community that would provide a good foundation for the few years we were together in Budapest. While the men worked, and studied within the faith, the women extended the network, one that would survive the war, badly torn, but firm. This gave rise to the hope that a community thus bonded through hearth and synagogue would weather the storm brought about by a group of viciously dysfunctional psychopaths in Germany who were lauded to the skies by the disaffected, the poor, the downright crooked and those out to take rather than make. For Leopold, through his muslin veil of optimism and trust in the coming Messiah, like many in the orthodox faith, he could see the day a-coming when the wrath of God would clear the path to the promised land. The rise of Nazism in Europe was proof positive. The opposition in the last days would crumble into dust under the feet of the Coming One. The spectre of the swastika was the illusion to be annihilated by the brilliant reality of God's love for his chosen people. Enough said. We went about our business, short on food and essentials, but sustained by each other, the community and the faith.

There was no disputing the oppression we were under, merely what the outcome would be. Many decided not to hang around to find out, and left Europe. This was becoming less and less possible as the world war proceeded, indeed, along with the Hungarian citizenry, the men and younger women of the Jewish community were called up for war work. Technically, we boys were now trainees in the military, under orders to turn up for a training programme geared, tailor-made, to subject 'The Jew' to the toughest of regimes. Brutal. Yet, in the midst of work-for-survival, 'military' training and hostility in the streets, Leopold had Munky and I attending the local yeshiva with devoted regularity for Talmudic study and Hebrew. Three hours at a stretch each evening, except when Hungary called and Father had to step back.

Apart from this conscription among the young, many men were taken to forced labour camps. At times, they were allowed back, then as time progressed, this occurred less and less, until little if anything was heard from them. From around 1941 this had gone on, depleting the community and also leaving relatives in the worst of limbos. By 1944, the sense of impending doom and sudden absences had more than rumours and propaganda to feed on. Street beatings became commonplace, as did the followers of a Hungarian fascist, Ferenc Szalasi, who had brought on to the streets a mutation militia made up of farm boys, bad lads, gendarmes and anyone gullible enough to believe that the Jews and the Niggers were conducting the war against Hungary.

These were the Arrowcross. They wore calf-length boots, olive shirts, beige trousers, bomber jackets or, in the cold, greatcoats. Their 'rig' was topped off with a wide-brimmed hat displaying cockerel feathers. Their armband insignia, to ape the Nazis, was a cross of arrowheads where, at one with the Nazis, a swastika sat. The swastika seemed like a moving object frozen in time that would at length turn, whereas the Arrowcross seemed forever fixed. It represented a particular group of people who had adhered to Szalasi from the late thirties, when they gained a reputation after grenade atrocities at the Great Synagogue. Budapest fascists of several stripes became the main political opposition to President Horthy who, in October 1944, was subjected to a coup by Szalasi, backed up by Hitler who saw Horthy as a vacillator. Admiral Horthy, in spite of increasingly draconian anti-

Semitic legislation and the ruthless deportation of Polish Jews to their fate in the death camps, had been 'loyal' to Hungarian Jewry. In the last days of the war, Hitler needed to step up the killing. With Horthy removed and Eichmann installed to oversee, Szalasi became a de-facto Führer and went about his business of savage persecution and murder. His private army, earlier despised and laughed at as impossible dolts and poseurs, in 1944 had the run of the streets. Only the Russians put a stop to their blood orgy.

By the time the madness was hitting the streets, Munky and I had become official firewatchers; the Russian air raids had started, and even we were called on. After one particularly hair-raising night of playing the hoses on an inferno, we had no time to go home and wash up for Sabbath *shul*. We went covered in dirt and ash, giving off that bitter odour that comes only from yesterday's smoke. In the extremity in which we all found ourselves, nobody quite knew whether to laugh or cry when we made our appearance. Laughter won.

Back in the autumn of 1943, not long after Charles and Max had been sent to a work camp, Father started to frequent a different *shul*. In our turn we two lads took our tuition at the Tiferet Bachurim. When there was spare cash we would take in an opera or concert, a rare and a real treat. Father wanted me to join a choir, partly because he felt my voice needed the practice, and also because there was a measure of payment involved in being a chorister. No-one would touch me as my voice was breaking. The received opinion was that the voice should be rested and not worked until it had changed completely or damage would occur. Although Father continued to disapprove of Zionism, seeing it as a secular and therefore political movement, Munky and I would sometimes sneak off to the Mizrachi *shul*. Munky's interest in Zionism was deepening, leading to a friendship with a young man called Gyuri Morgenstern. Where his interest would take him, I couldn't guess, but for now I was along for the ride, but Gyuri had loosened our brotherly bond.

Father had been taken by the beautiful Yiddish oratory of the rabbi at the Polisher *shul* and, come Saturday, would grab his hat, coat and us to hear this paragon. Munky said to me in jest that we should drag Leopold to the Mizrachi as a quid pro quo. Max had heard the man some time before when the rabbi officiated at a wedding he had attended in the village of Munkacs. Though ultra-orthodox, what he had to say was balm to the spiritual wounds received away from the synagogue. Men destined for the camps would kiss his hands and ask for a blessing before departure. He was a beacon in our darkness. I would get a smile from him when quickly calling in for prayers on my way to work first-thing. His beliefs adhered to the certainty of the imminent arrival of the Messiah, which would return the evil poisoning of the planet to its 'native nothingness'.

On Saturday afternoons his followers would sit with him at table for the third, compulsory meal of the Shabbat. To obtain *Shirajim* – acquiring leftovers from the master's table – was a great merit gained. We, as ordinary mortals were confined to the pews to watch the disciples in action, gaining their crumbs of comfort. It was such a Saturday, nearly at the end of 1943, Father, Munky and myself were in our usual place, when we noticed a strange look on the rabbi's face. He had started to rock backwards and forwards, saying nothing, looking upward. The rocking motion was slow, his demeanour trance-like. Was he communing with the almighty? It seemed to go on, and on. The daylight was fading fast. The synagogue lights were switched on, and still the man did not come out of his state. The congregation, even the devoted with him, had become disturbed and concerned, the time for going home long passed. We continued to sit as muted whispers began. Night had fallen, Shabbat was over. Without warning, the rabbi threw his arms skyward, bellowing, like a wounded beast, a plea to God:

'What are you waiting for? If you do not help us now, it will be too late. Your children are dying at the hands of the Evil One.'

He was in tears, clutching at the empty air above him. His voice rose a panicky octave. In total despair, he continued in an almost incoherent shriek: 'We are losing our trust ... help us believe in you again ... show yourself now ... Have you deserted us? You have deserted us ... We are betrayed ...'

We were all very frightened by this man's breakdown; our shocked eyes met each other to confirm that we were watching such a scene. A trusted rock was crumbling before us.

'Wait no longer, I beg you ... please, please, wait no longer, our God, Our Messiah ... Come now.'

He collapsed. Those with him helped him to a back room. A shocked silence ensued, enveloping us in a deeply embarrassed gloom. God the helpless, God the impotent, God hiding from the Nazis. No Messiah coming to the rescue, maybe nothing existed but a profound eternal silence. I could hear my father quietly weeping, and now we were all shaken and could no longer look at each other, the nagging sense of betrayal hanging like vapour in the house of God. A Chassid who had been sitting near the rabbi broke into the tune of grace that would follow the third meal. Near to tears, his powerful voice filled the void with religious fervour and hope. We joined in, and our chorus was strong against the tide of doubt that threatened to drown us. Our fate was sealed, a horrendous reality faced us in our mortal future, with the prospect of no immortal intervention.

We walked home, Father holding our hands as we made our way through Budapest's darkened streets. He recited prayers of forgiveness for the rabbi who had dared to put God on trial. The great silence was not to be questioned, only the rabbi's loss of faith and its effect on us. Neither Leopold nor any of his fellow-believers in the congregation had been awakened by the rabbi's agonized outburst at the prospect of death camps, the pistol held to the temple, the rape, the torture, the disease, the rumble of tanks, the howl of aircraft, the searing pain of fire. We were choking in the stench of Nazism, and gripped by its tentacles. Nowhere to go and no Messiah to save us. 1943 ended in spiritual darkness.

PART II
CAPTIVITY

6 Transition

In March 1944, the Germans invaded Hungary. Munky and I had to go twice a week for military training in the youth section of the Hungarian army called the *Levente*. It was compulsory, and to skip training incurred two days' imprisonment. The *Levente* started out as multi-denominational, but by the time we were called up, a special Jewish division had come about. Segregation had become necessary; as social pariahs, no one would train with us, a measure of the success of propaganda planting seed on the fertile ground of popular superstition about us. Never liked, we were now loathed and subject to attack. Run by pro-Nazi Magyars, the training regime set for us at this camp on the outer suburbs was as provocative as it was brutal. One of the training days was set for the Sabbath, which meant we had to walk to the camp, a hefty hike which left us all tired before the start of the exercises, set for us specifically by our Jew-hating squad leaders. The workouts led not just to the usual abuse handed out by army trainers, but to vitriolic language guaranteed to sting and provoke to response, which when it came was brutally battered back into submission.

The sergeant who had charge of our squad was a cruel disciplinarian whose actions, when he was crossed, ran to criminal extremity. With no one to restrain him, physical damage was frequent, as with Munky. The push-ups that particular day had gone on longer than most could endure, but the sergeant's boot happened to be closest to Alex who received a couple of body kicks to the stomach that later caused him to cough up blood. As a result of this incident, and Mr Scher the pen maker not wanting to release me for the mid-week training, Munky and I decided to quit going. Mr

Scher was certain nothing would happen, that the threats over non-attendance were just so much hot air. I had my doubts, having felt the breeze the couple of times that I had skipped, but the camp's regime was unendurable.

Scher was wrong. We were summoned to appear in court. Munky, whose attendance record was better than mine, got off with a stern warning, whereas I, who had not helped my case by delaying my appearance for sentence, received four – not two – days' detention. A family council was called to decide what should be done.

Therezia: 'Four whole days in Mozsar prison. Anything could happen to him in there.'

Fritz: 'It's just token, Mother. Community service. Washing up in the canteens, floor cleaning, that sort of thing. That's what I've heard. What d'you think Papa?'

Father shrugged. He certainly didn't want me inside Mozsar, but he had no opinions, nor, as he saw it, any choices.

Munky: 'What if Ernest doesn't go at all?'

Fritz: 'No. With the Germans watching their every move, at the slightest provocation, the authorities would be at our door. It would be best if Ernest just went and did his time. We don't want this to blow up in our faces.

The matter was decided, I was to go.

On the morning of Thursday, 13 April 1944, I was sent off to Mozsar, with a rucksack stuffed with kosher food, along with underwear and socks, lovingly packed, unpacked and re-packed by my mother, anxious that I should not go short inside. In the end Father took the rucksack from her.

'Leo, I'm just making sure he's got everything he needs.'

'It's all there Therezia.'

Father took hold of my hand, pulling me through the front door. Mother did not turn. Her back was to me as we left the apartment. Her boy could not be going to prison. I had had a hug from her and the others moments earlier, but this parting moment did not exist.

At Mozsar police station, we found our way through the entrance door, along the deep shiny lino-floored reception area to a desk behind which sat a uniformed sergeant. Glancing at the piece of paper my father handed him:

'Right Mr Lowy, you can leave your son here.'

The voice was matter-of-fact, not once had he looked at me. Leopold was reluctant to leave. Though I had just turned 19, I was still his little boy.

'Mr Lowy. You may go. Your son is in safe hands, safe as houses.'

The sergeant could never have realized how wafer-thin such a reassurance would be to a Jewish man who had lost his property to legalized thieves. Father let go of my hand.

'I'll be back for you in four days, Ernest. Behave yourself now.'

His trying to act like the stern parent of a delinquent fooled neither myself nor the desk sergeant, who smiled broadly.

'On your way home Mr Lowy.'

Father made his way slowly to the door, slightly bowed. Before leaving, he turned, smiled, gave a little wave, and was gone. It was the last I ever saw of him.

No sooner had Leopold gone through the doors of Mozsar and out into the activity of the street, than I was escorted below to a large holding cell where I stood watching the guard lock me in. I was alone. Benches for the detainees ran along two of the walls. I made use of them. I had a book and it made sense to try and read, though my heartbeat made my eyes throb and the print became blurred at moments. Time went by, voices came and went. Laughter came from behind closed doors, teasing my imagination. I was a few pages into the book when doors swung open with a bang, and footsteps clattered along the glossy lino floor. The cell door was unlocked and, escorted by a guard, a young street girl was bundled into the cell. The officer escorting pushed her on to the bench opposite, leaving her with a warning to leave the kid alone and keep her butt on the bench.

With the guard out of the way the heavy door slammed shut, she was by my side and up close. Ilyes would have spent all his meagre wages on this one. Taller than me, and, to my eyes, stunningly beautiful. She put me in mind of Angel; as young, as pert and forward as my sometime friend, her golden auburn hair tousled, carelessly tumbling over the fox-fur collar of her camel hair coat. Beneath it was an emerald velvet dress with white buttons along the front, the lower ones open to reveal a pair of the most beautiful legs I had ever seen, even from the workshop window.

'Maybe you should sit over there like the man said,' I stammered, 'I don't want to see you getting into trouble.'

I was no deterrent. More, I seemed to be a magnet. She began to play with my hair, twisting it around her fingers; 'Don't be like that, sunshine. Such an innocent, so young.' She breathed this into my ear. 'I'm Klari. You are?'

'Ernest, Ernest Lowy.'

'What are you doing here, Ernest Lowy?'

'I skipped *Levente* training.'

She laughed a musical laugh.

'Can't say I blame you. Tough was it?'

'Very.'

She looked deep into my eyes.

'How old are you Ernest Lowy?'

'Nineteen.'

'Me too. Twenty next week. You don't look 19. You Jewish?'

I nodded. She continued idly playing with my hair:

'I don't hold with what's going on against your people. I like Jewish men, you're much more appreciative. I get to feel less like an object. You are with me in the bed, not trying not to be there … know what I mean?'

I didn't, but nodded anyway. She kissed me full on the lips. The shock was pleasurable and embarrassing in equal measure. A key turned in the lock and, before we could separate, the door opened and the guard entered supporting a drunk. Pushing his charge on to a bench, he reached over to drag Klari back to where he had placed her, cursing her roundly, impugning her virtue.

The drunk, heavy-set and middle-aged, bloody-nosed with

swollen eyes glazed over, slid from the bench to the floor, and, all of a heap, settled into a foetal position to begin snoring a loud room-filling racket.

When the guard had gone and she was sure he wasn't peering through the spy hole, Klari returned to my side.

'Want to know why I'm here? Customer grassed me off. Said I'd stolen fifty *pengo* from his wallet.'

'Did you?'

'Yup. He was crude. I didn't like him. He resented paying. I'm up for a body search. Ernest, would you hide the money? They won't search you. You can get it back to me later.'

The drunk stirred, woke and started coughing. His back was to us. From beneath her dress Klari produced a small bundle of notes, lifted my trouser and slipped it into one of my socks. Before I could object, the drunk was fully awake and staring at us. Grunting, he stumbled to the cell door where he started a banging that went with a loud shout that he 'needed ... a piss, you bastards.'

The door opened abruptly. Two guards stood there.

'About time you gits.'

One of the guards grabbed the drunk and dragged him through to the reception area. We were ordered to follow on. Klari gave me a re-assuring wink. In seconds we were being herded into a police van, already occupied by a catch of whores, a couple more drunks and a very shifty-looking character who was holed up in a corner of the van. I was puzzled by my removal from Mozsar, but was swept along with this tide, my protest barely formed.

'Stay clear of the boy, slut.'

This from the guard as he shut the van door on us, but, within seconds of the van leaving the kerbside, she was on my lap wriggling her butt and snaking her arms round me, laughing with the whores that I was theirs once she was done, but not to hold their breath. The guard had joined the driver in the cab, which had a spy hole shutter. He drew this back and saw Klari at work on me. The van screeched to a stop, the guard dashed to the back of the van, threw open the doors, and leapt in. Misjudging the height of the van, furious, he jumped in, his head striking the top of the door frame, all but knocking himself unconscious mid-leap.

He fell back into the street. Instantly Klari was at his side, helping him, nursing him. No thought of making a run for it, she used her handkerchief to staunch the bleeding, helping him to his feet like a doting mother, then for her pains was bundled back into the van by her patient. The thought crossed my mind, did they know each other? The thought vanished as the van resumed its journey. I learned from the others in the van we were headed for Mosonyi prison; a bad location. What was my business there?

On arriving, the men were separated from the women. Klari's parting words were: 'Listen Ernest. As soon as you have done your bit of time, your first call will be to Madame Clarisse on Kiraly Street. We can close our little deal, and for you a little of my time for your kindness. I guarantee you won't regret it.'

The men surrounding me made crude remarks in a 'lucky bastard' tone; I had by accident gained a little kudos among the drunks. We were all marched to the 'Mousehole', the name given to a common cell; *'Egeres'* in Hungarian. Within minutes of arriving, my kudos was forgotten, my rucksack manhandled out of my grasp, raided for the food, then tossed back to me, underpants and socks still intact.

As the hours ticked by, more people were shoved into the cell, already crowded. One newcomer, a lad my age, aggressive to those around him, took it on himself to 'Jew-bait' me. I was glad he was handcuffed. I tucked myself into a corner as the evening wore on, making an attempt to sleep in the midst of low conversation, sudden swearing, loud coughing and a chorus of snores. Around midnight, there was a lot of noise in the corridor. The cell door part opened to the sounds of a distressed altercation between the guards, a man and a woman. Craning forward, through the part-open door, I could see a couple; he quite old, tall, well dressed, elegant. The woman, younger, expensively dressed and like him, elegant, in deep distress at the separation taking place as the man, her father, was about to be shoved into our cell. Her cry of protest was ignored as the man hit the cell floor, the door shutting on him, her voice, now muffled as she was dragged away. Even the floor could not rob this man of his dignity, but his shock of being there at all, his distress at the brutality of separation brought on a sorrow about the eyes that cast fear into my senses. I realized that prior to this moment I had been more excited than anything; now I was plain scared. He was Jewish, of obvious wealth, of probable influence … and here. He stood in the middle of the cell, isolated, with nothing around him familiar. He looked round at the bundles of humanity on bench and floor, and began to weep quietly. A space was made for him on one of the benches.

The next morning, before most were awake, I put on my phylacteries (two small black boxes for prayer, one to the head, one to the heart). I stepped carefully over sleeping forms to gain a clear space in which to pray. The elegant old man caught my eye. With a whisper, 'Pray for me also.'

I smiled, willingly nodded. He tried a smile in return. At that moment, the cell door opened. A tall middle-aged officer called the old man's name:

'Ledermann!'

He looked up at the officer. Confusion was taking over. Seemingly in a daze, he rose, following the officer out and away from the cell after his name was bellowed a second time. Everyone was now awake, but I was able to finish my morning prayers in spite of callous ridicule from the youth in handcuffs. I prayed for Ledermann and his daughter for good measure. Not long after, the same officer returned to call me out. I took one last look at the cell with the half-interested faces of my cellmates, creatures of the Budapest underworld, staring my way before the door shut and I was led away. We walked along a corridor. The officer informed me I was on my way to do communal work. As this was what I expected, I wasn't ready for the 'trick'. He stopped and stared as if examining me. In a voice half-kind:

'Breakfast. You want to eat kosher, son?'

I was Jewish, so what?

'Thank you, that would be grand.'

The 'trick' had happened. I was still not connecting, my stomach was rumbling. Twenty-four hours since I had eaten and Therezia's lovingly prepared food had gone down the throats of scoundrels, not mine. The guard led me into a large hall where Jewish families were seated. As the door closed, I heard the key turned in the lock. I went to the counter to get some breakfast. On my way I spotted Ledermann and the girl together again. When I had finished queuing for my food, he called me over.

'Don't tell me, you were asked if you wanted to eat kosher.'

I nodded. Ledermann laughed joylessly as he asked me to join them. He introduced me to his daughter, Eva, and in conversation it transpired that he and his family had run a chain of exclusive cinemas in Bratislava, places I had used back then. They had no idea why they had been dragged in off the streets along with these families who had obviously been at the receiving end of a planned operation. With their hastily packed cases and bundles, it took me back to our deportation from Czechoslovakia. Now the Germans were here in Hungary, anything was possible. Labour camps loomed as a possibility. As for me, communal work seemed increasingly like a 'red herring'. The Ledermanns and I seemed destined for something more sinister. The food became dry, heavy in my mouth and I reached for the jug of water in front of me. I was no longer excited or scared … I was terrified.

At midday we were taken into a yard at the rear of Mosonyi prison where we were all lined up in ranks. I became separated in the crush from Ledermann and Eva. As we stood in the bright sunshine, the crowd from the night before, who had been dealt with or released, were filing out. They stopped to look at the Jews. Among them was Klari who, instead of smiling and waving, was sobbing at the sight of us. What did she know? What had she been told while inside? She looked over to me giving me the tiniest of waves. I still had her money in my sock. I doubt that she even cared.

Mounted police force-marched us through the streets of the capital; a parade worth turning out for on such a beautiful spring afternoon. From their horses, the police, in an effort to impress the German uniforms dotted about the place, lashed out at us indiscriminately. This was Rome? This was Egypt? Budapest with its pavements lined with jeering citizens, laughing among themselves at the humiliation of the 'damned Yids ... and good riddance'. Then there were those who, like Kraijchirovich, our neighbour barber in Bratislava, just stood, smiling. Klari was the only one who had shown either concern or pity; but then what do whores know? The march of shame came to a conclusion at Keleti railway station where the mounted police left us standing in rows under the streams of sunlight beaming in through the high arched windows. Waiting for us were Germans in SS uniforms who, armed with rifles, and holstered Lugers at their belts, yelled and barked orders which echoed round the station hallway as they herded us all onto a waiting train. Several soldiers had snarling dogs on leashes, and these they let snap at the legs of those standing in line, terrified.

The train was made up of cattle trucks with their side doors open. Each truck held around eighty people at a pinch. Everything went smoothly for the Germans. No one objected, the scream of collective terror was muted by the terror itself. Panic was in everyone's eyes, not least mine. I tried to catch sight of the Ledermanns as I was bundled aboard, shouldering and being shouldered by those around me, but no sign of them. The doors were slid shut and sealed. Apart from the children asking questions and the odd baby crying, there was a stunned silence broken into by coughing. Slowly, but slowly, people began to speak to each other, at first in whispered tones, then more volubly as our eyes became accustomed to the semi-dark of the unlit wagon. One beam of sunlight shafted in through a tiny paneless window, up high and fringed in barbed wire. The train lurched suddenly and everyone stumbled against everyone else; the clanking of the wagons as the jolt of movement went down the train in a chain reaction was loud against the hollow-sounding shouts of the SS men on the platform. Someone near me started to pray, a woman wept close by, and round the carriage various noises of discomfort became the norm for the journey. One old man began to moan, and his moan seemed to cut into my thoughts for most of the journey. It went on until he died, twenty-four hours later.

The rail truck was packed tight with people, standing or sitting. The crush led to reactions all round. As long as they possibly could, my fellow passengers on this journey to God-knew-where kept the veneer of politeness and mutual concern. Classes and different income groups had been thrown together. Rank and expectation were melting in the heat of terror and discomfort. As the train rattled along, the heat of the day, and the lack of good ventilation, made the air hard to breathe as did the increasing smell of urine, as bodily resistance to natural function began breaking down. As with order. There were scuffles over space, arguments about the behaviour of children, especially the whines and crying that grated on the already frayed nerves of the adults. The kids were the first to defecate but, as day turned to night, at points when the train stopped and nobody came to let us out, people with deep shame, gave up. Increasingly the stench we collectively produced became repellent.

Thirty hours later, the train slowed for the last time. I peered through a gap in the truck slats to see a station with a Polish name. I was relieved that this seemed to be the end of the journey, as the hostilities inside the truck were getting close to boiling point. The train gently stopped, then after a brief pause, jolted into reverse and moved backwards along a fresh piece of track. Those anxious to know peered through the cracks to establish our surroundings, countryside which seemed grey and desolate. The station name was Auschwitz.

Eventually the train made its final stop. I squirmed my way to the edge of the truck to get a better view through a space in the wood panelling. Outside, across in a distant field, my eyes struggled with an image of what seemed to be thousands of small red flowers fluttering in the breeze. I was to learn later that these were women, all wearing red headscarves, working away in the fields beyond. What was in the immediate foreground grabbed my attention. Men in SS uniforms, with snarling dogs on leads, running along the platform, sliding the wagon doors open, shouting and screaming for the occupants to evacuate:

'Raus! Schnell!'

This was repeated as a dark mantra, punctuating other orders shouted at us while the dogs snapped at whatever came close. Those who were too old or too young to hurry were dragged and hurled from the trucks onto damp, hostile concrete. Standing terrified on the platform, I became aware that, though I had left behind the smell of our shit, some other deeply unpleasant odour had taken its place; a sweet-sour otherness which, though inescapable, was in equal measure, unbearable.

A group of four immaculately dressed SS officers swept up in an open-topped Mercedes, and, leaving the vehicle, began the process of dividing up the several hundred bedraggled Jews standing before them. A particularly erect officer gave off a particular aura. The set face had a cold, distant look. He carried a whip. The name I later learned was Josef Mengele. Why these officers were splitting us up I couldn't tell. Again, later I was told we were being selected for work detail, or death in the gas chambers. Families were being broken up, wife from husband, relatives separated from each other and hit with riding crops or bitten by the dogs if resistance was shown. Small children and babies were allowed to stay with their mothers, we found out, to prevent early panic before being taken to the place of slaughter. The fact that healthy men were separated from their families saved their lives as they were isolated for work camps. No amount of begging or bended-knee-pleading would deter the SS officers from their tasks. Loved ones went, protesting, their separate ways while their tormentors laughed and joked with each other, apparently oblivious to the misery in front of them.

In midst of all this upheaval and chaotic emotion, Ledermann. A being possessed, he tore in and out of our column, a tornado of panicked action. He had snapped.

'Eva … Eva … my daughter. Where is my daughter?'

He didn't see me, his possession was total. A couple of guards tried to nail him but his madness gave him speed. Finally, in despair, he threw himself to the ground pounding the concrete, calling Eva's name. His beautiful daughter was nowhere in sight, maybe separated here or Budapest, I couldn't tell. The guards dragged him off the floor, his nails scraping the ground. He was taken out of sight, just one more being sick with grief in a weeping mass. He was gone from my eyes.

After being pushed, bitten by dogs, kicked, shoved and generally screamed into place, I found myself with a group of around 500 men, all of whom looked fairly young, fairly fit, but scared as hell. Those men separated at the platform from their loved ones were locked into an almost catatonic remoteness. The old, the infirm, the very young with their mothers had been herded away out of sight. Me, I stood clutching my rucksack containing my change of socks and underwear. We had been selected to live and work. None of this we knew, as around six in the evening we were marched into the camp at Auschwitz. Our 500 had become several thousand, as more trains had earlier disgorged yet more bewildered, frightened beings to undergo the agonies of separation brought on by this relentless mechanical sifting, devoid of compassion, with which the very sky, in its unremitting greyness, seemed to collude.

This darkness, this murky underside of 'The New World Order', something entirely strange to us, was brought home in stark fashion. A man in our line stepped out of it to ask a Jewish kapo about our immediate fate. His approach was polite, not aggressive. The kapo's face contorted. With the truncheon that he was holding, he beat the man to the floor, bent over him continuing to club the unfortunate about the head until all resistance departed, his life oozing away with the blood that now puddled the concrete floor and flecked the kapo's truncheon, face and hands. Sated, he looked up and into our horror-stricken faces.

'Want some?'

The kapo. I would come to know and mostly despise this breed. Mainly Jewish, mainly convicted felons, given interesting things to do around the work camps by the Nazis. As the war dragged on, they gained more and more licence to give vent to all manner of atrocity, usually vicious beatings, wanton mistreatment of prisoners involving starvation, male rape, exposure to the elements; murder. Essentially, though fellow inmates, their status was to be in charge of the day-to-day activities in the camp; to maintain discipline and be answerable to their Nazi masters. That killing was my introduction to violent death and I would see so many more die in front of me in the coming months. Being the first, the moments involved in that beating remain sharply clear to recollection. Hundreds of men stood helplessly by as this unhinged act took place, planting them squarely in the nightmare realm of the impotent victim.

We were marched in parties to a badly lit blockhouse and told to undress. Our clothes and belongings were taken, my change of underpants and socks gone forever; the book, the rucksack, away, and Klari's fifty *pengo* grabbed with a grin. We were kept standing together naked for what seemed hours, then abruptly we were marched into a large hall where each man was compelled to jump onto a little platform. Other prisoners then proceeded to shave every hair away from our heads and bodies; the razors they employed were blunt, scraping our skin, leaving cuts in abundance. I stepped down from my platform, cut all over, deeply offended and ashamed, exposed inside this mass madness. The next step was to be shepherded through an archway into an annex where more prisoners waited with sponges and buckets of disinfectant. I was liberally doused in the stuff. It went into the cuts, my eyes, my anus; it seared my balls. My entire nervous system reacted to the massive stinging. Tears of pain filled my eyes. 'What next? Dear God, what next?'

The shower room was next. Herded in and packed tightly together, unable to stand apart, we were huddled together in an intimacy of pain and fright. Minutes passed. Taps then burst open and we were attacked by boiling hot water from every side. Nowhere to dodge as the scalding took place. A collective jig of pure agony as our torn skin reacted to hot water that was almost steam. We could only jump like monkeys. I shook terribly; like the others emitting sharp cries of pain. Looking around, I was participating in something beyond the ridiculous. Laugh or cry? My body decided to turn my screams into laughter. For several minutes I lost it totally and was, for that short period, completely insane.

The day was coming to an end. The Sabbath over. Exhausted, we had been kitted out in a uniform, black-and-white stripes, not unlike the pyjama but in a coarse fabric. The kit had been shoved at us whether it fitted or not. As a little time passed, by exchanging, the right sizes were found; even so, we looked ludicrous with our ill-fitting 'pyjamas', scabby heads and scratched faces.

By degrees, the uniformed presence of the German guards lessened, though they were present for our various humiliations, had happily cheered the killer kapo, for example. Now we were 'dressed and ready for bed', the kapos were more in evidence, their sneering insults accompanied us to block eleven at Birkenau. Eleven had no toilets. For forty-eight hours I had held on; since Mosonyi. Even now, try as I might, I could not join in the collective pissing that went on in that block. Ankle deep in urine, the floor was no place to fall. Some had fallen. People had just let go. The place stank, the dominant smell being ammonia combined with excrement, combined with that strange smell of otherness. Completely exhausted, I fell onto a bunk where three others were trying to rest. I must have slept. Suddenly I was awake to hysterical giggling laughter. Eyes open. On the other side of a ventilation grille just above my head, faces were pressed against the bars. A scene from a Bosch painting. Polish Jews who were completely unhinged, 'long-termers' who somehow, like rats, had impossibly survived in these hostile surroundings. One of them shouted in Yiddish:

'Worry not boys, you'll not be here long. You'll be able to escape up the chimney.'

Laughing, they pointed through the long block windows to the tall chimneys billowing smoke in the day's last light. One or two older men fell to prayer:

'Praying won't help. God's got nothing to do with it. No escaping the chimneys. Kiss your life goodbye.'

First night in Auschwitz. Just two days before, our lives were as normal as warfare and social hate would allow; now here we were, bruised and bloody ciphers breathing the tainted air of human misery. Those grinning nitwits catcalling us through that grille had given us the dreadful message that the smell permeating the entire camp was the stench of incinerated beings who, in their thousands, had been fed into the furnaces since God knew when. I looked at the little metal tag which had my personal number on it and realized that this was my only identity. No hair, no name, no dignity, no hope. We were at the mercy of madmen, people who could do what they wanted with us. Darkness had truly fallen.

The following day, still unable to relieve myself, bowels bound tight and body bent double, along with the other hundreds, I was called out to pose for photographs taken by the SS. Under pressure, I was amazed how straight I could stand. We were archive material, something for the Führer to gloat over and the thousand-year empire to proudly display to its young. For several days we did nothing, except drink thin soup and ruminate on the gossip passed on from the mad Poles whose crazed utterances let us into the chaotic, panic-sodden world of the prisoner. Our other initiation was the orgy of kapo violence provoked by the Nazis, who got a kick out of watching Jew torment Jew. The guards were present but were content to let the kapos deal with us, to sit back and enjoy the show.

After nearly a week of enforced idleness, a rumour flew round that block eleven was up for a 'selection'. The word was a euphemism for a time of 'wheat and chaff'. The wheat would be selected for a work camp, the chaff would go to the gas chambers, thence to incineration, cremation and release from this profound mental torture.

In spite of my evident discomfort, my life was spared, being selected for work camp, pushed to the right side by an SS officer's whip. Several hundred of us were singled out to leave Auschwitz. Forced labour 'commandos' were needed in another camp, and we were it. I could not believe my ears. It was parole, it was pardon, it was release. It was not certain death.

Once again, on to cattle trucks, this time away from Auschwitz, feeling light, even able to straighten up. God forgive me, I found myself kissing the splintered wood sides of the dirty truck wheeling us away from the place of death. We were en route to Wustegiersdorf, a small labour camp in Upper Silesia.

7 Wustegiersdorf

In 1944, Wustegiersdorf, a small attractive Silesian town about 60km from Auschwitz, lay just on the borders of Czechoslovakia and Poland, a little Ruritanian patch tucked away in an industrial region fattened and expanded by the needs of the Third Reich. The train ride found us a short walk from the camp on the edges of town.

We were marched through the main gate in the barbed wire perimeter fence – which was interrupted by sentry lookouts and pillboxes – to a large three-storey building, formerly a textile mill. Its machinery had been ripped out to make it habitable. Beyond the fence were some smaller outbuildings where the guards and their officers had their quarters; alongside these, factory workshops. After our period of terrified silences and furtive whispers in the idleness of Auschwitz, during the train journey camp to camp, there came from us relieved outpourings; faces became more familiar and names became known. Relationships began to form. This labour camp was going to be tough, but we were not yet on a conveyor belt to extinction. Our home for the duration was to be this mill with its red-brick exterior and tall narrow windows, arched and attractive, almost the height of the building. Through them we could see movement. As the latest to arrive, we were billeted on the third floor. The ground floor was taken up with Polish prisoners who, being long-termers, had had plenty of time to mutate into dehumanized aggressive grunters, and who gave us plenty of invective as we made our way up the wooden steps from their level to the next where Hungarians, Germans and Ukrainians subsisted in crowded conditions. Their stares, as we filed by, told us nothing, and apart from odd comments passed to each other, nothing was said as we clattered our way to the floor above. So, it was the Poles we had to watch.

The power pyramid in the camp was fairly straightforward. At the apex was *Obersturmbannführer* Seidel, a man we hardly saw, a high-ranking SS officer in charge of several work camps, whose word was law. He and a few subordinates were the seat of power. His second-in-command at Wustegiersdorf was another SS officer, *Lagerführer* Shwarz, whose contact with us was usually painful. He suffered from the endemic complaint among the Nazis of erratic mood swings. It was not good to be on the receiving end of his displeasure. He was deeply feared. Known affectionately as the 'Phantom of Dusseldorf', he had flame-red hair and his porky bulk was stuffed tight inside his SS uniform. He had at his beck and call a small number of young SS officers and a larger number of Wehrmacht guards who, though never a soft proposition, were not twisted round by the special indoctrination handed out to the SS. Further down the pyramid were the kapos, along with trusted prisoners with special status, our representatives. A token status, but one for which there could be uses, especially with someone like Messinger, our *Lageralteste*, a giant athlete of a man in his mid-thirties. Prematurely bald, he nevertheless cut an imposing figure around the camp. A well-known face, he had been a famous footballer in Bratislava and was held in general respect. Although the kapos were not bottom of the official heap, to us they sank without trace. These were souls, mainly Jews, who out of cowardice, fear of death, revenge or pure criminality, would deal out pain on behalf of their captors. They were there to keep order, and had increasing licence, as the war closed in on the Nazis, to maim and kill Jews. Finally, us, at the base of the pyramid, along with the east Europeans and the Gypsies.

As this was a labour camp, we received a minimum measure of daily food, never adequate for young men engaged in heavy manual labour, but sustenance nevertheless.

I saw, more than once, a Polish prisoner unselfishly pass his ration to his teenage son. The lad worked hard enough for both of them, but even so it was a big risk for the father, as food supply was so sparse, every morsel was needed by every man. The pair were devoted. Naturally, a black market existed in the camp, and I quickly learned that my cousin Leo and his pal Zoltan, both of whom found me on the first day, were leading lights in the movement of illicit goods, mainly food, around the camp. Again, even with this conduit at large, malnutrition eventually overtook us all, except the soldiers.

The contact between ourselves and our keepers was at arm's length unless a kicking or a clubbing with a rifle butt was felt to be due a prisoner. Apart from Leo and Zoltan, my close companions were those with whom I shared age and outlook. Walter, at the outset, was my closest companion, a Viennese who had opened a philatelist shop in Budapest. Our common love of the city got the relationship going, and I quickly became 'Ernesti', the confessor and confidant. Nobody could work out why, but he had been allocated a bunk bed on the ground floor with the Poles whose kapos gave him a hard time due to his strong-man reputation. Stocky, heavily built, Walter had enjoyed some success in the world of amateur boxing.

I would like to have known *Lageralteste* Messinger better. In spite of his camp obligations, his innate compassion was barely held in check. A *Mensch*. The tension between him and *Lagerführer* Schwarz was an ever-present excitement for us. Two very big men who had to function together, in spite of one's indoctrination and the other's 'victim' status. Outside the confines of the madness, they were well-matched for a fight. A typical example: already in an invidious position of being the man to administer any flogging for breaches of camp rules (not something any thinking man could relish) Messinger trod a dangerously fine line. This particular morning, as usual, we, the work kommandos, were lined up to witness a punishment. The minimum number of lashes would be a survivable five; however, with the maximum of twenty-five lashes, the prisoner invariably died. With the prisoner forced over a bench and held in check by guards, Messinger had his orders to whip the unfortunate. It was evident the victim would not withstand many lashes at full strength. Messinger pulled his strokes and Schwarz noticed. In spite of the agonized whimpering of the prisoner, Schwarz demanded that Messinger use his strength.

'Do it properly or I'll do it for you.'

Messinger's overall policy was one of passive resistance, but here he had to lay into a victim whose infringement remained unknown, but whose destiny was all too clear. Even so, Messinger did not use all his strength and, though Schwarz knew it, he kept his council. Because he was useful in containing the prisoners through his fame and imposing physical presence, the Nazis back-pedalled slightly when it came to Messinger's insubordinate attitude. Witness the day of the hanging. The young Polish lad with the devoted father had made a bid for freedom when on a work party and, after failing in this, would hang as an example to us all. Berger, a young SS officer, one of Seidel's mobile group and Schwarz's immediate superior, was overseeing the execution. In terms of sadistic cruelty, this man had the edge on his underling and had no time for diplomacy around Messinger.

It was a midsummer Sunday evening and we were returning from our work detail. There, erected on the *appelplatz*, was the gallows. Lined up in front of it, we were at a loss to know who had today incurred the wrath of our young SS, known to us all as the 'smiling assassin'. When it turned out to be the Polish boy, our reaction registered with young Berger who, with a sense of theatre, had arranged for Beethoven's Fifth Symphony to be played loudly from the gramophone in the officers' quarters. The symphony rang round the *appelplatz* and, just as with Hitler's hijacking of Wagner's music, it deeply pained those of us who loved music that other devotees should use art as a weapon against us.

The father was made to stand near the gallows. The son was escorted from one of the outbuildings, his face puffed and blue with bruises. The older Pole wept at the sight of his lad. The boy was taken to the gallows where a coarse noose was placed around his neck. Like a lot of us not prepared to witness this murder, the father cast his eyes helplessly to the concrete and stared at the lengthening shadows thrown by the evening sunlight. The young officer caught the moment.

'You would look at the floor while your child dies? What kind of parent are you? Look up old man, face death. That goes for the rest of you. Look Up. That is an order.'

The officer waited. Slowly faces lifted, along with that of the reluctant father, whose chin had been raised by Berger's riding crop. When satisfied we were all facing the gallows, the boy was placed on a stool. There was a second pause when the music stopped and the record had to be turned over. The young officer looked across the *appelplatz* toward the clouds gathering around the sunset. The condemned lad was bathed in a warm orange glow; we collectively cast long, thin shadows towards him. The officer nodded to Messinger to kick away the stool. Nothing. He didn't move.

'The stool, Jew.'

Messinger didn't move a muscle. The officer had no patience.

'Are you deaf? Kick the stool, you bastard.'

Nothing from Messinger. The young man became livid. The drama was under threat from farce. The needle on the record advanced towards a second pause. He stepped up to Messinger.

'You have one minute to do this, or every tenth prisoner will be shot through the head. Your decision.'

He checked his watch while the strains of Beethoven's Fifth continued unbearably. The minute came and went. The officer by now was purple with anger. He had been denied, his sense of theatre, along with his ego, was challenged. Schwarz was apoplectic, but unable to step in and administer a brutal resolution to this impasse. Berger then made a crucial mistake. He escalated the threat. His screaming anger was directed at all of us.

'After two minutes every fifth prisoner will be shot, starting with your *Lageralteste* Messinger, who appears to be struck dumb and paralysed … and therefore better off dead … unless one of you sees sense and kicks away the stool!'

Time passed. The record ended but no-one put the next disc on. Silence ruled. It seemed an eternal moment. The boy whimpered, the father sobbed, their eyes forever fixed on each other. Two or three prisoners could not stifle bad coughing. A Polish kapo, a quiet man, detached himself suddenly from his group, ran the short distance to the stool and kicked it away. The rope was too long and the boy's toes could brush the ground. Eventually, after much choking and facial contortion, the boy gave up the ghost. A fellow prisoner stepped across and helped the old man, now in a state of collapse. The young SS officer turned on his heel and, red-faced, left the scene. Schwarz stared at Messinger balefully, then dismissed us all. Somebody in the outbuilding put on the next record in sequence of the symphony. The sound echoed around the emptying *appelplatz* as the body of the boy was removed and the temporary gallows dismantled.

Humanity depends on ritual. In a Nazi work camp, ritual was at times mutual, at times exclusive to a group and, where possible, an individual. Our keepers, for example, subjected us to early reveille and roll-call like clockwork. Any morning prayer had to be performed in a reduced, whispered moment, in no space, in the semi-dark of early day, or before sleep. My companions were, by and large, believers, so they too would try to snatch their moments with the Father of the Universe. Even the work itself had a ritual quality, though sometimes a blank aimlessness, when we were just shifting rubble, seemingly for no good purpose. Our activity was couched in a common awareness that the days of this gross, mentally unsustainable period, were, one way or another, coming to a close. For the prisoner, the expectation was death by beating, starvation, disease or latterly, an Allied bomb. Jew and Gentile alike had little expectation, little hope except that, come nightfall, some sleep might be possible, and maybe the following day might yield a little more substance in the gruel or, joy of joys, a long awaited shower bath, a collective affair, but an eagerly awaited luxury.

Friendships engendered endurance and pleasure. The French doctor, Georges, with whom I was to share great moments in the coming months, was central to our regular Sunday night soirées, where he, a cellist, would vocally imitate the cello, and I, an aspiring singer who could imitate a trumpet by piping into rolled-up paper, would entertain. Others, like Toby, my rival tenor, would join in. It became a popular moment, when recollected pieces were performed, songs and religious works sung, stories told, humour and laughter shared. These were the pearls beyond price, some of the reasons to endure the horrors of the week, so that we could return to the times wherein lay the best of us.

The bonding within our barrack was inevitably put to the test by the stresses of day-to-day life where the work alone – often backbreaking effort in the open – would force weakening men to their knees. Add to this the brutality of the overseers who, spotting weakness, would often prey upon it, death the inevitable outcome for the prisoner. This served as an incentive for the others neither to show nor confess weakness, or become slack. A rifle butt to the face or body – and if a prisoner should fall to the ground – a boot to whatever got in its way before the final target, the genitals, would usually take care of those on their last legs. Betrayal for gain was rare, but there is betrayal and betrayal. All of us were, morally, 'up against it'. For myself there were moments of deep shame and regret, where, for survival's sake, I fell.

Walter and I had become inseparable pals. We were an odd couple. Before the war, he had been an amateur boxer. Camp life hadn't got to him physically at this stage, except around the eyes. Fairly short and stocky with a bustling rough-tough exterior, he was in fact very unsure of himself, which is I guess where I came in. We were very much each other's 'minder'. He had bailed me out, more than once, from difficult

101

moments of camp conflict, a couple of times risking his life. One Sunday, he stumbled up the stairs and on to our third floor billet. He stomped over to me, gathering up my belongings and blanket.

'Ernesti. Come. I need you downstairs. I am bored being by myself among those ugly Polish peasants. You can share my bunk. I have no one to talk to there. You come, keep me company.'

I had not been able to say 'no' to this '*Palooka*' since meeting up with him in Auschwitz. His shock provoked by the place and his predicament had filled him with dreadful foreboding about his fate. Others entertained hope, but Walter remained caught like a fly in a web and in deepest dread. Reluctantly, I followed him downstairs. The ground floor was empty, disconcertingly quiet without its occupants.

When they returned, it became immediately obvious that we had made a huge mistake. They surrounded the bunk. Walter stood to face them. One Pole made it his business to skirt round him and confront me nose-to-nose while speaking across to Walter.

'What's this doing here?'

'He is a friend, keeping me company. None of your business.'

Walter's defiant attitude incensed the Pole who lashed out, catching him unexpectedly full in the face. The Pole had not moved from confronting me, the blow landed as Walter had turned. The next moment Walter was under a belligerent mound of anti-Semites eager to have a collective go at the Jewboy boxer, who, on his back, was still managing to hurt a few. Seemingly from nowhere, Messinger was into the fray, hauling bodies away from the struggling Walter, who, suddenly liberated, was on his feet, but through blind instinct he threw a 'haymaker', catching Messinger full on the jaw. The big man staggered backward a few steps. Walter froze, realizing the significance of his action. The Poles stood panting and very quiet indeed. Nobody knew how Messinger would jump. In a one-to-one he could do a lot of damage, even to Walter. Under camp rules, Messinger could decide life or death. We waited. Feeling his jaw, he ignored Walter. To me, evenly:

'You, back upstairs.'

He then turned and walked away. We would come to call these, 'Messinger Moments'. His even temper and unassuming, quick thinking saved many from a beating and worse. He never descended into the petty squabbles of survival. Seemingly aloof, his own man, he walked the thin red line of camp survival within his own authority. This containment of the situation with or without status didn't come to many. Schwarz didn't have it. In spite of his SS uniform and the absolute power he had over all the prisoners at Wustegiersdorf, the conflict in the man left him dangerously unstable. He had pledged his heart and soul to the Nazi cause. Where that political indoctrination rubbed up against his earlier upbringing, together with his awareness of the Eastern Front moving inexorably westward, and the Allies making inroads into Western Europe, the man must have felt exposed to a threatening future. Both individuals had degrees of power, and these allowed their respective qualities to emerge. We were the underclass, our power and degree was stripped away. Where there were strengths and weaknesses within each man, these showed like beacons on a dark hilltop.

Vazsonyi Janos, an outstanding man in his own right, was born into a political family. His father had been a finance minister in one of the governments of pre-war Hungary. In his late thirties, Vazsonyi arrived at Wustegiersdorf in a pathetic state. Still recoiling from similar experiences to those around him, he found comfort in his new companions. He was a great asset to our Sunday cultural gatherings, contributing much with an able mind and a natural authority derived from knowledge rather than opinion. We would listen and learn. Our living conditions dragged him down, however, with his singular weakness, an inability to resist hunger. This led him down paths of desperation. The effects of hunger later, finally, took him beyond our reach.

103

There were no toilets in our barracks, so we had to use buckets which were situated on each floor. 'Slopping out' was a shared activity run on a rota. Each prisoner would take his turn on what proved to be a roughly two-hour shift. In that time all the buckets on his floor had to be emptied and rinsed three floors down. Any paper and rags had to be removed to avoid clogging the drains. Everyone took their turn; no one liked the task and the temptation to throw up was ever present. It was my turn on this particular morning. Vazsonyi noticed that earlier I had hoarded away a half-slice of bread. He stopped me as I started to lift the first bucket, offering to do my shift in return for the half-slice.

'Please Vazsonyi, don't ask this of me. Don't do it to yourself. A bread slice. It's not worth it.'

'Ernest, you'll be doing me a favour.'

His eyes were begging for bread. After a moment I offered him the slice.

'Here, take the bread. Forget the work. It doesn't matter.'

He took the bread with a slight snatch, his eyes showed eagerness and gratitude.

'It matters. Now I'll do your shift.'

He pocketed the bread and took the bucket from me. I suspect Vazsonyi had done this kind of exchange before. It was painful to watch this well-educated, well-connected man gradually decline. As with many, hunger contributed to his death on the long march, a dreadful time yet to come. Like Vazsonyi, all of us had our beliefs, loyalties and scruples challenged on a daily basis. A day dawned when I would be challenged, heart and head.

Schwarz had gone on leave. In charge was the young SS officer who, at the hanging of the young Pole, had had his usual leering grin knocked sideways by Messinger's defiance. Unlike older soldiers like Schwarz, this youngster was pure Nazi, brought up inside National Socialism, trained and indoctrinated in the Hitler Youth and now, a full-blown member of the SS, performing his Führer's primary ambition of ridding the future of the Jewish plague. The fact that his hand had been stayed from outright mass-killing, here and now, frustrated him. Orders were orders. The vermin in front of him at reveille were required hands and backs on work details. Better them than the gallant soldiers dying on the Eastern Front, or the good citizens owed a Jew-free future when Bolshevism and western Jew capital were laid low in abject surrender. Berger. I never did learn his first name.

We were stood before him in straight lines.

'Grossrozen needs electricians.'

The mention of Grossrozen was enough to strike horror in all of us. I felt the chill hand of terror on my heartbeat. Walter was an electrician. Grossrozen was a camp nearby where a free hand had been given to a regime of brutal kapos. It had become a killing ground, a place where nobody would willingly go. It suited the other camps to have such a place down the road to send offenders. This and other forms of duress kept rebellion at bay, though God knows, as weeks went by, weakness from hunger was proving enough to keep us under.

'*Elektriker austreten.*'

Berger repeated this a couple of times in a sing-song voice, the smile never leaving his face. He loved the effect this simple request was having on us, knowing, as we all did, our fellow prisoner, Walter, the boxer, my friend, was a 'sparks'. He had used his skills around Budapest while stting up as a stamp dealer. Berger walked the lines smiling all the while, softly calling as if to a cat: '*Elektriker austreten.*'

The smile had us on edge, a real menace. His pale right hand fingered his gun holster. We well knew he could easily produce that Luger to put a bullet into one of us, to bring on the required response. He took his time though, slowly moving, periodically stopping to stare into some unfortunate's face.

'Electrician?'

Head shaken, he would feign temporary sorrow, then face someone else into a terrified response, smiling all the while. The delay seemed endless. He stopped at the end of the last line.

'Sorry, gentlemen and Jews. I cannot believe that among all

of you there is not one person who can tell positive from negative. You are having fun with me.'

One of the kapos pushed Walter forward.

'Come on you.'

Out from the rest, he looked very alone and frightened. Berger approached him.

'Memory lapse?'

Walter didn't reply to Berger. Instead he looked my way. He gave me a desperate look and begged: 'Ernesti, come with me. Come.'

Berger looked my way. I was struck dumb and rooted to the spot.

'Is Ernesti an electrician also?'

Walter shook his head.

'He is my friend.'

Berger understood.

'If your friend wishes to join you in Grossrozen, he is very welcome.'

He turned to me.

'Well, Ernesti?'

I could not step forward. I tried to tear my gaze away from Walter, who was now tearfully and silently pleading to me. Berger shrugged. To Walter: 'Looks like Ernesti prefers it here. On your way.'

He nodded to a kapo, who took Walter by the arm. He resisted.

'Ernesti; for God's sake come with me.'

His voice had become a pleading whine. The kapo pulled, he resisted. Berger struck Walter across the face hard with his riding crop. The fight left him. As he was led away, he called back to me:

'Ernesti ... Ernesti ... come ...'

His face was a picture of sorrow and disbelief; mingling with his tears, blood from his nose. I felt an intense urge to run after him, but my animal survival instinct kept me in line with the others, from whom came no murmur, as the young Nazi officer taunted us while Walter was dragged off. He strolled up and down our ranks half-singing, '*Maurer austreten*? More masons? We want electricians too too too.' Rumour had it that this youngster had been shell-shocked on the Eastern Front, and we were his playthings while he was on leave, recovering.

Right? Wrong? Inside, I remained in turmoil over Walter. I stood more chance of staying alive at Wustegiersdorf. Would he have followed me to Grossrozen had the situation for some reason been the opposite? Who knew? I am ashamed of this moment in my life, but realistic in that the choice was 'here' or 'gone'. It felt like betrayal. Was I giving in and becoming immune to the suffering of those around me? A certain hardness had to develop, as did the need to fight one's corner, but essentially my compassion stayed in place. I would endeavour to keep faith with myself and my neighbours; my loss of Walter strengthened that resolve. No one knew his fate. Like so many who passed my way in the camps, I never saw him again.

Humanity and identity were central to survival, together with food and water, which coincidentally were the province of two individuals who brought me insights and excitement, my cousin Leopold and his friend and partner-in-crime, Zoltan. On the outside, these two would have been underworld overlords. Here they had quickly felt the pulse of the place and worked it to their and our mutual benefit. We loved their daring, their ability to work the kapos and influence the guards. Magic was at work in these two, surely not the hand of God.

Leopold Pozsonyi, my second cousin, was a well-built, handsome lad. His mother and my father were cousins. I had first encountered him when our family was evicted from our home and thrown out of Bratislava. One of the places we visited on our brief odyssey to Budapest was the small Hungarian peasant village of Paszto. Leo must have been 16 or 17 at that time. His father dealt in animal skins and fur, which made him top man in the community. The family managed to bring a little Hebrew refinement to the place. The synagogue, I remember, was rough-and-ready, small but very tidy; probably the feminine touch. I remember a lot of laughter and liking this older relative. Then Wustegiersdorf.

I bumped into him, literally, the day I arrived in the labour camp. As new boys, we had arrived and were seated on a slope outside the camp in our striped 'pyjama' suits with matching *Mutze* (pill-box caps), manifestations of weird bureaucratic detail, typically German in its finicky oddness. In heavy rain, the caps were useless, though in hot sun they helped. Nobody was paying us much attention, so somebody suggested saying the afternoon prayer. At the end of the *Amidah*, a standing silent meditation, I moved back the obligatory three steps and fell over a prisoner who had finished his prayers and was seated. Leopold.

'Mind yourself, zealot.'

I picked myself up. Our eyes met a moment.

'Ernest Lowy?'

A nod, a tearful embrace, a lot of catching up. Neither of us knew the fates of our families, but it was a certain fact that dear Uncle Hugo and Aunty Ilonka from Fulek had been hauled off to Auschwitz, and there had perished. I was introduced to Zoltan Merer, a roughneck whose smile and twinkling eyes gladdened many a dark moment. In the short time they had been there ahead of us, they had established themselves in the camp. They had provoked envy and admiration in good measure. The SS had them in their sights, but as much as it was possible for him to like anyone, they had found Schwarz's soft side, despite their being Jews, and in Messinger, a natural ally. Apart from charm, something special was at work. Like many 'criminals', these two engendered trust and confidence, were intensely moral, but could steal, kill and walk away smiling. Somehow these likely lads had wangled their way into the food-store kommando which, of course, meant access to special provisions on occasion, along with smuggling, sometimes on a grand scale.

One Friday, I returned to our floor after a hard day in the

open, soaking wet. In the bunkhouse, much excitement and a knot of inmates surrounding something pleasing. I pushed my way through the cluster of prisoners to find Leo and Zoltan dispensing herring to all from a barrel. Pickled herring. I stood open-mouthed, and out came a shocked cry of laughter.

'Shut your mouth Ernesti or you'll catch a fly. Here, make your Sabbath a good one.'

The Sabbath without fish, once unthinkable, was in the camp, normal. This was a minor miracle.

'How?'

I stared at the pair of them, their grins a mile wide. Big men, their pleasure at our pleasure made them seem like little boys. Zoltan replied: 'Don't ask.'

I persisted. 'Leopold. This has got to be dangerous for you. What if the guards discovered the food is missing?'

'Ernest. Stop fussing, I've sorted it.'

He waved me away with a laugh.

'How?'

Zoltan cut in.

'The guard in the food store is a woman – a German woman.'

He smiled to himself. A couple of inmates laughed. I didn't get it.

'So?'

Leo replied: 'So I've sorted it, is all. Arranged to our mutual satisfaction. Give a little, take a little?'

'What did she take?'

'You mean what did I give her?'

Leopold drew me to him, a powerful arm round my shoulders. He whispered into my ear: 'What d'you think, little cousin?'

He then gave me a playful kiss on the cheek. The penny dropped. As realization dawned on my face, the two rascals could not contain themselves and doubled up, as blushing, I met the eyes of my bunkmates who were grinning broadly.

8 Requiem for the Living

By September 1944, Leo and Zoltan had deals going on all over the place. With Schwarz, who had a large frame to fill, it was 'extras', as he held no sway in the food store. They corrupted the corruptible at all levels in the camp; consequently they had an 'untouchable' aura that added to their appeal. They even worked a deal for me. Summer was coming to an end, and the prospect of working outside with inadequate clothing and limited food intake scared me. Leopold stepped in and after a heart-to-heart, said he would work something for me. I was gladdened by this, for in spite of the weather still holding good, it would worsen, and I'd had enough. Working on the outside was pure misery. Whether you were Pole, Ukrainian, Jew or Gypsy, you were a target for the brutality meted out in the daily 'routine'. It was a killing ritual based on 'slow down or fall down and you die under the boot or rifle butt'. Both were incentives to getting up again, but, if you could not, they despatched you, Nazi-kindly, to the world beyond.

There was little quarter given, though the Poles were not meant to be killed unless they went out of their heads, or were too weak to bother with; so their status was token. It was obvious from the rumours and unguarded comments from the kapos and soldiers around the work areas that the days of the Third Reich were numbered.

This was terrifying and, of course, full of promise that for some of us at least there would be a tomorrow. The immediate problem was that the panic such stories engendered in the Germans would rebound back on us, which they did. The killing atmosphere went from brutal to vicious. All across

1. The author, a young man ready to live life after the war.

2. My grandparents, father and aunt, 1905. My grandfather, father and aunt all perished in the Holocaust.

3. My sister Lillie, 1935. She now lives in Glasgow, very close to Kathy and I.

4. Mother with Elsa and her son Ian. Ian also lives in Glasgow with her family. Elsa sadly died just before publication; she was a great support to me when I first arrived in Glasgow.

5. Alexander, or Munky, my dearly beloved and closest of brothers. Sadly, this is the only photograph of him that has survived. In 1944 he was forced to dig his own grave and was then shot in the head by Hungarian fascists.

6. Father in his robes as cantor, 1936.

7. Mother, Tertza, 1946.

8. Grandfather Eliezer Lowy, Cantor of Papa, Hungary, 1910.

occupied Europe, where there had been cold bureaucratic dispensation of efficient mass-murder, inexorably this declined into wholesale blood lettings carried out by disenchanted soldiers, along with crazed SS. All were caught up in the paranoid maelstrom that was destroying their belief and drowning their leader in blood. Outside the camps, civilian militias, such as the Hungarian Arrowcross, gave vent to their blood lust in an ad-hoc killing of Jews that could only be partially laid at the door of a mad Führer. It had so much more to do with a madness about us that had festered for two millennia, sired by religious untruth and plain, old-fashioned superstition.

A section of humanity was indulging itself in another orgy of self-induced destruction, something that over time it is prone to do, when the unknown brings the human into conflicts of uncertainty posing as Science, Religion or Philosophy. As so often before, Jews were among the 'fall guys'. But we were experiencing at first-hand an altogether new dimension, an escalation of cruelty without compunction in a supposedly civilised context. Hitler's strut upon the stage had eliminated conscience and bleached away guilt. As 1944–45 was the endgame for all he stood for, the injured beast he had roused from the depths of the human mind assumed a terrible stature. The word 'survive' resonated in our heads and hearts like a perpetual tolling of a bell, as it had for centuries.

In the middle of all this there were moments of great revelation and hope. For a while I had had my eye on a Wehrmacht guard who stayed aloof from his fellows. Unlike young Helmut, another guard who had become to us a lifeline and source of information, this man haunted the place, showed no sign of friendliness, did his job – just – but had not yet raised fist, boot or rifle butt to any one of us. He appeared not to mix well with the other guards. I was curious about him, so were we all. My chance to gain contact came one sunny afternoon. The work party I was in had been labouring outside the camp, just on the other side of the wire. Taking a break, we were allowed to sit on the grassy slope near the wire. The sun had shone most of the day. I was laid back, eyes shut, my companions were close by talking to each other in low tones. As usual, for me, in a drifting moment, my mind danced around thoughts of family and old times. Where were they all? Had they survived? How did they look?

A sudden dig in the ribs from Slomo Braun roused me. He pointed to the *appelplatz* where a pathetic assemblage of new prisoners was being marched into the camp. Standing in two lines, they looked more dead than alive, their bodies drooping like marionettes, arms dangling straight down beside their bodies. Even we, by comparison, showed more life when lined up, so I felt. The bright afternoon sun projected their shadows, long and angled, across the parade ground. Georges the French doctor, and Toby, another singer, like me a tenor, both shrugged when I asked who they were. Davide, another of our group, wandered across from having a furtive word with Helmut, our eyes and ears.

'From Warsaw via Auschwitz. Professional choir.'

We turned to look at Davide, who settled back down beside us. He gave me a little push.

'One minute you're singing for your supper, next you're here in an abject state, eh, Ernest?'

'I know. I wonder if they were any good?'

Georges looked across to the *appelplatz*. 'Odd that they're being kept standing around.'

I smiled at him. 'We were, remember? Their guards are checking in.'

'If they're joining us, you two can take a break and we can enjoy some fresh voices,' Slomo teased.

'A change is as good as a rest,' Toby responded.

We chuckled at the thought. Truth to tell, the inmates had heard our repertoire a few times over, though we were still getting requests, and to some extent Toby and I competed in extemporizing to add variety. It was fun. Talking among ourselves, we had taken our eyes off the standing group.

An explosion of sound brought us to surprised attention.

The air was full of the choir's singing. A wonderful noise erupting from emaciated frames starkly shadowed in the afternoon light. We listened astonished as the world beyond the work camp was returned to us, a world of art, beauty, simple humanity couched in melody. We had no words between us to recall the absolute purity of sound that bathed our souls that day. These beings were as emaciated as ourselves, if not more so, yet they produced a hypnotizing journey through heaven, hell, slavery and liberty. They sang of the future, the glorious possibility we all shared of a tomorrow. One by one from the nearby mess, tins in their hands, the Wehrmacht guards stepped out into the sunlight to see what they had been hearing through opened windows, this little concert on the *appelplatz*.

As suddenly as it had begun, it was to be over. Life seemed to desert the two lines of singers, their heads drooped to their chests, thirty automata with the clockwork run down. A despairing silence followed. At a window across the *appelplatz*, on the other side of the wire, Schwarz had appeared with his superior Seidel; they were talking animatedly. Seidel had his hand on Schwarz's shoulder. In the yard all was silent. As one or two guards began to move back toward the mess door, and while we were still looking at each other through tear-filled eyes, a sudden burst of singing seized all of us: 'Libera Me'. A requiem mass, a lament about fate, destiny and death; a cry from the heart about the absence of hope. A cry understood by every prisoner there, held entranced in the lengthening afternoon.

Keeping watch over us on that work detail along with Helmut, our friendly Wehrmacht guard, was the 'loner'. He had been standing by the gate listening intently. I felt this was a moment to approach him. Having discussed this possibility with my companions, they realized when I stood up what I was about to do. They weren't keen on the idea, and Davide tried to grab me as I stood.

'Ernesti, no. Get back here.'

I was up and approaching the guard who, as I got closer,

looked up from his reverie and laid his hand on the strap of his rifle. Summoning my courage I stopped, slightly out of reach: 'May I speak?'

He knew me. He had caught me looking his way more than once. 'Go ahead, son.'

My entire body was shaking with fear and animated passion. 'These singers, these artistes. You have been hearing great music. Doesn't that sound from their throats touch you? Doesn't it cry out to you?'

He looked at me for several seconds, then finally looked away. From his uniform pocket, he produced a couple of large biscuits which he proceeded to eat. I persisted, tears filling my eyes.

'Don't you feel like crying out loud? For all of us? For the destruction that's coming?'

He looked at me again and continued eating.

'Get back to your place.'

I received no answer. He had not lashed out, shouted or cursed, but his complexion had darkened, the pulse in his neck and temple expressed the emotion the uniform forbade. The choir's escort emerged from Seidel's office and marched them back out through the gates. As suddenly as they had arrived, they were gone. Weeks later, we learned their fate.

9 Anton

Leo was as good as his word. As September progressed, I found myself assigned to one of the factory workshops situated just beyond the camp gates.

'You cost me two bottles of champagne, Ernest.'

'Who got them?'

'Schwarz, of course.'

'Was he hard to convince?'

'Yes.'

Schwarz was a drinker. It helped persuade him. I gave my second cousin a hug.

'It's not all one way. You're meant to be skilled.'

My first morning found me very scared, standing in front of the man in charge. Short, stocky, middle-aged, with a brown uniform too tight for him, his Nazi armband added to the incongruity of a fellow so obviously an engineer first and party man a long way second. A draftee in the *Organisation Todt* (the 'state enterprise dealing with military infrastructural construction and maintenance'), he hardly fitted the image of the glowing Aryan engineer with utopian vision. Anton Sturmer, one of nature's gentlemen, decked out in a Nazi shell. He greeted me quite formally and without edge.

My first detail proved disastrous. A skilled metal job involving a huge axe and an eight-metre lathe. I had a little engineering experience, but this was beyond me. Hands on waist, Anton watched my vain struggle for a while smiling, then stepped in to avoid further punishment.

'My office. Five minutes.'

I stood alone by the machinery, desolate. Every eye in the place seemed to be on me. The minutes dragged, so that by the time I knocked on the door to his office I was shaking in my shoes. I entered. Anton was half-sitting, half-leaning against his desk. In the office with him was an older prisoner, waiting, hands behind his back.

'Though I should send you back, I don't want to see you spread-eagled on the *appelplatz*. It wouldn't make my day. This is Sandor, Ernest. He'll show you how to use the heavy stuff. I take it you approve.'

Approve? I could have flung myself at his feet and kissed them. Reprieved. Sandor Grossman from Transylvania was as skilled as they come. I quickly learned and made myself useful around the place.

As time went by, Anton's stature among the newer prisoners continued to grow. Though many of the men working under him were not properly skilled, he presented us all to the SS as essential labour. Eighty men, of varying quality, were there to maintain and repair mainly military vehicles, though from time to time other stuff came our way. He had full autonomy in the workshop, and inspections were rare. He used our first names, seeming to enjoy our company, more engrossed with the tasks in hand than exacting petty discipline; all of which made our days in the workshops, relatively speaking, a pleasure. For a while we were back in touch with our humanity, unlike the poor souls who had to endure winter in the open, under the whip. His motivation remains a puzzle to me, even today. When recalling him, I like to compare his actions to some other people at that time who could wear the uniform, '*heil*' the '*heil*'; yet, as if thinking with two brains, be themselves. Like Anton, they were natural humanists, they could stand apart from the hokum foisted on them by the political climate, the war, and just be themselves. It was high risk, but he didn't seem to care.

He had his little group of favourites in the workshop, those with proven skills with whom he could function in the engineering tasks that war damage brought about. With these prisoners he would sometimes discuss the war, and was early in letting us know of the Russian advances. Apart from this, he kept himself pretty much to himself. A private and modest man, but available to us; something Leo and Zoltan 'cottoned on to' in no uncertain fashion.

Food smuggling was a hazardous enterprise, but Leo and Zoltan had it down to a fine art. It all appeared ingeniously simple, something to laugh about when the danger had passed. Part of my job was to carry large pipes into the camp. They were used to repair the stoves in the barracks and guards' quarters. An immense amount of wood was burned in them, and replacement was frequent, due to heavy coatings of soot and other debris choking the flues. The replacements that I carried in were two metres in length with a U-bend.

Leo's bunk bed was next to mine. One night he was seated on it, handing out little parcels of food to a queue of hungry inmates, when he touched on the subject of the pipes.

'One of the stoves downstairs is blocked again.'

I yawned and pulled my blanket up. 'So?'

'So they'll be sending you in to replace the flue pipe.'

'Probably.'

I covered my head with the blanket. A pause.

'How often do those things clog up?'

'One flue a week about. Why?'

Another pause. The last man received his little parcel. We were alone.

'Would anyone think it strange if two, maybe three stoves clogged up weekly? It is winter.'

I pulled the blanket from over my head and sat up. He was smiling broadly. My eyes narrowed at him in the semi-dark.

'Where is this going?'

'Nowhere if you don't want it to. Are they heavy to carry?'

'Fairly, but I don't have to take them far, do I? What?'

'If we had stuff packed inside them, could you manage the extra weight?'

'What stuff?'

'Why, food, Ernesti.'

He was humouring me. Zoltan nearby chuckled.

'Is that why you worked so hard on my transfer?'

'On my life, no it wasn't. But the thought crossed my mind when I saw you fixing the stove up here. It would be a whole lot safer than stowing the stuff in our clothing.'

'Let me be clear. You want me to risk my neck smuggling food into the camp stuffed into flue pipes.'

My voice was raised. Leo looked around.

'Keep your voice down. Well?'

'A favour for a favour.'

'If you like.'

I stared at the rafters and pictured myself at the end of a rope.

'The food's for us all, Ernest. Zoltan and I couldn't carry such a quantity in safely. We could try, but the guards would rumble us because of the increased activity. The odd barrel of herrings is one thing, little parcels, well okay, but only you can increase the intake by using the pipes.'

I glared at my relative who had me over a herring barrel.

'And if we're caught? Grossrozen?'

'If we're lucky. Look, I won't blame you if you say no, but see it my way. You're just a boy, a nice boy. Where's the harm in you? It won't cross their minds that a slip of a lad would ever be involved in a scam like this.'

I was silent for several moments. Leopold lay back in his bunk.

'You need time to think. Let me know when you decide.'

'No need Leo. Of course I'll do it.'

'You're a *Mensch*, little cousin.'

I glowed with pride in the privacy of the half-light, the danger put to one side in the excitement.

We needed Anton's help in all this. The following day Zoltan and Leo were in Anton's office. Through the glass, I could see the smile on his face as the two rascals explained what they wanted. He was peeling an apple in his usual way, using a Swiss army knife. Slowly, painstakingly, from the top, he created an unbroken spiral, until the apple was stripped of skin which, that day, he handed to Zoltan who, laughing, consumed it while Anton devoured the naked apple; flesh, core, all but the stem which went in the waste bin. I watched him do that each morning, and to this day, I peel and eat my apples that way in memory of a remarkable German.

The deal was done. Whether he was rewarded in some way, or whether, as I suspect, it was done out of solidarity, I never learned. I was called in and told the plan. The smuggling involved mainly tinned food: pilchards, anchovies, sardines, mainly from Belgium. Anton helped in the packing, sealing the tins into the pipes with rough rags, stuffed in so tight, they could not slip out. Only once did Schwarz stop me. Asked what I was up to with a ladder on one side of me and the metal pipe on the other, I explained about the stoves.

'You can do mine, it's beginning to smoke. How come you can speak such good German? Where d'you come from?'

'Budapest.'

'You are Hungarian.'

'No. Jewish.'

The big man looked down at the little lad with the stovepipe and the ladder and with a barely hidden smile: '*Alhauen* – disappear.'

We were so successful that I became careless. We were getting cheeky and going to the limit. One evening, I returned to the mill from the workshops loaded with food. I all but clanked when I walked. I had on two pairs of trousers, the inner pair tied tight to the ankles. Inside the trousers a large quantity of dried yellow peas, cookable in the bunkhouse. Around my waist and torso were tied more cans of food. It felt like armour – and like armour it limited my ability to bend.

As the work party approached the gates, the whisper came down the line, worker to worker, '*Hippish*', Hebrew slang for trouble, which in this case was a body search at the main gate.

I was in line, no retreat. Schwarz was overseeing, Messinger was sharing the task with three kapos. I couldn't step out of line. In terror, I manoeuvred toward Messinger who must have sensed I had a problem, for when a kapo called me to him, Messinger clicked his fingers and beckoned. I shrugged to the kapo and stood in front of the big *Lageralteste*. He put his hands over my torso and momentarily paused to look at me. I mentally shrank into a little ball. Schwarz noticed the moment.

'What's going on there? Trouble?'

Messinger hit me very hard across the face and sent me sprawling. I could swear I clanked.

'Kid had a penknife in his pocket.'

Punishable but not lethal. In that split second, Messinger had saved me from death. I staggered through the gate and headed to the mill, realizing in horror that somewhere, probably after being cuffed to the floor, the string around one of the inner trouser legs had loosened and I was trailing peas. My fellow prisoners were on to the problem and kicked dust over the tell-tale line. By the time I was unloaded by Leo and Zoltan, I was a ball of grease, haunted by what might have been.

The smuggling continued through the winter, right up to January 1945 when, to our deep regret, Anton was replaced. One morning, everything stopped when Anton appeared in the company of a man much older, also from *Organisation Todt*. Probably in his sixties, the grey hair going white, his two front teeth were metal which gave him a menacing appearance. Quite tall and slender, the man had a slight stoop which gave him a sepulchral feel. Anton spoke.

'This is *Oberlieutenent* Ostwald who will be taking my place. I am returning to the Fatherland.'

Our shock registered to both men. Anton continued: 'For the co-operation you have shown in your labours, I thank you. Oberlieutenent Ostwald?'

The new man turned on Anton.

'Are you quite mad? It's soft-hearted idiots like you that are costing us this war. You thank these vermin for not dragging their feet?'

His voice had risen to an ugly high, his facial colour heading towards purple. I couldn't resist.

'*Wir danken, dem Führer.*'

I was parodying the customary German response of thanking the Führer instead of God. My voice carried further than intended. I felt like the brazen boy at the back of the class.

'Who was that?'

The new man was furious. Anton looked concerned. Ostwald looked through me. He was making a point. I didn't matter. Everyone held their breath.

'Stand to one side, boy, I'll deal with you later.'

He glared at Anton.

'What is this? Are we running a holiday camp for Bolsheviks? They're overfed and rebellious.'

He walked slowly round the workshop, eyeing each one of us with a cold, cold stare.

'Far too well-fed. I'll bite through your gluttonous gullets, you Hebrew parasites. That will stop you eating.'

Anton had his hands on his hips and his head slightly to one side.

'Ostwald, perhaps you could enlighten me. What crimes have these men committed?'

'Their guilt lies in the fact they brought the war on us, idiot. Don't you know that?'

Anton looked away from this Nazi ranter, smiled at us, shook his head and addressed the middle distance.

'If you honestly believe that, you're a bigger fool than you look. I pity these men in your hands – and I pity you, when the end comes. Report me. It won't matter.'

Ostwald was incandescent and strode away from the workshop. Anton followed him, but not before turning to give us a final wave before disappearing from our lives. We were left standing with mixed feelings: elation at the news that the Germans were losing, sadness at losing our friend, and fear at the manic behaviour of our new overseer.

I had been forgotten in the heat of the bad-tempered exchange. Anton's last act had let me off the hook. I never learned much about him or his family, but, like the others, I felt close to the man. Our thanks went with him. My abiding memory is the smiling man with the knife, carefully peeling and munching his way through his morning apple. My family laugh now when I peel one Anton-style.

10 Obersturmbannführer *Seidel*

One afternoon in October 1944, just a few weeks after my transfer to Anton Sturmer's happy band of engineers, I was tidying my bunk bed when, abruptly, a booted foot landed on my backside with such force that it propelled me to the edge of the bed and on to the floor. Frowning, I picked myself up dusting off floor dirt, and turned to face my assailant. The broad grinning face of Janck, a Polish kapo, met my temper and quelled it.

'Messinger wants to see you, now. Move it, you miserable little son-of-a-bitch!'

The *Lageralteste* had his quarters on the mill's ground floor at the far end beyond the Poles' bunks, which meant I had to run a gauntlet of hostility before reaching his hideaway. Making the bottom of the stairs and looking down the long hall, it was not difficult to imagine the looms back in place and working amid clatter and storms of cotton fibre. The long side windows with their arched tops, evenly spaced, ran down both sides of the building, offering generous amounts of light. On the sunshine side, the brilliant afternoon shafted in at a steep angle, creating a high contrast of light and shade within the building. In the path of the giant sunbeams, dust and flecks danced and floated, mixed with the curling smoke from the odd cigarette being enjoyed by a lucky few. The raucous chatter of these reduced men changed when they caught sight of me about to make my way through their ranks. On my way I was blocked, held up a few times and called a Jewboy; as if I didn't know. I was told I had no parents and if I should convert and become a good Catholic, I would still be a Jew, that couldn't be helped, but I would eat better and live longer. When somebody pushed me in the back sending me on a forward stagger, I felt my fists tightening. On top of all the frustrations around the camp, we had to put up with these idiots. Eyes filled with angry tears, I turned to face my tormentors, to shout and swear at them, but they were just silhouettes haloed in sunshine brilliance. My fist was raised. Their laughter seemed remote from their forms; tricks of the light and bounced sound.

'No Walter to back you up, ratface.'

'Skinny little runt thinks he's Schmelling.'

Reminded suddenly of Walter, my shame returned, and my fight went. I turned back toward Messinger's little room.

'Get lost, Polaks,' I grumbled.

There was a collective roar of disdain, then they fell back to their own affairs as I got closer to the door. Messinger's den. Knock on the door. Back came the deep rich voice of the *Lageralteste*.

'Who's there?'

I opened the door and edged in. The small space was full of men and tobacco smoke; half a dozen Polish prisoners and a couple of guards. Everyone turned to look at me. Over their standing frames I could not see Messinger. Where?

'Ernest Lowy, *Lageralteste*,' I stuttered, feeling small and not a little threatened by the hard stares I was getting. I stood, frozen, in the doorway. A big hand reached through the group and pulled me further into the room. Messinger. His tall frame towered over me.

'Wait here, Lowy.'

He dismissed the prisoners, then he and the two guards went into a corner for a huddled conversation, words beyond the reach of my hearing. I stood shaking with anticipation and fright caused by the healthy, well-fed menace radiating from the trio as it murmured away to itself. The two guards shouldered their rifles and left. Messinger called me across.

'I am given to understand you would be able to fix a fountain pen.'

Cousin Leo had been talking. I could put money on it.

'Maybe.'

He insisted: 'Not maybe. Certainly.'

'I apprenticed in a pen workshop in Budapest.'

'Is good. *Obersturmbannführer* Seidel is having trouble with his fountain pen.'

I blanched. Not only was Seidel the head of Wustegiersdorf, but he was also in charge of several other labour camps within range of Auschwitz. Messinger read my face: 'He's not one of the worst. Don't worry. I'll take you to him. We go now.'

I followed him past the Poles, 'So long Schmelling, nice knowing you', and out into the *appelplatz*, through the gates to one of the side buildings, quite close to my workplace. Outside the small building that was Seidel's lair stood a young guard. Standing alert and imposing, his SS credentials were not only his uniform, but the lad had the bearing that shouted 'elite'. Messinger explained who I was and why Seidel wanted to see me, then, after giving me a friendly push, walked off. The guard opened the door and led me up the few steps beyond the door, through a shiny lino reception and up to Seidel's office door. As I was ushered in, I got my first look at *Obersturmbannführer* Seidel, the master of my destiny.

A small man in his fifties seated behind a large oak desk. Immaculately uniformed, his grey hair centre-parted, perfectly lacquered. As we entered he was shifting papers, maybe for show. He spoke without looking up.

'You speak German?'

'It is my mother tongue.'

I tried to cover the shake in my voice. Seidel looked up; our eyes met for the first time and, for a moment, held. He smiled to himself, looked away and from the desk drawer he carefully brought out a beautiful, very expensive fountain pen: 'This pen I love for personal reasons, a gift from my wife. It usually works so well. Lately the ink isn't running cleanly, tends to flood with the ink going everywhere.'

He fixed me with an intent stare.

'Can you restore it?'

From me, a sudden burst of self-assurance. 'Yes. I can do the job.'

He looked at me doubtfully. 'You are sure, young man?'

From the same drawer, he lifted out a Luger pistol and laid it on the desktop, its dull gleam increasing its menace. 'It would be unfortunate for us both if any harm should come to it.'

While my heart pounded against my rib cage, a smile played round the corners of his mouth as he placed the Luger back into the drawer and closed it. How bad was the worst?

'Well?'

All I could whisper was: 'I'll need some cork.'

The smile threatened to return. 'Cork, eh? Where am I to find cork?'

In the corner of his office sat a very well-stocked wine basket. I pointed to it. 'You could always open a bottle of wine.'

I was just being helpful. He met the comment with a wide smile, no longer the patronising smirk. 'You're a brave young man.'

Moving lightly, quickly, Seidel left his desk. From the basket he pulled a bottle of wine, from his pocket a penknife with a bottle opener. In seconds I was handed a fragrant cork.

'Will that do?'

Nodding vigorously, I took the cork from his pale hand. I noticed that his nails were manicured. The pen was still on his desk.

'May I take the pen, *Obersturmbannführer*?'

'A moment.'

From a bureau beside the basket of bottles, he brought out two wine glasses. He half-filled both and handed one to me. Trying desperately to gauge the situation, I politely refused. He insisted: 'Don't start with me, boy. Your refusal would be offensive.'

A glass of beautiful fragrant white wine was placed in my trembling hand.

'Pinot from Alsace.'

I gulped down my first taste quickly, then slowly, in a

confusion of moments made strange by the delicate floral dryness of the wine as it raided my senses. While I lingered, momentarily, over the taste, Seidel wrapped his pen in some tissue paper and handed it to me.

'Take good care of it,' he warned and patted his empty holster. I nodded furiously.

'Wetzel!'

The young SS guard snapped into the office, eager to do the bidding.

'Escort young Lowy back to barracks. No rough stuff.'

'Sir.'

I gulped back the last of the wine as Wetzel ushered me to the door.

'Lowy!'

I froze. He held out his hand.

'The glass?'

I returned the glass to him, half-saluting, half-bowing.

'You'll also need this.'

He handed me a small bottle of blue ink. I pulled a little face as if to say 'stupid me'. Mutual hate had been tempered by moments of mutual gratitude and a little humour, adding to the surreal nature of the lives we were leading.

Wetzel was silent as he escorted me back behind the wire. At hundred-metre intervals around the perimeter of the camp stood little sentry pillboxes, along with strategically placed lookout towers. We passed into the camp, just as one shift relieved the other. I noticed Helmut was about to take his place near the main gate. He looked at me quizzically as if to ask, 'what have you been up to?'

Wetzel noticed the look: 'Friend of yours?'

'He was often the guard on work-party details when I worked in the open.'

He seemed satisfied with this, finally leaving me on the *appelplatz*, standing alone in the waning day. The wine had taken temporary hold of my senses and had created in me a velvet warmth. I went and sat on the bottom step of the fire escape outside the mill to think back over my encounter with the man who had ultimate power over life and death in these parts, trying in vain to equate the man with the job. Dusk was falling, the odd lights came on as I dwelt on the taste of the wine and the memory of its flavour from the vineyards of Alsace.

Later that night on my bunk bed, in the pale dimness supplied by a few wall lights, without even contemplating sleep, I set about my job. Spreading my tools on the blanket, a razor blade, a large nail, converted by Toby into a drill of sorts, a matchbox for sandpaper and the cork, I felt the eyes of my comrades watching my labours. As night progressed, snores replaced their attention, and I was alone in the inner space of concentrated effort. For a while the task eclipsed everything else, including hunger.

Leo and Zoltan had some business on the lower floors, and by the time they returned it was dawn. I had fallen asleep on the job, but the task was completed, and when tested, the pen worked to perfection. A strange elation filled my heart. I was anxious to see the pleasure on Seidel's face as he tried the pen. What was this? Where in hate and fear was there space to please and delight?

At roll-call, I managed to catch Messinger's eye. He couldn't, however, take me to Seidel until later that day. I had wrapped the pen in the tissue paper and carried it about during the day's labours in the factory workshop. Even though I had secured my trouser bottoms with extra string, I couldn't resist checking my treasured object every available moment. Time dragged unbearably. Worse, when evening crept round the corners of the camp, there was still no sign of Messinger. Excitement turned to anxiety; inside I was jumping up and down. I gave up waiting. Nothing for it but to risk the Polish 'chicken run' and get to his room at the end of the ground floor. I could not get into an altercation with anyone, but their words and my temper were a volatile mix. The pen, Ernest, the pen.

'Hey Kid Kike, how's it going in Kikeville?'

'Who's on your list, Schmelling? Fancy me?'

'We've got a couple of bantams want to use you to mop the floor.'

127

The expected foot came out; a trip, a stagger. Hand out to break my fall against a seated form.

'Watch where you're going, small fry.'

A push, a staggering back. I felt my anger rise … the pen, the pen. From Messinger's little room came the strains of accordion music. If I could just get past these bestial Polaks, I could risk breaking in on whatever celebrations were happening down the other end of the mill floor. A call from the front entrance pierced the racket made by 200 souls.

'*Lagerführer. Lagerführer!*'

Mayhem. Everyone scurried to their bunks. A deathly silence entombed the whole ground floor, so much so that we could hear activity on the floor above. Just the strains from the accordion being played in Messinger's room entered our silence. I was alone on the long shadowy work floor with two hundred men either supine or seated at their bunks. I took to the shadows and pushed myself tight into a corner. All listened as *Lagerführer* Schwarz's boots rang loudly on the bare boards at the entrance and proceeded to make them creak as he walked heavily and slowly forward. In the dim light his bulk became clearer as he reached midway along the room. His ruddy complexion and flame-red hair seemed to produce their own glow. He stood halfway down the centre aisle between the bunk beds. Us he was ignoring.

'MESSINGER!'

It was a jungle roar. The place vibrated. A lion-shaming bellow. From the *Lageralteste*'s room, the music stopped abruptly. A pause. Messinger emerged. Fearlessly, he strode toward his 'boss'. Titan frame-to-frame with Titan. Former athlete and Football Hero versus the 'Phantom of Dusseldorf'. Two hundred Poles were mentally placing bets. In the shadow, I stood glued to the spot as Schwarz took a step forward and leaned nose-to-nose with the favoured prisoner. Almost like rivals.

'Have you been drinking?'

'No.'

'*Liar.*'

'Perhaps it is your own breath you are smelling.'

A deadly pause. Schwarz landed a sharp back-hander to Messinger's face. The rings on his hand broke skin. Messinger held his ground and his dignity by not flinching, but did not retaliate. He was far from being on a level playing field with the SS man. The fact he survived the backchat was a big achievement. Schwarz turned on his heel and beckoned Messinger to follow him. Noisily they left the building together. A murmur broke out down the long room. People rose and started to move around. Cards came back out, the odd match-light sparked, flared, did its job to waiting cigarettes, then died. Conversation rose.

'You still here, Schmelling?'

I gestured a wave and ran for the stairs before the bullying resumed. I needed my bunk and its anonymity. The pen was safe. Hallelujah!

At roll-call the next morning, I tried to catch Messinger's eye. The bruise on his cheekbone was quite pronounced; the cut, short, deep and raw. He didn't seem to be looking my way so, after a while, I gave up trying. A little later, he came into the machine room. From out of my view, behind me came his rich, rolling voice in a lowered confidential tone.

'Job done?'

'Yes.'

'I'll take you to Seidel later today after food call.'

Doubly good. Today we were eating.

When I found myself in his office later that evening, Seidel was wearing civilian clothing. He looked more ordinary, smaller, less fearsome. I reproved myself for being intimidated by uniforms every time it happened. I had become vulnerable, the old me had subsided as general physical frailty took hold. My mind was undergoing changes as this deeply damaging incarceration continued, along with hard labour and scant feeding. The thought came again. How much a man is altered by the wearing of a uniform. He appeared altered, but what about the mind behind? Had to be, but by how much? Seidel seemed reduced by the lack of SS regalia, but maybe just in my eyes and imaginings. The SS had his brain in hock and doubtless, his balls. What caught me was how much of his office had, in my earlier terror, escaped my attention. The large portrait of Hitler, the SS banner and the ever-present red and black banner bearing the swastika. After escorting me in, Wetzel left the room.

'So?'

'I managed to fix it, *Obersturmbannführer*. Good as new.'

'Excellent. Show me.'

I handed the pen over. He held it to his desk light, examining it closely for damage. He then leaned over to write his name several times on a desk pad. The ink flow held constant. He looked up and smiled.

'It is good.'

He went behind his desk and, from the drawer, took out two large chunks of white bread cemented together with a good helping of margarine. My eyes must have lit up as he wrapped them in a sheet of paper and handed the precious package to me.

'Here, take this.'

I was keen to leave but Seidel turned me around and sat me down on a red leather easy chair. My bottom had not felt such comfort since Budapest.

'What's the hurry? Why don't you eat your bread now?'

'Thank you, *Obersturmbannführer*, but I want to share this with a couple of people who helped.'

'Your skill, your bread.'

'They helped with the tooling.'

'Fascinating, such altruism shown. Typically Jewish.'

'Adversity makes us so. What touches one, touches all. What benefits one benefits all.'

'A truism. Don't forget I have met your traitors, but I take your point.'

The next question shocked me.

'What do you think of Schwarz?'

Without waiting for my reply, he continued. 'Not your place to say, of course, but you are on the receiving end of his

130

behaviour. He is an idiot, a dangerous fool.' He went on in this vein, as if talking to himself: 'I have never liked the man.'

I didn't know what to say or where to look. This was a disorder in the ranks of the Waffen SS, Hitler's own minions in the field of conflict, mortal manifestations of the god himself. This very senior officer was in his office with a half-starved Jewish youth, complaining about his second-in-command. If this kind of unpleasantness was happening elsewhere, it was an indication that the Nazi mindset was in deep conflict with itself. Maybe, on the other hand, it was that Schwarz was seen to be the '*klutz*' he was by one and all, not least of all his boss.

'Yesterday, I told him to cut back on the floggings and beatings going on in this camp. Far too many.'

I was hearing things.

'Time we came to our senses, I told him, things being as they are in the Fatherland. He just stared back at me as though I'd cut off his arm. His devotion to the cause will only be severed by death. He doesn't think. Avoid him.'

This I needed telling? Hitler glowered down from his portrait and the black swastika, like a foetus in its white womb surrounded by the blood of history, yelled out its silent rage at this turncoat. The future denied. He should watch Schwarz more than I should. Seidel crossed the room to stand by my side. Confidentially: 'Remember the choir that passed through a few weeks ago?'

I surely did.

'They were meant to come here, but Schwarz is tone-deaf. They would have antagonized the man, so I had them sent on. Could be you people thought I'd sent them back to Auschwitz. Wrong, wrong. I sent them to KZ Friedland. Things are a little easier there. The *Lagerführer* is a baritone. It should work out for them, maybe they'll last out the war. So might you and I, who knows?'

Throughout his confidences, I remained silent. I looked up once or twice, the boy cowed by the man, but intrigued by the introspective flow of his intelligence and the news he was leaking. My heart lifted at the prospect of surviving all this. An end to Nazi control? My God!

'You had better run along now, young Lowy, to share your bread with your comrades. Don't change your mind now and wolf it down alone.'

I got up and turned to leave. As I reached the door, he called: '*Du!*'

Shocked, startled at the personal form of address, I turned. Seidel placed his fingers warningly against his lips. Then, 'Wetzel!'

The door swung open, and the war was back on.

'Sir?'

'Escort our young friend here back to his barrack.'

'Sir.'

The heels clicked and we were out of Seidel's office. The door shut, his face now a vivid recollection; slightly tired of voice, dark around the eyes, the fine, slightly febrile hands nursing the pen. A smile with no hint of malice or madness. All the same, SS.

'If he's so enlightened, how come he's still letting Schwarz run this hell-hole on blood and bone?'

Slomo Braun heaved his body round on his bunk to join the whispered conversation that was becoming more and more intense behind him. Regardless of Seidel's injunction to keep silent, back on the third floor of the mill, I'd blabbed and blurted. Flopped back down on my bunk, I gave a blow-by-blow account of where I'd been, who I'd seen and what I'd achieved, to my little group of friends whose bunks neighboured mine. They were aware that I was fixing a pen, whose they hadn't known until this surprising moment in the night. They were now very awake. Davide was excited: 'So he thinks the Reich is imploding?'

'He wasn't that specific, but what he did say would imply they are in dire straits.'

Georges punched the air: 'Home time!'

The others laughed. Toby joined in: 'Reining in Schwarz says much.'

Slomo growled: 'Give me half a chance with that ginger freak.'

I looked at him. He had become our minder against the hostile Poles in Walter's absence. 'With respect, Slomo, you're half-starved and he's well-fed, overfed. As good a wrestler and street fighter as you really are, you are out of condition. He'd snap your neck.'

Toby again: 'Do you think Seidel was lying?'

Me again: 'Why should he? What's he to gain?'

Toby: 'Raising hopes and dashing them? Fun to be had there.'

Davide: 'The Germans have been agitated for months now, well before we got here. Things weren't going to plan, obviously. Now something's definitely up. For instance, why are they marching people everywhere? It used to be trucks and trains.'

Georges: 'Well, Seidel seems to be backing off. Emptying his locker.'

Slomo: 'It's still midnight where I'm standing; no crack of light on my horizon.'

I smiled broadly. Out came the trump card, two huge chunks of fresh bread and margarine. The smell was enough. It was a pleasure to watch their faces as we shared the feast.

'Reward or peace offering?' mumbled Toby, through a mouthful of fluffy heaven.

'Who gives a goddamn,' growled Slomo. 'Right now, I'd give Schwarz a go.'

The stifled laughter disturbed the sleepers around us. Through the tall mill windows, bright stars danced around a crescent moon.

I had seen in Seidel the flicker of a damaged soul seeking release, proof maybe that a being can be brought back from the thrall of evil thinking. I heard the echo of the choir of emaciated civilian captives standing in the late afternoon sun giving vent to '*Libera Me!*', and looked forward optimistically to the days ahead.

11 My Friend Georges

As dark as things were in Wustegiersdorf, the abiding sense that the Nazi days were numbered, bolstered by Seidel's confidences to me, and the day-to-day evidence of increasing collective neurosis amongst our captors, were seized upon by us as props to our fragile morale. Along with Georges, our morale booster.

If there was ever a splendid, delightful, amusing character in any situation in life, it was Georges Heim. In the camp, he was a godsend. Apart from his being a medical doctor – itself a boon, even without medicine – his natural optimism, wit, and simple humanity never showed signs of waning and were a constant source of light and heat in the cold and darkness of our concentration-camp days. Even Schwarz, the 'Phantom of Dusseldorf', camp commandant and outright son-of-a-bitch, found it hard sometimes to resist this man's charm, to the point where the occasional smile threatened to crack his rock-set face. Georges' mere presence encouraged conversation, smiles and sometimes outright laughter.

In his mid-forties, he hailed from Lyon. He had been arrested in Paris, mistaken for one of his brothers who were active in the French Resistance. The three brothers had a German-Jewish mother whom they adored to the point of worship. Her influence had therefore been considerable, but happily liberal, endowing her boys with an open world view and truly catholic tastes. Twenty years married to Edith, his beautiful *'petite poupée'*, they had a son studying in the US. I was 19, he was very much our senior, but we youngsters saw in him not so much a father figure as a pally uncle. Music was our personal link, me with my ambition to sing, he with his cello playing in a 'semi-pro' chamber orchestra in Paris. We needed no excuse to talk music, walk music, sit music, be music. Where outside, this would have taken on proper social proportion, in the camp it was a skylight to the sunshine of sanity. Others thought us a little crazy in our pursuit of this single aim whenever we could, except Toby who was my singing partner and loved to join in.

Georges liked my 'trumpet' playing. The instrument was made of a sheet of paper. My voice was still 'in the break' and with my 'trumpet' it could produce a passing fair simulation of this and the French horn. One evening, with Georges sitting on my bed, I was playing him one of my favourite pieces, Bach's '*Kom süsser Tod*' ('Come Redeeming Death'). Georges used a couple of lengths of wood as his cello, his fingers working the invisible strings, the invisible bow easing through the air with graceful accuracy to his own 'celloish' vocalizing. Smiling, we floated our way through the heart-moving chords and lines of Bach's little masterpiece. That was followed seamlessly by the dignified moving tune of the *Kol Nidre* prayer, the way I learned it from my grandfather. While we sat in our reverie, the bed had become surrounded by our neighbours who called persistently for more. By the end of the little session, we had them in tears. It was the beginning of our regular Sunday evening 'socials' which brought the sanity skylight to the barrack and better morale for Monday.

Tchaikovsky's 'Song Without Words', Georges' favourite tune, will always return me to a day when we were on a detail together, in the back of a truck heading for a yard to pick up sand and pebbles, to take to a building site near Oberwustegiersdorf. He was humming the melody quite loudly against the diesel engine, and I was helping. The young POW driver, a Frenchman, had a call of nature, pulled over to park and, after getting a grunt of permission from the half-awake Wehrmacht guard, took off for a brief vacation. We had stopped at a pretty little place called Scharlottenbrunn. The guard ushered us down off the truck for a requested leg stretch. Our striped pyjama uniforms, not yet replaced by more weather-resistant clothing, created an instant response from the few locals around, mainly elderly, who quickly dispersed and disappeared.

We were standing in a lovely town square, because of us now deserted. Georges was commenting on the beauty of the place and the privilege of being lucky tourists to stop here courtesy of French bowels, and I was giggling my agreement, when suddenly, on a bicycle, a man in his middle years wearing dark blue dungarees, large bag over his shoulder, and a pot of paste dangling from his cycle handlebar, fast-pedalling swept into view. He meticulously parked his bike, pedal-to-kerb, close to the public toilet, the outside walls of which held wartime information posters and Nazi propaganda. From the bag came a gigantic poster, bigger than the man himself. He had trouble pasting it and, consequently, had our amused attention. When he finally got it into place, our jaws fell open, as did the young Frenchman's who came out of the toilet adjusting his trousers and looking round to see what had caught our appalled gaze. The poster portrayed a Jewish man in the manner of the stereotype caricature that could have come straight out of the Nazi newspaper, *Der Sturmer*: ugly, hostile, about to eat the world and pocket the money. Beneath it, the legend, '*Der Jude, Kriegsverbrecher, Kriegsantiffter*' ('The Jew, War Criminal, Warmonger'). Great! We were to blame. We stood. We stared. I snapped. I called out:

'What are you anyway? You Nazis. You see that piece of propaganda, and you see us standing here. Where are you coming from? You're not human. Throw that junk in your bag into the rubbish.'

The guard mumbled a warning for me to behave. The man looked up, and as if seeing us for the first time, squinted our way. Slowly, deliberately, he wheeled his bike and walked toward us, offering me my reply; 'Not a chance sonny. Everyone has to know the truth. You need to know the truth about yourselves.'

I gestured to his bag. 'Give me one.'

'You want to put it on the camp wall next to Betty Grable?'

His snigger was repellent.

'Just give me a poster!'

He reached into the bag and handed one over, smiling wickedly. It was obverse folded. The man mounted his bike.

'Enjoy your likeness, Jewboy, *Heil Hitler!*'

Both he and the guard saluted, though the guard's '*Heil*' and '*Hitler*' seemed muted to the point of indolence against that of the enthused civilian who parted the square with the shout;

'*Juden Raus!*'

Georges looked at me holding my prize. 'What are you going to do with that? Paint a moustache on it?'

'Make myself a better trumpet. Several.'

He nodded. It seemed like a good idea.

With the truck later laden with sand and pebbles, our little party was on its way to the work site to unload. The Wehrmacht guard, though fierce-looking, was, we had found out long before, quite docile and very lazy. We could tease him and his response to the bait was the odd 'shut up' ('*maul halten*'), usually mumbled as if we were disturbing his sleep. He was a little disappointing. As the truck rumbled along to its destination, he sat on top of the driver's cabin, rifle between his legs, swaying to the vehicle's movement. Georges and I lay back on the pebbles, staring up at our guardian and trying him on.

Georges: 'What kind of political system gets itself into a war it can't win, then wastes its dwindling resource on paste and paper to propagandize against a racial minority which is unarmed and helpless?'

Me: 'I don't know. Which political system gets itself into a war and does what you said?'

'The German *NAZI* party, stupid.'

'Never heard of 'em.'

'*Maul halten, maul halten …*'

The Wehrmacht guard was surly. He was miserable, he couldn't laugh, not because he shouldn't have laughed, but because the poor bastard agreed with us!

Later that night, amid the snores and groans of the sleeping barrack, Georges opened up about the circumstances of his arrest by the Gestapo.

'I was about to embark on a clandestine love affair.'

In the semi-dark of the barrack, he laughed at the shock on my face. I had learned from him his devotion for Edith, and the man himself seemed completely within his integrity. In voices lowered to suit the sleeping.

'A what?'

'A love affair, an extra-marital relationship.'

'Why?'

'There is a plane where souls meet and converge that exists clear of the conditions we impose on ourselves. I stumbled out on to that plane, briefly. If it wasn't for my brother Davide and the Gestapo, who knows, I might still be on it with Paulette.'

He had met her socially in Paris. A stunning beauty, intelligent, softly spoken, given to café life, talking dangerously and chain-smoking Gitanes; a typical Parisienne of the period.

'An intoxication, Ernest. Before you marry, enjoy a little café living. Explore.'

The prospect seemed remote.

'But you were married.'

'Nineteen years; all your life. As happy as any beings could be. Devotion personified.'

Georges had a successful Parisian practice and a wide social circle. He had encountered Paulette several times at parties and gatherings where the bohemian, the loyal and the politically dangerous cocked a snook at their occupiers and enjoyed life anyway.

'Quite apart from Edith, I could feel my passion for Paulette growing. I indulged myself in the adolescent sense of helplessness in the face of the magnetism she exerted upon me. My temptress.'

I wanted one. He continued: 'Second rendezvous at a Paris street café. Outside, a warm day. Hand-in-hand across the little table. A car pulls up. Three men in leather overcoats. Gestapo. Some poor victim was about to be dragged off. They stopped at our table. "Your name is Heim?" "Yes," I said.

"Papers," they said. I produced them, they looked. "Come with us," one said. So I had to ...'

He was silent for a few moments.

'Paulette tried to intervene and was warned off with the threat of arrest. In spite of my credentials there in front of them, they had their orders to bring in a Heim. I was it. It was Davide they were after, someone must have betrayed him. Being a doctor, I had enjoyed relative freedom in the city. I had become careless. Anyway, I endured the questions and the beating reserved for Davide. When they finally acknowledged I was me, they sent me on to Auschwitz anyway. One less Heim around the place. I hope my brothers continue to thrive, that Paulette was left alone ... Edith. One good thing from this Ernest, realising how transient my affair would have been and how I might have lost Edith. So in spite of death staring us in the face, I still hope to get my second chance with my wife.'

Redemption at the gates of Hell. The irony was not lost on me, and with Georges, I sat on the edge of my bed, in the night, musing on a future that seemed a futile pipe dream. The barrack snores and nightmare cries a dissonance against the melody of our thoughts. Georges again: 'If I do survive this nightmare, and be one day re-united with my family, do I thank the Nazis for saving my marriage? As much as I loathe them, they did that much for me.'

I objected. 'I think you would have probably called a halt to your relationship with Paulette.'

Georges nodded. 'Maybe so, but maybe not in time. The Gestapo did me a favour they didn't intend.'

Me: 'Then your gratitude would be wasted on them. They deserve nothing.'

Georges: 'Here in the camps, I've rediscovered my self-respect. To take Edith in my arms again with a clear conscience is my single greatest incentive to survive, and for me, the greatest thought I can have on this earth.'

We fell silent again. Eventually, he rose, placed a friendly hand on my shoulder and wandered back to his bunk. I laid back and imagined Paris; the laughter, the music, the gaiety, the cafés full of fragrant smoke, wine and vivid conversation. And a beautiful mistress. Down the barrack in the damp dark, someone shrieked in sleeping panic.

We lost track of Georges after the camp had to be evacuated when the Russian advance from the east became uncomfortably close. We had been split into groups to attempt escape from a winter storm, as we fled on foot ahead of the military advance. It wasn't until early February 1945, towards the end of our long march to Belsen, that our little group found ourselves together again in a batch of about 200 prisoners. We were billeted in the local theatre in the beautiful town of Hildesheim. Georges and I hunkered down on stage in front of the heavy, red velvet stage curtain, very tired, very low. We managed to give account to each other of the time of separation. It was so good to see the twinkle in his eyes undimmed.

Toby, Slomo, Davide and a bosom buddy of mine, Joe, were resting in the area front-of-stage. Through the rear exit a Wehrmacht guard known by us veterans of our long walk as '*Die Ratte*' stomped in looking for trouble. He looked like a rat – apologies to the rat – and behaved like one cornered. It was his habit to kick out at his prisoners as they lay resting. With their spare frames and his heavy boots, the damage was often bone-snapping, often lethal. He made his sadistic way down the centre aisle. Passing us, he aimed his rifle butt at me. I rolled. He turned his attention to a sleeping prisoner a bit spread, and in his way. The kick was rib-breaking and he followed it up with a very sour curse. As he passed Slomo, their eyes met, and the Rat averted his gaze, not seeing Slomo's outstretched foot. The Rat tripped, stumbled and fell on his rifle. With blood pouring from his mouth as he yelled out in pain, he was finding it impossible to get up. He had twisted or broken something and was helpless on the floor in front of his charges. The place went silent except for the screams and shouts coming from the Rat. Two guards came to his aid and pinned between them, they helped him out of the auditorium, shoving prisoners in their way. Next morning, on our detail, no Rat. We had to struggle on without him.

We were working on the rail line at Hildesheim. It was early afternoon when the sirens sounded. The town clock showed two. A brief pause. Everybody started to look at everybody else in a great unasked question that was almost immediately answered by a huge, deafening roar as an Allied aerial bombardment began. The question of how close the ground forces were came into my mind as a bomb tore into the track a few hundred metres down the line, throwing debris and bodies upwards and sideways. A prisoner beside me panicked and ran. In the whirlwind of his panic, the spade he had been using was hurled to one side and hit me in the face. Another bomb blasted the station buildings. We ran. Blood was pouring from my nose so that breathing became choking, followed by my stumbling, coughing and doubling up in agony. Georges stopped me and put me down on a ramp. Prisoners were pushing by us as this brave man applied simple first aid instead of joining the general panic. Breathing was still hard, due as much to the smoke and dust of the dying town, as it was to my blood flow.

My face was numb, Georges and I came up from the track and stood watching the town disintegrate around us as the planes went about their business. We simply didn't know which way to go. Flames seemed to be shooting from every other window, buildings of Gothic beauty had fast become shattered, smashed. From some windows people were hurling their belongings into the street. Women and children were running hand-in-hand away from the town centre and away from the direction of the bombardment, their fear and tears etched in the pale dust that covered their faces. We had been joined by other prisoners. Having nowhere to run, and being prisoners in mind, as well as body, we made our way, almost disciplined, towards the theatre, now in flames. We were on the wide pavement with people milling on and off the kerbs. A one-legged soldier on crutches hobbled towards us. He was horrified on seeing us. In spite of the explosions all around, he upbraided us and called to the deafened world at large:

'For Christ sake, somebody get these Jews off the pavement. These mongrels should not share our walkways. Get off! Vermin! Off!'

We rushed past him, left him gesturing impotently at us with one of his crutches. I turned, paused and looked him in the eye: '*Maul halten* you mad idiot.'

It was as if I had knifed him. Open-mouthed, his eyes followed us as we hurried toward the theatre.

'Poor bugger. Conditioned. Dead hand of fascism,' muttered Georges.

Like all good sheep, we were nearly all safely gathered in by nearly all our complement of Wehrmacht guards. After a fitful, sleepless night in a cold village church away from Hildesheim, we made our way, let's not call it a march, more a hobble, to the concentration camp, Hannover Ahlem, where kapos held sway. Mainly Austrian, mainly 'released' convicts, they had acquired a free rein to do as they pleased with the camp inmates, and did. We had a little cover from the Wehrmacht who had come with us, but, with the increasing threat from the Allies, they were ready to run. After ten harrowing days in mortal danger from all sides, the place came under bombardment, and those of us surviving, captors and captives, joined the existing inmates of Hannover Ahlem for a final hike away from the Americans and the British to the disease-ridden death camp known as Belsen, where thousands were dying daily from starvation and, latterly, typhoid. This, to our cost, we would soon discover.

It was at Belsen, in the days of liberation, that I contracted typhoid. By the time I had recovered, Georges had gone. With repatriation proceeding apace, he had again become lost to us. The little group who had held together so tenaciously through the last and worst days of the madness missed him badly. We hoped for the very best for our friend, that he had survived, that he had found his family intact. I would, in time, hear that indeed, all he had prayed for came to him.

He and his family were reunited. My friend Georges, a charmingly warm human being was given his second chance. Heaven had smiled on him.

PART III
THE LONG MARCH

12 Slomo Braun

Back in time to Wustegiersdorf. After Anton left, we in the workshop got a real taste of the new man's cruelty. Ostwald quickly earned his nickname, 'The Beast'. Screaming anti-Semitic insults, he prowled the workshop looking for trouble. For no particular reason he would lash out with his boot at anyone he was near, almost out of habit. Add to that he was liable to report anyone to Schwarz for quite minor breaches and, therefore, the inevitable beating or flogging was delivered to the undeserving. As the working groups began to suffer at his hands, so productivity dropped and his bad moods increased, the cycle of mutual dysfunction becoming ever more vicious.

Apart from being a close friend in the bunkhouse, Slomo had become a bit of a father figure. Younger than Georges, he acted older, and because of his wrestling and street-fighting days, his face had acquired less a lived-in look and more a jumped-on look, complete with cauliflower ears. Even after months at Wustegiersdorf enduring limited nourishment, he was very powerful. Deeply loyal, like most roughnecks, he endangered himself on our behalf, very much like Walter. Unlike Walter, he was not terrorized by the place or the men who ran it. He held an uneasy peace with Schwarz, shared mutual respect with Messinger, and, as a real mark of respect, the Poles left him alone. He spent a lot of spare time on the second floor with the Ukrainians and Slavs where they had a couple of chess masters. Slomo wasn't the greatest but he played well and enjoyed their company, which in its turn, kept most of the second floor off our backs.

From the day their eyes met, a singular animosity developed

between Slomo and Ostwald. Mentally, they circled each other for three weeks before things came to a head. In the bunkhouse we had all heard the story about Slomo when he was in the *Aussenkommandos* working in the woods outside the camp. Rumour had it that he and a particularly unpopular guard had fallen behind the work party and, seizing the time, Slomo had killed the guard; easy for a wrestler. True or false, it did his reputation no harm around the camp. Slomo found it very hard to conceal his contempt for this tall skinny SS ghoul, whom he suspected of the kind of cowardice that a uniform sometimes reveals rather than disguises. So when Ostwald picked on me for using 'good' wood for the workshop stove and breaking up valuable timber, the attack came from behind with a stunning kick in the back. I went sprawling. Slomo saw red and intervened: 'Leave the boy alone.'

Slomo hadn't left his machine. He had been sharpening tools on a grinding wheel. Ostwald noticed this and came over to him.

'None of your business, Jew scum.'

Without warning, he grabbed Slomo's hand, which was over the spinning grinder, and thrust it hard against the turning wheel, which tore at the hand then caught it in the struts at the axle. Somebody switched off the power, saving Slomo's hand which, now very bloody, he extricated from the grinder. Ostwald recognised suddenly that he was in mortal danger and gave a little cry as, roaring in pain, the wrestler turned on his attacker who was thrown to the floor and pinned down. With his good hand, Slomo forced Ostwald's mouth open and held his bleeding hand over the gaping face and let the blood flow into the German, who writhed and wriggled helplessly.

'Now you can drink Jewish blood, you lame excuse for a man.'

Slomo was pulled away before he did the man any lasting harm. Ostwald got to his feet, aimed a blow at Braun, slipped on the bloody floor and had to be helped from the workshop.

146

We never saw 'The Beast' again. We thought we had seen the last of Slomo too when he was taken off for 'treatment', but somehow Messinger prevailed in his intervention on Slomo's behalf with Schwarz. Suffice it to say that a very bruised Slomo Braun turned up on the day we began the 'Long March'.

Within days of Ostwald's disappearance from our lives, we were told that in around ten days the camp had to be evacuated. This seemed to confirm that the rumours which had helped keep us warm since November were true. Before the off, we were given our last barber treatment by the kapos. In the camp they had tended to just run a track down the centre of our heads, and from time to time, a head shave overall. This time we received the full shave so we could greet the world beyond the wire with clean chins.

The Eastern Front had collapsed and the Red Army was rapidly advancing. We had heard from Helmut that our destination would be camps on the other side of Germany; lacking transport we would have to walk a lot of it. In the dead of winter. In the dark of the barrack, our conversations were slightly hysterical, trying to fathom how we were to get across Germany alive. We were in a reduced condition, certainly not up to the exertion of such a march in the mud and ice of January and February. We had heard there would be an issue of footwear; camp clogs would certainly not be any use in mud and snow.

'It defies logic,' muttered the recovering Slomo.

'Why don't they just dispense with us in time-honoured fashion?'

Davide volunteered: 'Lack of ammunition? Auschwitz is in the path of the Russians, so they can't take us there. They're probably evacuating that too.'

Slomo: 'They could just leave us here and take off.'

I offered a comment: 'They are ideologically attached to us. We are needed to the bitter end as we are target number one in the endgame. We will be there to see the end, and besides, it's not over until it's over. If they have to surrender, we are a bargaining chip. Right now, we're their slaves and wherever there is work to be done, slaves are needed.'

There was silence for a moment.

Davide: 'Well, tomorrow's another day, full of promise and a golden opportunity for our German cousins to fulfil their familial tasks.'

We chuckled into the freezing darkness of the barrack room, while, away in the distance, the heavy crump of Russian artillery warmed our thoughts.

The day of our departure from Wustegiersdorf work camp started as usual with reveille and the roll-call. Lined up in the cold semi-dark of a grey morning in late January, we were informed the 1,000 or so of us were to be divided into two groups with different destinations in northern Germany, Flossenberg and Belsen.

Lagerführer Schwarz screamed this thin intelligence between thicker helpings of abuse. His eyes rested on Slomo and our little group. Slomo muttered his usual invective against this officer who had sanctioned the cruellest of beatings on his person, followed by five lashes. Messinger had prevented his execution. Rumour had it that nobody amongst the SS at the camp actually liked Ostwald, so Slomo was allowed his life and time to grumble on about the fat pig who ate our share of the rations.

'If that bastard's coming with us, he'd better not turn his back on me.'

Some of us looked furtively round, in case of a kapo overhearing this injured hero and ratting on him. The ice-cold wind caused us to hug our inadequate clothing tight about ourselves.

Slomo Braun didn't make empty threats; this I knew. About a week after arriving at the camp, late spring, early summer, he and I, with about a hundred others, were marched across to the nearby village of Oberwustegiersdorf, where we were detailed to work at a large timber depot. I didn't feel good that morning. My system had not worked

148

well since my being held in Budapest and put on that cursed train to Auschwitz where pride and determination prevented any release. From then on, the conditions were so alien to me that bowel function was in chaos and constipation the norm. Nervous retention. I couldn't shit, my hysteria wouldn't let me.

That morning I could hardly walk, let alone work. I was doubled up in pain. Slomo solved the problem by hiding me behind a stack of long planks, the idea being that when the shift was over, someone would come by to let me know. A sharp-eyed young guard, a zealot, found me in a foetal crouch, dragged me out on to open ground where I was beaten and kicked until senseless. According to accounts later, several inmates had hurried to help me but were given the rifle-butt treatment by the guards and held back until my punishment had been satisfactorily concluded. Apparently Slomo's anger had gotten the better of him. He too had to be restrained. The guard had been ready to shoot him dead then and there. Slomo's invective would have bitten deep.

I came to in what passed at Wustegiersdorf for a sick bay. My body ached, and my mouth was numb. My lips had swollen, there was dry caked blood around my face. I lay back groaning to myself. I closed my eyes, settling back for a moment. The bunk bed on which I lay was hard against my body. I sat up again, painfully. No doctor or nurse had made an appearance. Afternoon light shone in through a dusty window. I had seen this outbuilding often enough and knew it to be staffed, but where were they? On a bunk bed opposite, a sleeping form lay motionless in shadow.

A doorway at the end of the 'ward' led to a shower room, from which I could hear the hollow drip of water from a showerhead not completely turned off. I was filthy and stained from rolling on the timber yard floor. Easing myself carefully off the bed, I limped past the sleeping form into the shower area where I found a water closet next to the two shower spaces. A mirror had been screwed on to one of the walls, which when I reached it showed me just how battered my face had become.

Behind the effects of the beating lay a face I didn't know, a being who had taken my place, yet responded to my every inflection. Pulling my puffy lips apart, I was relieved and surprised to find my teeth all there; loose, but all there. My tongue was too swollen to run around the outside of the fronts. Apart from the blood, though, they seemed okay. At one of the washbasins, I found a sliver of soap and made best use of it in the shower under the cascade of, oh dear God, hot water. I nearly scalded. I let it overwhelm me and, in my body's response, my bladder let go. I think I may have laughed out loud. My sparse frame had come alive causing internal relaxation. A dense sensation in my bowels sounded an alarm that sent me from shower to water closet in one step. It was a deeply pleasant release, perched as I was on a grubby china rim with no paper to wipe myself, dripping wet and free at last.

Back in the shower, I luxuriated in the heat and clean sensation of the moment. I gave my clothes a wash. Quite soon after we arrived at the camp, we were issued with clogs and civilian clothing, more weather-friendly than the striped pyjama suits. The dirt that ran out from the shirt and trousers I had been wearing made me long for new, clean clothes. I thought suddenly of my father as I walked back into the 'ward', rinsed and wrung clothing over my arm; 'Praise and thanks to the Holy Creator, today and every day.' I could hear his voice in my mind's echo chamber.

A little later, still naked and glowing from the effects of the shower, I lay still listening to the sounds of summer coming in from outside; an abundance of birdsong filtering in through a wall vent just above the bed. From the vent, a single shaft of sunlight beamed onto the floor just ahead of me. In its light, the shadow of a leafy tree branch danced to a breeze. The window offered a shaft more of daylight, giving the room a warmth it didn't naturally have. By degrees, my body began to tell me it was hurting. Bruising was evident in several places, large boot-sized areas all over. And my genitals; my genitals were distended and the colour of damsons.

'*Ezek a madarak betegge tesznek*' ('These birds make me sick').

This came in clear Hungarian from the other bed. A figure in the shadow sat upright into sunlight which caught a craggy face with a hollow-eyed stare that met my eyes square on.

'Where do those little sods get off? It's all flit and twitter as if they're taking the piss out of misery, sounding so happy. What are they celebrating?'

I replied: 'The summer? Not being human?'

'Let them go and do it somewhere else, they're getting on my tits.'

I tried to smile, but my battered face wouldn't let me. My heart was full of tears from the pains of the day, and the great freedom of nature beyond the walls and wire. A song by Brahms almost came to my lips. A setting of a verse by Heine:

> Death is the cool night,
> Life, the sultry day.
> It is growing dark,
> Sleepiness embraces me,
> The day has worn me down.
> Above my bed rises a tree;
> In it a nightingale sings,
> Sings of undying love.
> I hear it, I hear it,
> Even in my dreams.

That night I had to vacate the bunk bed for some poor man who was violently ill and given to spasms. That found me on the floor on some worn-out rugs and covered with a thin blanket. The beating I received gave me a day off work. This I learned from the civilian doctor who put his head round the door at the end of the day. He promised the three of us that food and drink would be forthcoming. We waited for it all the following day, during which more walking wounded appeared, courtesy of the guards. The day ended with no food. We drank from the tap in the shower room. An orderly appeared to check nobody had died, also to apply dressings where bleeding failed to co-operate and congeal. In the dark the inmates talked incessantly, making sleep difficult. In moments of silence, a moan would break into the reverie that dulls pain but doesn't let it go. Thoughts of home were the only refuge, while prayer seemed somehow to enlarge doubt and fear, as though it and our plight seemed to be hand-in-glove, partners in a Jobian nightmare. Suddenly, I felt someone beside me. Thinking me to be asleep, the presence shook me hard. In an insistent whisper: *'Lowy. Lowy!'*

I rolled over and came face-to-face with a shadowy form. Vaganfi. Hungarian for daredevil, the name fitted him perfectly; the man had no fear. He pulled me to him, and, in a low whisper: '... in the half-dark. Nobody noticed a thing. Buried him and his fucking rifle under tons of heavy timber. He'll be bones by the time he's found.'

'Who?'

'Who do you think, Ernesti?'

In the dark my eyes popped. He continued: 'Good eh? Braun got him. The guy was beating on everyone, not just you. Bordering on the crazy. It was a case of a hit and a spit too far. Paid the price. Bastard!'

Vaganfi's chuckle drifted lightly across the room as he disappeared into the night. The place stirred awhile, then settled into the quietness of those trying to sleep and those whispering in wakefulness. I felt a cold shiver run down my back. If they found the body, we would all be questioned. Could I hold out? Would there be reprisals? Almost certainly, if they found him. A retaliating blow against the Nazis had been struck again; such moments were few and far between amidst the carnage. Something. An object had started to dig into my thigh. From under the thin blanket, I pulled out a thick lump of fresh bread. There had been a rare delivery and I was not to be missed out. The little group in the bunkhouse were thinking of me. Our protectors and friends, Vaganfi, Slomo, my cousin Leo and ever-smiling Zoltan, all of whom would, in a peaceful world, run the gauntlet of the law and social disapproval from my class. Here in the camp, they were heroes whose kindness and selfless acts on our behalf kept the collective roughly intact and partially fed, in this gruel-based regimen of heartless deprivation. We needed them there and then. If they survived into a future peace, what would become of them, apart from being forever locked in my affection and memory?

I had come to know what it was like to receive a beating from a Nazi guard. I had survived it. Slomo had responded to our distress by taking out a guard. In the months ahead, he would be there for us. He would go on to survive a foul beating and the lash, to walk with us to Belsen.

In that grubby sick bay I ate some of the bread. Along with that, I laid back through the levels of pain, so that sleep began to creep across my consciousness, laying a velvet barrier between me and the ache of my body. Drifting softly away from this world, the notes of Brahms and the words of Heine floated across my memory: 'Death is the cool night ...'

13 Helmut

He stood with the other guards, all of them looking utterly frozen and disconsolate on that grey-as-pewter February morning in 1945. The sky was leaden with the prospect of snow; the ice on the *appelplatz* in slippery petrified puddles made walking difficult. Helmut dug his chin into the upraised collar on his greatcoat and beat his gloved hands together. He looked across to our little group among the 1,000 assembled prisoners, and we could see the sadness in his eyes at the state of us, now made ready for the hike across Germany with our special issue footwear – from the dead at Auschwitz. And the civilian clothes that had covered our backs since the weather changed in the autumn, a gift from the murdered. We were also allowed to keep the blankets from the camp as additional cover; from the look of the sky we were definitely going to need them.

We were all waiting for Seidel and Schwarz to make their appearance. My eyes met Helmut's. From him a reassuring nod, from me a little smile as I shuffled my feet to keep warm. We needed to move, to create body warmth against the chill breeze that forced tears from blinking eyes.

My thoughts began to stray back to my first encounter with this kindly Wehrmacht guard. I cannot have been in the camp more than forty-eight hours from the train ride away from Auschwitz. I had hated using the bucket lavatories placed on each floor of the mill. For an orthodox boy to defecate, let alone urinate in front of others, was mentally out of the question; a step too far. Though I had 'been' during work hours, the combination of thin soup and what passed for a hot drink played havoc with my bladder. The days were getting longer as spring led into summer, so that particular day, I must have been easily seen in the evening light leaving the mill, having made it down three flights virtually holding my groin. I found a shadowy corner and let fly. I had just finished when I heard the bolt of a rifle and turned to face a very surprised guard. A tall young man in his thirties, snub-nosed and big-jawed under the heavy steel helmet.

'This is not a lavatory. *Du kannst nicht ausgehen.*'

The rifle was still cocked and pointed my way. He waved me away from my 'christened' corner, as he referred to it later, and indicated the mill door: 'Use one of your buckets.'

I lied: 'They're all full.'

He was struggling against laughter in the evening glow, his eyes gleaming and dancing. For the first time our eyes met. In that moment there was an evenness that, in spite of his Wehrmacht swagger, uniformed stance and rigid German discipline, informed me of a likeable man.

'You've got to the count of five to get back to your floor, after which I pull this trigger and shoot whichever part of you is still showing.'

I darted for the mill door.

The second encounter occurred quite soon after. A Sunday evening, and on our floor the usual gathering was together round a few bunks to sing, play our mock instruments and tell tales, sometimes of life at the bottom of the social echelons; sometimes, as with Vasonyi, life at the top. Most of us fell into the everyday middle, but even here, what before would have been mundane, proved an enormous source of nostalgic comfort and desire for its return. I was riding high with the horn passage from Tchaikovsky's Fifth on my trumpet made from thick rolled-up paper, when a voice called up from two floors down.

'Guard headed this way.'

We struggled back to our bunks expecting trouble, as guards did not normally enter the barracks; very much kapo territory. Hunkered down, blankets up, we waited for footfalls. Some feigned sleep.

Finally, on my bunk, I propped myself up while the others were ducking under. I was curious. In seconds the place was quiet as the grave. With my bunk at the top of the stairs at the entrance to our floor, I was able to peer down the staircase. First the sound of the barrack door banging shut echoed its way up to us, then the noise from the stairs as they groaned slightly under the weight of our visitor. I stared into the darkness until the large frame of the approaching soldier became a shadowy reality. For a moment I thought it might be Schwarz, but the outline of his rifle confirmed that it was a Wehrmacht guard.

It was a 'game' I played, sizing up the threat. With all the strictures and limitations placed on me, inside and outside the house through childhood, I had developed a rebellious edge which simultaneously startled and amused my fellow inmates when it occasionally came to the fore around the camp. So, unlike the others, I was looking straight at him as his head and shoulders emerged from the top of the stairs. I scrutinized Helmut's face, which was naturally on the kind side. Here he showed no edge in the shadows, more curiosity.

'Alright, who's got the trumpet?'

His voice did not match his boyish look. His question took me by surprise and I gave him the quizzical look. His deep tones resonated around the barrack. More forcefully: 'I asked you a question. *Wer hat die Trompete gespielt?*'

Gathering my courage. I blurted: 'Me.'

'Where have you hidden it? Hand it over.'

'I don't have a trumpet … as such.'

'Don't make me angry, just hand it over.'

From under my blanket, I reluctantly withdrew my rolled-up paper tube.

'My trumpet,' I declared with a smile, offering it to him.

His next remark carried with it an amused weariness, having stomped up three flights for a piece of rolled-up paper.

'Oh, for Christ's sake.'

He slowly turned and, chuckling, made his way back to the ground floor. We heard him all the way back down to the barrack door. After it had shut and someone had spotted him making his way across the *appelplatz*, we resumed our evening, a decibel or two lower.

The next evening at roll-call, Helmut recognised me. He was off-duty and stood back from the activity, a half-interested watcher leaning against the mill wall, smoking. He looked much younger, different from his fellow soldiers. If it were not for his size and mature, deep voice, he would come across as a baby. He kept looking in my direction, giving me re-assuring smiles, and it seemed he was anxious to talk.

When we were dismissed, he walked over as casually as he could. In a soft friendly voice: 'Your name. What is it?'

'It is a number. I used to be called Ernest.'

'Helmut. I never was a Nazi. You are a musician?'

His conversational manner had me puzzled.

'No, a singer, though you heard me imitating a horn.'

From across the *appelplatz*, a guard approached. We both realized the hazardous nature of the moment and broke off. He looked toward the approaching guard and murmured confidentially to me:

'We'll talk some more later.'

Then, before making a quick retreat, I felt his hand against my pocket. Surprised by the whole incident, I returned to the bunkhouse, found a quiet corner and checked my pocket. Two flat sticks of barley sugar nestling together in my pocket. I broke off a piece for myself, the rest I divided between Walter and cousin Leo, telling them, as they accepted the prize, about the young guard, Helmut, who had difficulty hiding his human side.

'You'll see, he's a *Mensch*.'

Over the next six months, until Wustegiersdorf was evacuated, Helmut and I got to know each other a good deal better through snatches of conversation stolen out of the rigorous working day. As he was not ideologically committed to the regime, the chances were that he had been conscripted, like many young men in the Wehrmacht. This proved to be so. He was caught in a cleft stick, obliged to *'heil'* the *'heil'*, but being at odds with the doctrine. He thoroughly disliked many of his fellow soldiers – steeped as they were in the gore of National Socialism's deepest folly – in not for a moment doubting the rectitude of the Führer's dubious passions. In all this Helmut felt powerless to do anything. Maybe talking to me would prove the catalyst in some final stand against the oppression of his uniform and the ethos that compelled him to murder. He had now become acquainted with a single human from the grey mass which he was under orders to guard, beat or kill as required.

My thoughts were jolted back to the present as a grey open-topped Mercedes, bearing the swastika on its side, swept in through the gates and pulled up beside Seidel's office. He, Schwarz and a couple of younger officers emerged, looked about them and stepped briskly across the *appelplatz* to a point facing the assembly. Schwarz and the young men looked menacing, Seidel, simply calm and matter of fact. He addressed the ragged ranks of shivering, half-starved victims: 'As you are aware, this camp is being vacated and you are to be taken north to camps Flossenburg and Belsen. The men escorting you are instructed to execute any man attempting to escape on the way. That is all.'

Seidel walked to his car, Schwarz nodded to the guards and kapos who started the process of separation, while he joined his superior. All four SS officers got into the car, saluted the guard, then took off at speed through the gates. It was all over at Wustegiersdorf.

In the process of separation, I was cut off from some of my companions, including Leopold and Zoltan, who were designated for Flossenburg. Slomo and the others were in the group Belsen-bound. Vasonyi looked drawn and far from ready for this endurance test. Joe Lorinz, a boy with whom I had become friendly since losing Walter to Grossrozen, became my constant companion on this long march, which we were soon to rename 'death march'. As we were herded into our designated groups, Helmut nonchalantly passed by and in a low voice, instructed me to stay as close to him as possible.

'That way I can keep an eye on you. Maybe get food to you while the others aren't looking.'

Sometimes this plan went awry, but largely Helmut kept me going where others fell by the wayside.

Just as our party was about to go through the gates, Leopold ran across, against warning shouts, to give me a goodbye hug and to thrust eight chocolate sweets into my jacket pocket. We were tearful, I was grateful for our time together, more than sad to see him go. With Leo gone, Joe and I were to become each other's lifeline. Whatever came my way from Helmut, half went to Joe. Georges, Slomo and Davide took it upon themselves to take turns looking after Vasonyi.

A couple of miles up the road, I felt energy coming back into my system, the body was responding to the adversity. I was lucky, my shoes were not giving me trouble. Those who were not fit or young already showed signs of discomfort. Joe seemed jaunty enough, and we spent a lot of the time discussing the unknown future, as the long column of grey beings made their way toward the Silesian highlands. The roadside edge had the icy remains of the last snowfall. Light rain gave way to sleet as the road climbed. Three hours from Wustegiersdorf and the sleet became light snow as the road rose into the hills. A shot rang out. We all turned. Someone had fallen by the wayside, and had paid the penalty. Vasonyi looked terrified. The day dragged on. Dusk with night slithered quickly in to meet the short afternoon. Finally, to our relief, we were able to hunker down by the roadside and huddle.

Enterprisingly, fires were lit and the guards allowed wood collection. That first night no food was available, so we just strove to keep warm. Roadside banking provided a resting place, though where there had been soft mud, now the ground was rock-hard, the grass crisp with frost. The snow hadn't provided more than a dusting before the clouds cleared, and as night fell, the temperature dropped.

Shivering under our thin blankets, the one massive consolation to Joe and I was the immensity of the night sky. It was, however, offering beauty and infinity to beings incapable of taking up the invitation, most not caring beyond the additional light the moon had to offer. Some guards wandered up and down the line, while others took their rifle-at-the-ready rest. I remember sleeping and waking at intervals throughout that first night. Joe and I were interested and alive to every nuance of this arcane journey through the limits of simple endurance. It was the cold which was the guilty party in the here-and-now of it all; a cold that shook you awake if your lids dropped, but not cold enough to lull you into the sleep of sleeps, though some did not see the morning.

Our standing ready for the march revealed the night's toll. Maybe thirty bodies we walked by as the day's efforts began. We were at the back of the line, behind us the road stretched back down to the foothills. As the day progressed the clouds came over and snow fell, causing the temperature to rise slightly. The snow became our water supply, making my teeth jump and sing to every mouthful. More fell during that second day. Slomo's injured hand was healing slowly, though the cold did it no good. Vasonyi looked out of it. Joe and I decided to give him a couple of the dry biscuits Helmut had slipped our way. The guards were making do with hard tack from the supply wagon that moved ahead of us. From this came also our dribble of food supplies, mainly hard bread. As the march progressed, we were joined by men from other camps. These poor beings were entirely wretched from what appeared to have been a complete reduction. At Wustegiersdorf we were kept in a better state because of the workload to be carried out back there, but here we would soon be allowed to rot into the abject state of those who had joined us in the snow.

The fifth day saw it become less of a march and more of a dragging of the half-alive through a pain barrier by a simple device – terror. To fall was to be left to die; the guards began conserving their ammunition. They only shot dead those they suspected of pretence, following orders to prevent escape. We were only a couple of hours into the walk when we were joined, some way back, by a column of women prisoners who were segregated from us by a distance of seventy metres. The female SS with them looked case-hardened and were a perfect complement to their male counterparts who, in our party, were a limited presence up front. The women came, seemingly, from nowhere and later disappeared just as suddenly. It made me sad to see them reduced to a level where I knew they had been subjected to everything we had, and probably more; where power and sex can determine destiny, where the tenuous intricacies of prison existence weave strange patterns. I had seen this in our camp. Great intensities came and went, sometimes even across the barrier of the jailer and the jailed. Such is existence where survival becomes all. I felt a primeval terror enlarged by the pitiful presence of our female counterparts. Unlike our column, the SS were up front and down either side, female guards to watch over progress and bring up the rear. But in spite of their dire circumstances, the women were maintaining a measure of dignity. For example, whenever one needed to relieve herself, a circle of bodies would surround her.

Joe and I had worked our way to the very back (some crazy notion of maybe making a break) where, by casting glances behind us, we watched the female column. A moment of 'electric shock' enlivened my being. At the front of the marchers a young girl had been watching us. In a moment of my turning, our eyes met. A heart-stopping moment. She looked a lot like Medy. Was she? My first love had kept the light burning with singular intensity in my heart through all these dark days. The last I had seen of her had been outside the Dohany synagogue, Budapest in 1942. Since then, she had lived in my dreams. The soft hair, the Garbo profile; she was the queen of my imagination, able to blot out the cries and moans that had echoed off the night-time walls of Wustegiersdorf for the months the place held me captive.

Joe spotted my disturbance: 'What?'

He looked round to work out what I'd seen.

'I think I know that girl.'

'Which one?'

I gestured as specifically as I could without arousing attention.

'There, the tall one, front row.'

Joe's eyes found her.

'You know her?'

I prayed that I did, that it was her. I needed to know. Then, what if it was her, what could I do? How could I help her when I could barely help myself? The chocolate sweets. Make a link, get closer, find out. I confided in Joe:

'I'm going to try and get close enough to make sure. Maybe slip her a couple of our sweets.'

Joe grinned very widely: 'It's official, you are crazy.'

'I'll stay back, pretend to tie my shoelaces. Easy.'

'They'll never fall for that one.'

Ignoring the comment: 'I'll slip her the chocolates, then run back.'

Joe was doubtful: 'I don't think this'll work. But, if it goes wrong, I'll create a diversion. That'll alarm Helmut.'

Sweets in hand, I fell back, crouched and started to do my laces. Quite quickly, the women trudged forward. I looked up at the approaching feet and legs. When they were nearly level, I stood and looked for the girl. Big blue eyes staring straight at me, puzzlement and interest at what this young man was doing. She was not Medy. She was, however, beautiful. My palm opened to reveal the sweets. She smiled and stretched out her hand my way. The sweets crossed over, I gave her my best smile before turning to sprint back to Joe and the line. I hadn't noticed one of the female guards waddling down the column, headed my way. I froze to her shrill call.

'What are you doing here Jew filth? Get back to your flea-bitten brethren.'

She aimed a kick that sent me sideways into the snow. Helmut was there in seconds.

'Leave the boy alone, you miserable bitch.'

Her attention turned to Helmut. I was able to slip back to the anonymity of the line.

'And you, you are such a Jew lover, you would melt down your bayonet to make a shackle for your legs? For shame. Traitor! You feel *sorry* for them? I don't believe.'

Helmut turned his back on her catcalls and rejoined us: 'That was very stupid, Ernest. Disappear into the group. She's likely to make trouble ... Was the girl worth it?'

'The girl was worth it.'

'Good. Watch your step. The pressure is telling on the officers.'

Joe grabbed my arm and dragged me into the grey mass of marchers. I turned to look one more time at the girl. The female SS guard was marching back up the line muttering, erupting into the odd oath. The girl seemed to be peering into the crowd. Catching sight of me, she smiled and waved as did two or three others. I felt good.

For three days the women were with us, then as quickly as they had appeared, they were gone, at some crossroads in the snow, in the semi-dark. Their presence had been considerable. Behind us now was the dark tunnel of their absence and white, silent country. After they had gone, the weather worsened. Three heavy snowfalls in one day all but stopped us. Some just could not continue. In spite of the screams and shouts from the guards, they were simply incapable of walking another step. Even with rifles full in their faces, they simply could not go further. Those beyond it, or seemingly so, were shot or left. This was not rebellion, it was a simple fact. With little or no food, the only water being from the snow, and major stress upon bodies already below par, this was a marching column no longer capable of taking the necessary steps into heavy drifting snow. Impasse.

The march was halted at the village of Kwalish. Our little gang was separated when the column was divided up. Joe and I were in the batch taken to a farm which appeared to us as a cluster of neat white outbuildings on a low hill, across a field. On the right, as we shuffled in through the gates, was the actual farmhouse; a long, low white building with carved black-wood decoration. From the ground-level windows in the dusk, casting across the snow, a warm orange light which spoke of domestic normality, of oil lamps and an open fire. As I passed, I felt my eyes fill at the unbearable closeness of mundane cosiness and the utter desolation of being in the outer frozen darkness. We continued past the seductive moment to our billet. Straight ahead was a small wooden barn with enough space for fifty. Two hundred of us had to fit in the place. Our guards requisitioned a couple of huts nearby for themselves. The barn had a loft that took a few of us. Somehow we were able to stretch. No light or heating, but from the weather we were sheltered. As we were herded into the barn, we caught sight of the farmer. A tall, well-built man in his early sixties with a big oval face and high rugged cheekbones. With his boots, cap, leather jerkin and cords, he was every inch a prosperous farmer of undoubted local influence. As we settled in, he was taking time out to speak earnestly with the guards. We picked up later from Helmut that this man's name was Max. Although he looked nothing like him, Max reminded me of Anton; something about the voice, demeanour, and later, as we realized, outlook, placed them side-by-side in my memory. True Germans.

The conversation had naturally been about us, and became fairly heated. It was quite apparent that Max was not cowed by the SS either in idea or uniform, and though his voice boomed, we could only catch fragments. Enough to know that he was negotiating for us. The word '*Kartoffel*' jumped through the air and landed sweetly on our ears. Potatoes. He wanted us to have potatoes.

The SS agreed, and so daily at three, sometimes a hungry four in the afternoon, Max would stand at a huge drum of boiling water and hand out 200 large boiled potatoes, one to each man. Initially, we accepted the gift with eager hands and tear-filled eyes. Later, the hands remained eager and tears were replaced by smiles and grateful nods to this benefactor in the leather cap and hide waistcoat.

To us a potato had become a luxury, a rarity in work-camp life, never to be seen in our soup except as renegade remains of an earlier meal elsewhere and slopped back into our share of the fare. So our daily miracle at the farm was a delicacy full of marvellous flavours, just as beautiful as a salt-beef sandwich with rye bread or fresh strawberries and cream. We relished our daily 'manna', and we thanked God for Max. So careful was this man that he threw out anything rotten or small. We were to have the good stuff. By and large, Max was able to rub along with the Werhmacht soldiers. He had trouble with the SS, for whom he seemed to have a particular dislike, so much so that an argument he was having with one of them boiled over. The SS man pushed Max away from him, so we saw. The big farmer aimed a random kick in return, which connected and evoked a yelp from the younger man who went for his gun, but was restrained by a fellow soldier. I suspect we were at the bottom of that quarrel too. The fact that Max wasn't gunned down probably depended on his usefulness and social influence beyond the remit of dying Nazism.

I say 'we' thanked God for Max. I was having a crisis of faith. It was the bleakest of periods in the year and though we were out of the misery of the work camp, we were out into a permanent cold, albeit holed up in a barn while the blizzards raged. After the blizzards, we were due for God knew what, as fear worked on the souls of the SS and the Wehrmacht. Supposedly, we were Belsen-bound. The question was, how on earth was this to be achieved? To get us north. And just where were the Allied land troops? We knew where the Russians were. Some of us felt that our death by massacre at the hands of our captors was a likelihood if fear took them over the edge, beyond their discipline. For me, my winter depression caused me to look God accusingly in the eye and demand revelation, or my back would turn in shame against this unchecked crime that he had allowed to spawn, grow and consequently consume us, his children of the covenant. I could not square it. My body, like the others, was losing muscle dramatically. Hallucination and dark imaginings associated with the condition were hard to resist when nothing about day or night gave it any kind of opposition. The oppressive cause of the condition had killed the Creator, in my heart. In the halls of Eternity, silence ruled. The hosts of heaven hid their eyes as the cohorts of the little Austrian corporal did his bidding, even as his personal demons called to him from the pit. I was losing my belief as I was losing my body mass. I was young. At 19, what future? Despair had to have a scapegoat. I could not kill Hitler; it therefore had to be God. I thanked Max for Max.

For him, the Nazis were a passing affliction that in time would go, like blight or famine; the land would be there long after their strut across the continent was over, and their temper-storm passed. He was obviously a man of faith, probably Lutheran, probably storing up virtue in his heart's barn by performing good acts. In that motive, most believers have a share. In him, though, like some others in any of the belief systems, compassion resided naturally; such people would go ahead and perform good acts regardless. He was a *Mensch*.

For me, even with a bright future, there could be no return to the old interpretations of what the Torah revealed. Those of us who had our young lives raped by the perversions of Nazism and primitive, people-based superstition, would demand a complete revision of doctrine. For me, there were aspects of Zionism and socialism that were pleasing and seemed to offer a way forward. Human progress appeared to reside in secular hands. As we had died in countless thousands waiting on the Messiah to deliver us, it was time to take up the cudgels.

Then there was the sardine tin.

During the day we were let out of the barn, out into the intense cold, so we didn't hang around outside for too long. This particular morning, I watched enviously as a young guard forked his way through a tin of sardines. When he had finished, he dropped the tin to the yard floor, almost completely sheet ice, and kicked it away. The tin skittered and skidded in my direction. He lit up a cigarette, looked me over, then strolled off elsewhere in the yard. The tin lay on the ground, topside up. Maybe there was something left in it, maybe. When no one was looking, I gathered it up and took it into the barn. I checked it. No fish, but a fair amount of oil; still good, still good. I was about to sup it down, when an idea struck. I had some string that I had found in the ice. By now it had dried in my pockets, so by inserting the string as a wick into the oil, I made a little lamp. I found Helmut in the yard. When we were able to speak, I asked him for some matches:

'Don't tell me, you're going to torch the barn.'

I gave him a look. He laughed.

'We're going to celebrate Chanukkah a little late.'

He handed me a few matches from his own box.

'If the barn burns down, I'll know where to look.'

He walked off, still smiling at the thought. How could he think I would cut my nose off to spite my face? Wait. I was losing my sense of humour along with my belief. How could that be?

Later that evening, in the darkened barn, the little lamp was lit. A group of us sat around the small, sputtering flame, spontaneously breaking into the Chanukkah tune, '*Maoz Tzur*'. Chanukkah 1944 celebrated in February 1945; what difference? It felt good to gather. I thought back to Wustegiersdorf and the prayers that reunited me with cousin Leo but somehow, this far down the decline, my prayers had a hollowness; a lack of conviction. Looking at the pathetically makeshift 'lamp', our single light, I saw suddenly that it was just a reminder of a childlike belief, a faith to which I could never return. Since November 1938, my relationship with God had withstood challenge after challenge but now, with more to come, my alienation was almost total.

Ten days came and went. On the eleventh, with the weather improved, we all took our leave of the farm. Max was nowhere to be seen; we looked. He was usually around the place and we began to wonder whether they had disposed of him now his usefulness had come to an end. To thank him would have been good. Instead, we were treated to a surprise. Just as we were leaving the courtyard near the farmhouse a woman, maybe wife, maybe daughter, stood outside the farmhouse door. Her presence was a shock to us as nobody had the least idea she existed. From the doorway, she shouted to us:

'If it was down to me, I'd have given you two potatoes a day.'

Over the noise of mass movement, Slomo shouted back for all of us: 'Never mind, you and Max saved our lives. You are good people.'

THE NIGHT BY THE ELBE

Helmut had been ordered forward, for what we didn't know, maybe somebody had had a word about his fraternizing to the officers in charge. We didn't know; but we talked. As the day proceeded under clear skies, our shuffle in the snow took us out of the last of the hills into the lowlands. By the end of the day we had lost one poor soul and linked up with more marchers; the potatoes had strengthened us, not to mention simple rest. By late afternoon, we arrived at a village – someone said they thought we were close to Dessau – where the guards halted the column and went into an animated huddle. We were then directed towards a building on the other side of the village, maybe a warehouse or a disused industrial shed, its rusting corrugated roof a mottled russet in the dying day. The double doors were flung open and around 400 wet-footed, tired, malnourished Jewish men and boys were ordered into a space that could not possibly hold them. Eighty at a pinch. We were among the first twenty or thirty inside, and facing the wide open doors, watched horror-stricken as the crush increased. It was a little while before close became too close, became uncomfortable, became difficult, became hard to breathe, became painful, became a need to protest, became a need to beg and shout for help. The guards continued to push bodies into the building. Hands, shoulders, well-aimed rifle butts to back and body compelled additional space where none existed, until 400 protesting souls were stuffed into the building.

'*Deutsche Werhmacht, Hilf!*'

The call for help remained unanswered as the doors were forced shut and bolts slid to from without. The realization we were pinned in and were there to stay overnight, or until we were all dead from suffocation, dawned on us as the struggle to stay upright and alive became first priority. Already several men had been crushed to death against the walls. When some were lifted off the floor as panic spread, fists flew and elbows dug as the crush moved slightly this way, that way. There was no light. The windows had been boarded up, and frightened men clawed and pushed, trying to break out. Frantic sounds from all round were to accompany the night as struggle and fight became killing. Joe and I survived through mutual aid. When I was dragged under at a fall-over moment, Joe hauled me upright. It wasn't long before we were moving over the dead and the dying. The movement of my feet evoked cries of pain, but the force of the mass compelled my feet to move, to stamp, to sometimes tread empty air. One or two men had made their way upward to try and batter the roof into submission and, though in places it bent, it would not break. Some called for calm, some prayed. I could do neither as I felt the edges of my sanity begin to give; I was becoming lost to this reality and had no other reality to cling to, except Joe who was also engaged in the fight to make it through to the last.

Someone's hand pulled at me as it sunk into the mass below. I fought it off, and stamped at the source to rid myself of Death calling me under. It happened time and again as Joe and I made it through the night. The words, the gasps, the unendurable grasping and pushing, the rib-cracking, back-snapping pressure to be wriggled away from in the hot thick air with its stench of body fluids released; virtually unbreathe-able and utterly inescapable.

Just after dawn, the doors were flung open to allow the survivors to stagger out gasping and coughing. Some emerged on their knees and collapsed, others fell on their knees in prayer. I would not look back, but Joe later described the shed floor covered in broken bodies, some bloodstained, many stifled to death. Over a hundred by his reckoning. He helped me to rally, but set against the relief of emerging alive was the numbness and shock of what had just happened, not to lift until the safety of peace time, when the luxuries of self-recrimination and moral outrage were allowed to take over the past. I have guilt, I have dreams and memories when that night returns.

I was relatively strong. I survived. The weaker went under, some by my hands and feet. So it was.

Now it was time for gratitude. Each survivor was given a large chunk of fresh-baked bread topped off with a large lump of butter, our reward for doing a good job for the overstretched Nazis in reducing the workload. I was in hysterics, made worse when Slomo emerged from the build-ing without Vasonyi and in tears, admitted to losing contact with him, only to see him a few moments back, face-down in the carpet of corpses. The bread had to be eaten; for some it was the last food before arriving at Belsen. The utter shock of the past night's events got to my core. I hung my head and cried for all of it, a full-scale release that the preceding months had brought about. Joe's arm was round my shoulder as the trudge away from the place of death began. Who would clear the corpses, both there and on the road from Wustegiersdorf? There were no Jews to do the job. Maybe the task would fall to carrion, who knew? Maybe the locals would take paraffin and torch the place. Who knew? Who cared? Inside my clear-ing head a swirl of dark images that the cold morning began to lift, and the rising sun reduce.

We were only on the road for around half an hour before we reached Dessau railway station, where we were pushed on to open cattle trucks. Other groups of evacuated prisoners had joined us by this time, so that the station platform was full to capacity with grey, emaciated men. Fifteen hundred, two thousand maybe. I was on ahead of Joe and wearily helped him up into the truck.

'Ernest!'

It was Helmut pushing himself hastily along the platform. Half a loaf flew towards me which I caught. It was instantaneously grabbed and ripped to pieces by others while I held it. All went except the bit I held tight. That just divided into two bits. Joe shrugged. The fact that Helmut had found us in that seething mass was truly remarkable, remarkable also that at this stage, he continued to care. By the time the train rolled out of Dessau, the day had clouded over and an increasingly heavy snowfall began. By the time the train drew to a halt at Aussig, we were covered in white. The few thin blankets shared by us all were caked in snow. Everything was white, including the tall buildings of Aussig station. During the journey, to keep warm, eighty to ninety of us had wriggled and squirmed to generate heat, and in the process of contact, lice from the prisoners from other camps transferred their allegiances to us Wustegiersdorf veterans. We quickly felt the unwelcome addition. Back at the work camp, the worst type of infestation had been rats; mercifully, lice had been rare. Now their movement added to our general discomfort.

In the evening stillness, the clouds dispersed and the night sky blazed its glory. The station buildings reflected pure white against the flowing blackness of the river Elbe. The moon seemed exceptionally bright. Looking around the truck, the pale glow made spectres of the wasted men whose scant breath appeared to freeze as it hovered around them in the still air. It was midnight, according to the station clock, when the guard in our truck was relieved by Helmut who climbed in and occupied the stool in the corner vacated by his grateful colleague, who disappeared over the side into the night. I sat close by Helmut. Joe was curled up nearby. Between us, wrapped in a thin blanket, an ageing Pole and his two teenage

171

sons with whom he quietly conversed in beautiful Yiddish. I hadn't been feeling so good. Helmut noticed I was clutching my stomach. He rose and bent over me concerned.

'What's wrong?'

'Don't know. Spasms. I think it might be diarrhoea.'

'I'm not surprised.'

I was doubling up. He offered me a hand.

'Helmut. I'm going to shit myself.'

His arms went under mine and I was lifted bodily. I tried to make my way to the truck edge. This was going to be impossible. I tried to climb. He went to help. I tried to stop him.

'It's okay.'

'No it's not. You're as weak as a baby. No arguments. Up now.'

He pushed me up to the edge of the truck and I managed to shift my trousers down out of harm's way before the flowing mass left me.

'You managing?'

Receiving no reply from me, he got up alongside and helped me support my weight.

'Really, Helmut, you don't have to.'

He simply looked me in the eye and said, 'Yes I do.'

So we sat perched in the moonlight, while the contents of my intestines were released into the night air of Aussig where they hit the ground and promptly froze. Every twenty minutes or so through the night, the ritual was repeated. The pages of a newspaper Helmut had about him served to wipe the mess. At one point I fell back onto the wagon floor, thanking him:

'I don't think even my brothers would do as much.'

'Sure they would.' A pause. 'You have brothers?'

I told him the size of the family, its background, the shifts in our lives through the 1930s and early 1940s, along with the fate, as far as I knew it, of all of us. We even discussed Father's strict orthodoxy. There was a silence.

'In the light of all this misery, d'you think there is a God?'

I made no answer. Another pause. He spoke again, quietly, sadly. 'I had a brother.'

'Dead?'

He nodded.

'In the army?'

'No, Joseph wouldn't have made it in. Lost an eye in an accident.' He chuckled to himself, then: 'We were a bit accident-prone in our household. Father had lost a leg when young. A glass eye and a prosthetic leg. Odd lot. Dad was a dentist, so we all have good teeth. I mentioned God a moment ago because he loomed large in our lives, and because belief brought us misery and argument. It caused Joseph's death. Religion, I've had it up to here. Nothing divine can preside over this carnage.'

He looked across the tracks toward the river. The moon etched the shadows of his anger.

'How did he die?'

'He killed himself.'

A brief silence. From me, almost a whisper.

'Why?'

He looked away from the river to me.

'Love. My mother, the Blessed Virgin and Hitler. Mother loved the man. She was a God-bothering Nazi, devout in both camps.'

'Your father too?'

'Played cards with his friends while she and her friends made Christ's life a misery at the church. Dad didn't go with her on the politics either.'

'Was Joseph a Nazi?'

'No. He was far from stupid; too sensitive though, prone to depression. Romantic. Fell in love with the wrong girl. Helga. Very beautiful in that doll-like way, you know, blue-eyed blonde. A Czech from the Sudetenland. Never met her. I had been conscripted by then. Anyway, her father was a resistance fighter, a watchmaker, widower. He was taken in by the Gestapo, so Helga was under suspicion and had to hide. She turned to Joseph who, naturally, went to Father who sympathised but was very straight and had to say no to taking her in because of Mother. Joseph knew this. She would have

173

betrayed Helga straight off. So, it had to be the shed at the end of our garden. She stayed there briefly.'

'Your mother didn't find out?'

'She was too taken up with parish work and the Führer's latest rant to worry what went on in the garden. So Joseph brought Helga food and she holed up in the shed.'

'How long did that go on?'

'Just a few days. Then Joseph took her food one morning and found a note. A friend in the resistance had found her refuge. Because Joseph was German, our mother, a Nazi, their relationship was considered too dangerous and had to stop. Logical enough. But it put Joseph on the tilt. Dad said he withdrew into himself. Wouldn't eat. Finally took his own life. We didn't have a mother, my father didn't have a wife. In her screwy world, God and Hitler were the objects of her devotion. Her family incidental and possibly dispensable. I'd hate to put her to the test.'

He gave me a world-weary smile:

'That's why I've had it with religion. If God exists, I feel sorry for him. His devoted followers are such nitwits.'

Helmut cast his gaze across the rail truck in which we sat, looking at the sad sight of men all but skeletons. Ragged, frozen, caught in the winter moonlight which gave them a leprous, spectral appearance. Their groans and coughing broke the vast silence of the night. Every so often, from the trees near the Elbe, an owl shrieked. My guts went into spasm again. In seconds we were once more perched at the edge of the truck.

'For us Germans the war is over, Ernest, yet this killing goes on. We have lost but we continue to perpetrate agony and murder. Look at this state of affairs right now.'

I responded. 'There is worse. I have seen it.'

I described Auschwitz to a man who had heard about it, heard the accounts, had chosen not to believe them, but was getting confirmation first-hand about the gassing, the inciner-ation, the all-pervading stench of the place. The spectre of thousands upon thousands forced on and off trains, being whipped into forced separation for execution or slave labour, rose before us. The very nature of the killing factory had eluded his imagination, a simple denial of what went on just out of the corner of his eye was home ground. I took this away from him. A last little light of humanity had gone out.

'There can be no God in this existence.'

I nodded in agreement.

'I'm sitting in this truck in the uniform of a criminal nation. I'm carrying a loaded rifle ready to shoot near-corpses should one make a break for it and stagger off into the snow. How do I escape my fate?'

Without warning, the train lurched and began to move. We almost fell back into the truck. Joe started, sat up and looked around him. I pulled up my pants. Helmut returned to his corner perch as the train's movement woke more people.

It must have been somewhere around four a.m. when the train rolled to a stop beside the unloading ramp at Bergen-Belsen. As we fell out of the trucks, barely able to move after the cramped journey, we were greeted by a striding figure, tall and ox-like in build, roaring and screaming high-pitched oaths at all around him. Joseph Kramer, the Belsen Commandant. He looked vast in the bright lights that shone in our faces. With a long leather coat, collar up against the weather and a giant bullwhip frequently slashing the air, he was everything we needed to know about our future. We were lined up to march from the ramp to the camp, a painful distance from the station, and one that had the guards cursing over the cold and kicking out at us as we were compelled into rapid marching along the tree-lined avenue to the death camp.

All along, Kramer had us moving at the double. The whip's crack could be heard loud against his shouts. Joe and I held hands. We were nearly running, breathing hard and unable to speak. The Pole with the two teenagers begged his sons to let him go as they were losing ground. People to the front fell or collapsed and were under our feet. This set off a series of falls which left injured men pleading from the icy ground as the thousand-man column stampeded over them. There were shots when men could not rise up. We were leaving yet another area of ground covered in the dead and the dying; this time for Belsen's inmates to collect in the morning and drag off to the pits specially dug for mass-burial. In this brutalised area of land, men, women and children were dying in their droves from starvation, dysentery, latterly typhoid, indiscriminate beatings and the bullet.

Eventually the two boys had to let their father go as exhaustion overtook their wills. Urging his reluctant sons on, the older man sank under the tread of the people behind him, the boys wailing into the early morning air. At the head of that 'endless avenue' were the gates of Belsen. An icy wind had sprung up and cut across the flatland, swirling and mixing the gruff shouts of some men, the piteous cries of others, the incessant barking of chained dogs and sporadic single rifle shots.

How he managed to find us in all that dark confusion, I don't know, but find us he certainly did. Helmut had made the effort to get to me, and running the great risk of being seen by the other guards, gave me water from his flask. After diarrhoea, dehydration follows. I had a raging thirst, and no way was I yet able to scoop snow. He didn't mind that my mouth was filthy, nor did he mind when on his nod, I offered the flask to Joe. As a lapsed Catholic, this was a pretty Christ-like gesture. He also produced some bread smeared in beef fat; dear God, we were so grateful.

Suddenly Kramer was on the scene. He demanded ten able men to return with him to the rail ramp to clear the wagons of the dead and the dying. I was singled out, but the thought of being separated from Joe and the others made me hesitate. I was desperately trying to gain eye contact with them when a sharp searing pain stopped me in my tracks as Kramer's whip slashed into my face, causing my right cheek to immediately swell into an elongated lump. I believed my eye to be blinded. Back at the ramp, several lorries were already piled up with corpses; the cold night had taken a sizeable toll. Through the racket surrounding the business of loading bodies, came Kramer's voice.

'Line them up and box them like matchsticks. Are you listening to me? Like matchsticks. You'll get more in. More space. *Do it then.*'

In the middle of all this commotion, almost as if a space had cleared itself for him, Helmut stood motionless. In the gathering light of day, like a lost child, he stood alone and helpless, engrossed and paralysed by the enormity of what was going on in the waking day. He had had enough. Kramer couldn't help but notice this stillness in all the action.

'Idiot, moron. Move! Don't just stand around.'

Helmut unshouldered his rifle and took aim, pointing it directly at Kramer who for a moment in time and space, was halted. The other guards stood rooted to the spot. Was this soldier going to shoot the feared Commandant? Helmut's expression was set, determined, the rifle cocked and ready. Silence everywhere, except for the noise of the train hissing steam. The sane man lost.

Kramer chuckled and stared back at Helmut, held his gaze, staring straight down the rifle sights into Helmut's compassionate soul. The chuckle became a belly laugh. The eyes blazed with the fires of death. Finally, with a dismissive gesture, he waved Helmut away. Turning his back, Kramer strode along the ramp. Over his shoulder, still laughing: 'Later.'

Helmut was left standing alone. The mad activity that preceded the moment went on. The other guards stared a little, and one shaking his head, ran his finger across his own throat, making it clear to Helmut just what 'Later' meant.

The gesture was heroic but suicidal. The man who showed mercy would be given none when the time came. In his humiliation was our own, but I could not be more proud of my German guard than I was at that moment. The rifle was lowered, Helmut looked my way, shrugged, gave me a little smile, and walked off alone, his hand half-raised, gave a little wave, and he was gone into the shadows behind the trucks.

BUDAPEST 1952–53

A recital of German *Lieder* given by the baritone Dietrich Fischer-Dieskau. As he came on stage, I felt a profound shock, for standing there, about to take his audience into Schubert's *Winterreise*, was a physical reminder of Helmut. The moment took me back immediately to the waiting rail trucks in the snow when dying men were waiting for their final moment, not knowing how or when. A starlit, moon-bright midnight when Helmut and I talked in the freezing stillness. I had spoken of how I came from a long family line of singers, how if I survived, that would be my chosen path to uphold the tradition. He put his hand on my shoulders and said, 'You will make it, Ernest. I believe so.'

In the brief time he had known me, there were always words of encouragement from him, even over the paper trumpet, the memory of which continued to amuse him. When he saw me down, his words would somehow lift my morale. Friendship from the opposition goes a long way. Our beings met in a no-man's-land of liking and stayed that way until he vanished into that grey dawn at Belsen.

He had said: 'I would give half my life away to be able to sing.'

Once he had quoted a saying that my mother would use:

Wo dass Singen ist, dort lasse dich nieder
Bose Leute haben keine Lieder.

(Where there is singing, there you should dwell,
Wicked people have no songs to tell.)

14 Belsen

I was given a ride back to Belsen from the station ramp in a truck loaded with the dead and the dying. As we approached the gates, we gave up pausing to pick up roadside corpses; these would be cleared by inmates, including myself, later. The greyness of dawn had yielded to a deep angry redness which lit up the road through the gates. The power of the sunlight turned everything to silhouette. My first view of the place was jaw-dropping. Row after row of black windowless barrack huts uniformly spaced in either direction, the black wood softened in the morning glow, the windows of the outbuildings reflecting the searchlight sun. The huts seemed pencil slim, low and very long, stretching back into shadow. Everywhere there were people up and about, people who moved very slowly draped in blankets and whose bodies were bent and skeletal. In prisoner stripes, some had the stupid caps still on their heads, poor substitutes for the *yarmulke*. Here there were still believers? Were they about to attend roll-call? They seemed to be going one way. I was about to jump down from the truck when a voice came from behind me:

'My name is Weiss, Doctor Weiss. I am a physician from Budapest.'

I turned to look at him, his grey face lit up in dawn's threatening glare. He was sitting bolt upright as if to greet the day. The moment he finished speaking, he fell back into the pile of neatly stacked bodies, of which he was a part, and lay motionless. Leaving the truck, there was no one around to control my immediate present; guards seemed in short supply, so I bolted to a nearby barrack to escape the infernal outside; maybe find a corner, get some rest.

'Ernest?'

I was standing in the semi-dark of the nearest hut, my good eye trying to adjust to the gloom. Joe grabbed me in a hug and drew me away from the door. Joy was unconfined. Our audience of men, seated and standing, stared impassively at this show of energy.

This state of relative fitness and liveliness singled us out for special work duties away from the camp. Kramer seemed to restrict his activities to the camp and immediate vicinity, so it was a happy release to be away from the dark atmosphere that this man, his guards and kapos had created. We were detailed to Hildesheim, where we found Georges, where we were all billeted in the theatre, where Slomo tripped 'The Rat', where we had to duck and run from Allied air strikes.

Just before that happy moment of meeting up with some old campmates, Joe and I had to help clear a train wreck. A truck was stuck in a bomb crater and to make the heavy vehicle lighter so that it could be dragged out, we were to clear the cargo. As we dug we discovered it to be a consignment of butter which, with rubble, was suddenly on our spades. Naturally we went for it wholesale and hungry, only to regret it later with raging thirsts when no water appeared. Thirst makes you a little crazy and very daring. I sneaked into the station building under the guards' noses, going from room to office looking for a tap. In the basement I found crate upon crate of empty bottles, which led to a tantrum of swearing. I ducked out of the station building and made it through a back door into a commercial kitchen where two large women in their fifties turned in surprise as this young man in Belsen stripes pushed past them and buried his head in a full sink of warm washing-up water.

'*Nein, nein, nein!*'

The women dragged me from the sink.

'You musn't do that.'

I was thirsty, they were horrified. As we stood staring at each other in a moment of frozen indecision, a couple of guards who had missed me were heard coming down the steps to the back door of the kitchen. The older of the two women realized my danger and tried to push me into a small cupboard. That was not going to work properly, so she hid me behind some sheets and towels draped over an indoor line, hurriedly adding to the 'screen'. It wasn't perfect but it did the trick okay. The guards did no more than scan the kitchen before making off after the 'prisoner Jew bastard'.

One of them doubled back: 'Where did he go?'

'Who?'

'Jew prisoner. He came into this courtyard.'

The younger woman was quick. 'Put his face to the window. Scared. Ran off through the side door into the street.'

The guard looked carefully around, almost reluctantly left, and joined his colleague. The younger woman watched them through a small window until they had left the courtyard.

'All clear, you can come out now.'

I left my hiding place: '*Dankeschön.*'

The two women looked at each other, then me. The older one with a slightly impatient wave of her hand: 'Disappear, son. Go!'

'Wait.'

The younger one held me back for a moment. From a cupboard she brought out a stein mug which she filled with fruit juice. In seconds it was down my throat. It was so sweet. It tasted of raspberries, a flavour which to this day echoes a few minutes of madness and kindness with the two women in their pinnies and flower print dresses. Their smiles were shy at my appreciation and I made myself scarce fast, back to the unit, joined later by two angry guards who took time out to threaten my life, but were unable to prove I'd actually been anywhere but where they found me.

There had been no lasting damage to my eye. As the whip-wound swelling receded, I found vision unimpaired. On the afternoon of the heavy air raid, when Georges treated the spade blow to my face, the theatre that we all returned to like so many tame sheep was in flames. Our billet gone, the guards rounded us up and marched us further down the road to Hannover Ahlem where we were put to work in a mine. The camp there was a lot smaller than Belsen. The Germans were excavating the mine to install a munitions factory which, hundreds of feet down, would be immune to air strikes.

They must have known the war was lost. With some, that knowledge had the effect of producing a feverish work pace, as if that alone somehow, magically, would reverse the bloody tide headed their way. Others became uniformed sleepwalkers, going through the motions for want of something else to do pending surrender. Either way, the prisoners were at the receiving end. Entering March 1945, we could not believe our situation, or hope to hope that down the road the Allies would be marching our way.

At the mine, my unit worked the night shift. As we went down in the cage, we saw the other prisoners coming up in theirs. Dutchmen, they looked unused to manual labour. This, and the scarcity of food, had a telling effect on their faces and bodies; they looked like phantoms, grime-covered, lost and bent low. So how did we look? As for the contempt of the guards and kapos, this had ever been thus. It was very possible to think of ourselves as the Dutchmen. Self-esteem had long since faded into the dream of a past life, an existence that wasn't this. Maybe the Dutchmen were our true reflection.

In these first years of the twenty-first century, it is still easy to conjure the memory of those years of fear and darkness. At times, they present themselves uninvited, especially as humanity continues to wreak havoc on itself over and over again. Each atrocity across the globe opens the old wounds, as news of human suffering revives the suffering felt by us then, and consequently by association, now.

Most of the corridors of the mine were roughly head-high and the width of a narrow country lane. Water dripped incessantly down the walls of the rock face and, not long into each shift, we began suffering the effects of extreme cold and damp. Because explosives were being used below ground, alcoves were strategically placed for shelter. Throughout the tunnels ran a waist-high iron grip-rail, very useful when engaged in a coughing fit brought on by the smoke and dust in the aftermath of a working explosion. Work then had to stop in the asphyxiating air.

One evening, just at the start of the shift, I was shovelling rubble when a young guard came over to push me on:

'C'mon, put your back into it.'

'*Ja mein herr.*'

The guard stared at me. 'You said that with no accent.'

'At home, we spoke German.'

Maybe a chance to speak, gain his good side. He had that solitary, slightly lost look reminiscent of Helmut who had vanished from our lives.

'And where's home?'

'Bratislava.'

Surprised, his face broke into a smile. He wanted to talk. 'Me too. Did you follow the football there?'

'Sure.'

'Which team did you support?'

'SK Bratislava.'

'Me too.'

We started a 'same-time, same-place' conversation that grew animated and friendly. His rifle came away from his shoulder and he rested it against the tunnel wall. Behind him, and headed our way, was the smallest member of our shift, Mr Klein, a prisoner in his middle years, gentle and very formal with everyone. He was trying to control a wheelbar-row, much too large and heavy for him with its load of hardcore. His progress towards us was zig-zag. He was being followed by a guard who was, in turns, laughing at and cursing Mr Klein's erratic progress. This particular guard had quickly gained a reputation with us for a gratuitous violence that was downright ruthless. He was older than the guard with me, and taller. The younger guard shouldered his rifle as the couple approached. We were standing on a slight slope and Klein lost control of the barrow which, though he tried to dodge, caught my guard on the leg. The young soldier turned on Klein, furious, but seeing the poor little man cowering in terror, hesitated and took no immediate action. The older soldier laughed in derision at his colleague, who, with embarrassment and anger, blushed deep, seen by all in the uncertain light of the tunnel.

'So. What are you going to do with your Jew midget?'

The two guards stared at each other in the silence of the challenge. The silence spread either side of the little group suspended in the moment. Klein stood there, a small, terrified mammal. The young man unleashed a series of rage-fuelled blows at Klein's head with the butt of his rifle. Though Klein tried to fend off the blows, the force was overwhelming and the poor man slipped to the floor inert.

I moved silently away from the scene, horrified that the friendly young German could so easily turn. One moment we were into 'easy speak', and the next, Nazi conditioning, prompted by goading, broke the surface of normal behaviour to do its worst. Being 'untreated' proletarians, the women of the kitchen had shown all the right instincts in helping me; distrust of oppressive behaviour, the need to save themselves, yet helping a starving youth with a raging thirst. This young soldier, my age, a killer on demand, had received the full benefits of the most brutal of training regimes with the Wehrmacht, an organization where recruits would die not making the grade. From childhood, he had been told of degrees of racial 'type', where Aryan beings were destined to reign supreme. Jews were to be destroyed as vermin, Poles educated into serfdom along with the Russian proletariat, and the rest of the human sub-species across the planet to live under a universal Reich; a thousand-year empire whose future was to out-shine Rome.

Poor Klein's body was dumped on top of the hardcore and wheeled away by a large prisoner who, in his turn, with the additional weight in the wheelbarrow, zig-zagged his way past cheering guards and silent prisoners.

Within ten days we were marched back to Belsen Camp One. As we passed through the forbidding gates, a man, skeletal, shrouded for warmth in a blanket, gasped deliriously: 'None of you will get out of here alive. It's typhoid. The place is infested.'

Belsen had, over time, sunk into dark anarchy. A wasteland haunted by the barely living and the desperately afraid. Discipline was breaking down among the Germans, desertion had begun and civilians would not go near the place. Kapo domination had virtually taken over. It must be remembered that the vast majority of kapos were Jewish. Just what mental gymnastics these people had to perform, just to play supervisor over their own during the Nazi years, didn't relate to anything known by us. It was new. Jewish people, traitors to their own. Jews had been known to be exploitative of each other and there had been great animosity between Jews from the east and Jewish Germans. Also there existed a certain distance between American Jewry and the European diaspora. There were the rivalries due to orthodoxies, along with the growth of Zionism. There was assimilation. All these were natural consequences of being spread across the planet by the winds of history. But there had never, ever, to my knowledge been a mutation such as the one brought on by the terrors of Nazism where a being's very soul was signed away in the blood of his brothers. Hidden away in the recesses of hell, afraid to come out and show his face, lurks the rogue Jewish kapo.

In the darkness of Belsen many kapos plumbed the depths, but even they could not outstrip the killing effect of typhoid, which had taken hold. The camp had no fresh water, it had to be shipped in. During the last few days supplies had broken down so that many resorted to drinking from puddles around the camp. Into these ponds raw sewage found its way. The pollution poisoned thousands, and thousands died, covering the ground wherever the eye would rest. Those of us whom nature allowed to survive had the task of burying the dead, in spite of our increasing hunger and consequent weakness.

A PRESENT MOMENT, APRIL 1945

I am just 20 and I have a job. My task is to haul the bodies of my fellow inmates to one of the several giant pits, where later lime will be added to quickly reduce them to a chemical slurry. With typhoid rampant in Belsen, their failure has been so rapid, they have been left where they expired: some luckily in their beds, others over sinks, in the barrack yards, food queues, wherever the moment took them. In their wake, a trail of defecation and vomit. These beings had been starved, worked, beaten and exposed to disease-carrying water, their deaths a certainty due to neglect and insanely vicious cruelty. They were artisans, dealers, rabbis, lawyers, doctors, musicians, street people. Just like me, Jewish in the main, but dead. Somehow I'm surviving where younger and sometimes fitter are falling. My faith is hanging by a thread of spider-silk thinness. Where is He, the God whom I used to thank? Not here raising the dead, that's for sure. Call to heaven and a guard or kapo turns up to beat you senseless for crying out; either way it is a Belsen brute, a being whose mission it is in the *Third Damned-Forever Reich* to eliminate me and mine. In these last days, the pride of the Reich has been dissipated, lost by having to share the midnight of despair with us slaves. We, the prisoners, languishing, hardly able to move, waiting for death from disease, overwork, neglect or violation; he, the SS soldier, Werhmacht guard or kapo, waiting on the fast-closing military vice.

I am so much less than myself that to carry or drag a body is a mammoth task. Normally, I'm not so big physically. In a year I haven't eaten properly so I'm down to bone, with very little muscle. I wear the Belsen stripe and spend my day on corpse detail since the return from the mine, which now seems a haven. It's drag rather than carry, and by the time I reach the edge of the pit, there's no energy to toss the body over so it gets rolled over the edge. In this work detail, we're alike in our exhaustion. It has led to a build-up of abandoned bodies near the pit's edge. Even when we work in pairs, the energy can't be found to send them very far in. My effort with this one is making me gasp. There is a heavy pulse behind my eyes. The day and the objects around me darken as it impairs my vision. I feel dizzy. Must breathe. Just, only just, I get the body rolled in, but it has hardly travelled at all over the edge. I look down at an awkward agglomeration of oddly positioned carcasses, a random pile of skeletal beings, some naked, some in their stripes. A spring breeze wafts through the stench that permeates everything. A fleeting, almost imagined, bouquet of early flowers and wood smoke threading its light, delicate way across the stinking reaches of Belsen, mired as it is deep in the marshes of Hades; with me in the midst. I am a child. I want my mother, my father. I am lost.

A Wehrmacht soldier hardly old enough to wear the uniform, with his kapo ape in tow, has appeared, is ordering me to get down into the pit to shift the bodies from the edge to the shallower centre; a reasonable-enough request, at gunpoint. I step over gingerly into the communal grave. Some of those I am treading on to do this are not yet dead and give up little cries of protest. My fellow inmates are getting careless in checking for signs of life. It's no good, there's no power left in me. I can't haul these bodies around any more. I'm supposed to drag off their clothing, but that's an additional task beyond my capacity now and evermore. These bodies seem stuck together by rigor mortis. I have fallen to one side and can't focus for a moment. The guard has let his gun drop to his side. He can see my state and, in the indolent spirit that is now Belsen, judges me a horse not worth the flogging. As he and the kapo leave the edge of the pit, the kapo looks over his shoulder and spits in my direction. Time passes.

Alone in the pit, surrounded by hundreds of dead and dying; the odd moan breaking the silence. The afternoon light has softened from iron grey to rose pink, casting a gentle light across this singular scene. I am done. Enough. I must try to reach the edge and climb out. Each time I try, an overwhelming weariness places a heavy weight on my being. To reach out, to grasp, to hold. Noise, diesel engines. Trucks. Pulling up by the pit. Soldiers unloading more bodies. Dear God, women. Young girls. Thrown as if weightless, past my blurring vision. Focus. Wake up Ernest. These young girls are not starved and they still have their hair. Can't be from Belsen. Against the noise of the engines and the shouts of the soldiers, I am hearing two men talking. Two guards, just above me, within reach. Look up. An older Wehrmacht guard is leaning on his pedal cycle talking with a younger soldier and watching the trucks being unloaded. They don't know where the girls came from but the scene has upset them.

'This is grim. What have we done to the world?'

The older man responds: 'Waking up, Werner?'

'The retribution for this will be terrible.'

'Not a hiding place to be found, lad.'

The younger man nods. I gasp for help but, in the noise of activity, I go unheard. For just a moment, rest. Sit, recline, become one with the welcoming cushion of the bodies. The soldiers are gone, the trucks driven off, leaving their exhaust fumes hanging over the pit in the greying stillness. I am another piece of coral building this reef of cadavers. Eyes close, just for a moment …

Awake. Eyes open. It is raining hard, blowing gusts. Water splashes my face. Mouth open, I take the water gratefully. The bodies around me shine with the wet. Here and there, a little steam rises from the still living. Day is almost over. I need to climb out. So close. In rising, I fall. In falling, I go into the groin of some poor being. This is beyond endurance. As if in a dream, waking seems out of the question. This condition is it. My soul screams for release. I try to rise and cannot. Finally, up. To step over the few bodies between me and the pit's edge, a tangle of arms, legs and torsos. There is no God. There is just this eternal dusk of despair. I cry out and all I hear is a cracked gasp. In tears, I sit back and weep with the rain. I think on my father. I lean back, mouth open, to receive the rain. It helps my mouth taste less metallic, eases the soreness around my gums. The haze of sleep is gathering round my brain, wiping out thought. Absent in fleeting thoughts, dreams of yesterday, of family and summer warmth. Of Medy.

One eye open. There's bright moonlight beaming down on the mass of bodies. All, all silent in the naked white light, grossly interlocked in a hellish leprous work by a bestial sculptor. I strain to rise from my cushion of bodies. A strong gust of wind brings on gooseflesh. Someone, very close to me in the moonlight is sitting bolt upright, eyes wide, staring straight at me. George, my dead new friend, a Romanian carpenter. I'm choking on my words.

'George. We thought you were dead. Come on let's get out of here.'

His boyish blue eyes are staring straight at me, intent on a wordless message. I am terrified, something is so wrong. Gasp another question. No response. A sharp gust catches George, causing him to lean grotesquely sideways and become fixed at an impossible angle. My terror is absolute. From within somewhere, panic sparks movement and I am able to scramble upward, my hands reaching the pit's edge. No strength to scale it. Stuck. Dead beat. Eyes closing. Go now and leave it all and just slip away to oblivion; the land of no more.

A sudden sharp pain across my head.

'*Lebst du noch*? You alive or dead?'

Eyes open. Look up. Torchlight. I am being poked at by the end of a stick. I try to fend it off.

'*Ja, ich libe noch.*' I manage to gasp affirmation.

One hand on my collar, the other bruisingly under my armpit.

'You're out, pal. Back to barracks. Now.'

Nod mutely, thank him, my moonlight saviour, my dark benefactor, this anonymous raiser-up of bones, as into night shadow he disappears. I have to cross the muddy spaces between here and the barracks, gaunt, low and stark under the moon. From the guardroom comes the sound of drunk men swapping songs. My last days seem bound in theirs, maybe I should try to live a little longer to celebrate with them the ending of this monstrousness, this hypnotic tragedy of living evil that has kept us enthralled over the years, and in which we have all played our parts so effectively.

Acknowledge their existence with a little nod as I stagger and weave past the glowing warmth of the guardhouse to a part-occupied wooden palette awaiting me in the darkened barrack.

PART IV
LIBERATION

15 Schreiber

Everything had gone into slow-motion, an awful dragging nightmare where day and night seemed to merge. Friend and foe sharing a common fate; a grindingly distressing morass of persecutors and persecuted drifting around in the habits formed by having nowhere else to go, and nothing to be done but wander aimlessly into each other, until whatever end was to befall us, did. I felt it was only moments away, my death. Along with all my fellow prisoners, I was starving. Desperation for food led to insane behaviour and that had meant the end of loyalty, morality and anything else that might stand between a being and a crust. And yet, and yet. Decency lived alongside cannibalism; the very extremity of man's fall from grace was God's opportunity to reveal the divine quality still resident in some. Selflessness and compassion were in evidence, even at the last, as the sewage that was fascism flowed over us and down the Styx to Hades. Not so with one man.

We knew him as Schreiber. Apart from typhoid and starvation, he was the principal cause of the death toll around me in those last days. A kapo, the *Block Alteste* (Barrack Superior Kapo) who had in his hands the future of several hundred frightened, starving beings. Jewish. Schreiber was Jewish, like many kapos. All we knew about him was that he came from Warsaw. After time in Auschwitz and Birkenau, he had found himself in the blind alley of Belsen, a death camp without him, a killing ground in his presence. Like most kapos, Schreiber was out to please his masters by running to excess.

Just up Kramer's street. When the Third Reich was a going concern, Schreiber's activities were met with patronizing approval; now in the last days of the 'Thousand Year Empire', nobody gave a damn, except us. Kramer was probably in camp two anyway, where disease was less.

We feared Schreiber. It was physical. His madness was manifested in acts of outrageous cruelty that led to the death of his victims, sometimes sudden, sometimes protracted. What really made him unusual was where all his venom was coming from. All beings are meant to have a redeeming centre that can be reached, or at least spotted, by some; but in this man we had nothing but a dark hole where his soul should have been. He was like foul smoke, pervasive, choking and deadly. How, in our dying days, we dreaded this usher to the mysteries of the great beyond.

A short, stocky man in his mid-thirties, broad featured with dark thinning hair, he didn't exactly promote terror by his appearance. It was the power he had acquired in the camps, the heavy club he kept ready to use at all times, and this atmosphere of malign intention that made every malicious second of his day an opportunity to inflict pain and death on his helpless charges. When he made a 'kill', the wide grin on his square face manifested the pleasure he gained from his addiction, along with evidence of a dire need for dental attention. He would celebrate a kill by doing a little shuffling dance step. He truly was a king among the kapos in their competitive niche of our confined world, our herdsmen, our keepers, our torturers; from us, but no longer of us.

Schreiber's 'cave', his headquarters in our barrack, was a little set-up in the corner of the long hut short on windows, where only a tiny door at one end let in any appreciable daylight. His bolt-hole was separated from the rest of us by hanging blankets nailed to the wood ceiling. In the cramped space by his bunk bed sat a small table. On the other side, a stool, in front of which a cooking pot containing a permanent supply of turnip soup resided like the Holy Grail. When boiling, the smell would drive us mad with desire. Leaning against the pot was Schreiber's means of dispatching his randomly chosen victims, a club with a narrow handle bound with black tape, broadening as it extended, resembling a baseball bat. The pale wood had been darkened by human blood. It was the 'Dragon at the Threshold'.

He was definitely unhinged and therefore victim to massive mood swings. There were 'normal' periods when he was just plain nasty, but approachable. Being sensitive to him, we had quickly worked out the symptomatic moments that would lead to his brainstorms. From behind the curtains we would hear him muttering loudly to himself, and replying with little whinnies of laughter. Or he would wander up and down the hut, chin into his chest, looking intent, as though trying to remember an essential something, wander back to his cave where we could hear his pallet creak heavily as he threw himself onto it. A silence would ensue. If we heard a snore, we all relaxed; if, on the other hand, no snore came, we waited. Even at night, with eyes wide open. Waiting. Schreiber owned our very heartbeats.

When the desire to kill overwhelmed him, the curtain would part dramatically. He would stand there, club in hand, scanning the length of the dim-lit barrack, a villain straight out of a German melodrama, an Alberich looking for satisfaction. The helpless, the weak and terrified beings that haunted his every waking hour, he would reduce by a few powerful swings of his club. Those hit when standing collapsed in a skin-and-bone heap, some dead before they hit the floor, some eased away from mortality after a bout of agonized twitching. Those on their beds died bloodily where they lay. Depending on his mood, a few would die or he would take out to double figures. In our reduced condition, how could we resist? We waited on his convenience. When the brainstorms abated, he would pause, look around him as if coming to, then turn on his heel, leaving the dead and the dying to those of us able to move and drag the corpses outside to the pits. The floor of the hut was a cold, damp, stony place, the beds, lice-ridden and filthy. These, my fellow beings, bade their farewells in this environment, this cheerless state, their bones smashed, their flesh torn open by being warped out of shape by a satanic hand. Those of us with a remnant of belief, or who had known love for others, managed somehow to hold on. We saw it in each other's eyes. Those we had known who had no such belief or hold, tended to go under. It wasn't an absolute – nothing is – but it tended to be that way in the camps, in the last days.

Schreiber had a new game to play. He had taken to waiting outside the hut and, with the help of a fellow kapo who would forcibly herd us through the small door, he would wield and swing his club at the head of each person coming through it. Some, like me, small, young and even in weakness, fairly nimble, could duck and run. The worst I got was an agonizing bruise on my shoulder. The pain was excruciating and lasted until my eventual hospitalization, but I was alive. Others, who had to be pushed into the daylight, died from a couple of savage blows, staring at the day across the grey expanse of the yard, past the deep pits soon to be their final resting place. A protracted bloody affair it became, to get the diminishing numbers onto the parade ground for a headcount, a daily ritual which went on to the end; something for all to do, other than club or be clubbed.

One day, Schreiber's penknife went missing, disappearing from his table. He stepped out into the hut minus his club and stood in the middle of the long narrow building looking around him. I was near to him. We all smelled bad, but this man radiated a mixture of a rank, peppery odour mixed with the kind of smell associated with a rendering house. I coughed involuntarily into the silence and for a moment his eyes fell on me. I looked back. There was no insolence in the look. He looked away and round the room. In clear Yiddish he addressed the room:

> Somebody here doesn't love you any more. Somebody has my knife. It has a pearl handle. It is my little treasure, and one of you has it. Now we could turn this place

upside-down and scare the rats. We could hold every one of you arse up and shake and shake, but after careful consideration, here is my proposal. On average I kill ten, maybe twenty of you by the day. Here's the offer. Return the knife by tonight, on my table, I promise not to peep, and I won't up the number to one hundred. A little longer to live and enjoy your labours. The benefits are obvious.

Schreiber pointedly left his lair during that day and, naturally, the penknife was returned. The killing, however, was briefly stepped up anyway; because he could.

On a detail to drag corpses across the yard to spill them over into the pits, something slipped out from the clothing of a dead man I was dragging. Tobacco, in greaseproof paper. I instantly hid the little package from prying eyes and examined the prize later; the stuff was dry and, on the outside, would have been thrown away, but here it was gold dust. I picked a time when I calculated Schreiber's killing streak was dormant, took my life in my hands and parted the blankets to his private space. He was sat reading an old American comic as I sneaked in. Entering his space was strictly forbidden, so that he looked up at me more than a little surprised. He half rose and reached for the club. I cut in quickly:

'I've got tobacco. I'll trade it for some soup.'

He gave a contemptuous chuckle, cocked his head to one side. 'Is that your soup tin, you cheeky little whelp?'

'Yes.'

'Pass it across then.'

Though there was no flame under it, the soup was still hot from an earlier boiling, the aroma of which made me decide to risk everything for a ladle of it. He passed the filled tin back to me. The warmth and the smell of it made my body shake with anticipation. I handed him the package. He opened it, smelled the contents, rolled some in his fingers.

'Nice. Got any more?'

'Maybe. Later.' I lied.

197

'You're a brave little shrimp, coming in here without permission. Keep me supplied and you live, with maybe some soup thrown in. Miss out on the supply, bye bye. Deal?'

I had painted myself into a corner. I would pay for my cheek with my life or supply the mad bastard with tobacco I hadn't got. I nodded my assent to his insane proposition and made my way out into the hut. Before I was able to raise the tin cup to my lips, it was snatched from me by those nearest to the alcove. My tin was returned with just the dregs to taste. We had become a pack of dogs. I cried bitter tears at the loss of my treasured food. My friends, Joe, Slomo and Toby couldn't help. Nobody around had tobacco and if they had, would not part with it without a valid trade. A day went by, the killing went on apace, and we, the survivors, had the usual task of dispensing with the bodies. Though I frisked every one of my tasks, not one carried tobacco or anything else of value. Then I had a desperately crazy idea. By the barrack walls, weeds grew. I picked the dry ones, remnants of the previous year, and broke them down to resemble tobacco, which they didn't, and mixed them with tobacco that I had held back from the first stash. It was pathetic. All of this I wrapped up in the remnants of a paper bag and handed them across to Schreiber when the time was right. He poured my soup, which I put down me there and then; lukewarm, gruel-like and heavenly. Schreiber laughed at my rapid intake.

'I see you're not taking chances like last time. No Jew like a hungry Jew.'

Did he consider himself no longer Jewish? Had the Jew in him died along with his victims? He started to open the packet. Oh God. I froze. I had prayed that he wouldn't, yet. I knew he would discover the deceit but I had hoped to hide by then. He looked at it, then he looked up and across to me. A slow smile spread across his wide, square face. He reached down for the club.

'Thank you for the tobacco, but the weeds I can live without. Where would you like to die? In here? I know, out there in the hut with your fellow vermin looking on.'

He dragged me by the ear out into the hut. All faces were on us. Club in one hand and me held by the other. 'This little bastard thinks I am stupid. Weeds for soup. Not a fair trade.'

The talking was my chance. I kicked out hard and caught him high on the leg, aiming for the groin. It was enough to gain release. I ran and felt the wind of the club's swing. It missed the back of my head. I ducked and dodged, made it beyond the passive onlookers and out into the yard. Schreiber was screaming abuse my way in Yiddish. There were no guards to be seen; disappearances and desertions were well under way. Another kapo half-heartedly gave chase in response to Schreiber's demands. He had fallen over a couple of bodies in the yard and was screaming mad. I eluded both of my pursuers by cutting across to a storage shed. Stumbling in, I found the place neatly piled end-to-end with bodies stacked high to the level of about two metres. I scrambled to the top and ran across the bodies the length of the shed to an end door. Where I came in, framed in the light of the doorway, the other kapo stood. He didn't venture further into the darkness. I stood in deep shadow, panting and aching with effort, hoping the kapo hadn't seen me come in. He went away and I slid down to the floor and slipped back out into the daylight, just in time to see Schreiber disappear, making for the other side of the block to catch me there. I just ran blind in the opposite direction, winding up in a section of the camp area into which I had never ventured.

Grey ground gave way to uncut grass through which celandine was starting to bloom. A metal railing, spiked, green-painted and rusted, ran in a gradual curve for some distance. Behind it, some way off, were some handsome, red-brick, single storey buildings in a cluster. I slipped through the fence at a gap and made my way in sun-dappled shadow under trees through cool long grass. I was tempted to rest there and then, but the thought of Schreiber urged me as far away as I could get. Maybe help lay ahead, somewhere to hide at least. I was functioning on fear and nervous energy, little else was holding me up. I came up close to the side of one of the buildings and tried to peer in through a barred window. The lower half was frosted, so that even on tiptoe, I couldn't get a look. Jumping up and down was beyond me. I edged round the building looking out for a guard. None was there. From way over back in the grey barrack area, I heard Schreiber's distant curses and shouting. For the moment I was out of sight, I was also fully aware I could not go back to that barrack hut. Would I be able to find a safe hideaway? I put my ear to the open barrack door to hear female voices, in Hungarian what is more. I called out from the doorway:

'Lowy. Budapest. Who is here?'

The women hauled me in. I went from person to person looking for a familiar face. Maybe my mother, my sisters. Medy? I cast around with no result, but as a consolation I was given food and drink from their scant stockpile. I must have looked at death's door, for though they were thinned down and hollow-eyed, tears were shed at my appearance. As I ate, they told me that in numbers they were several hundred, all of whom were under the protection of the Red Cross who had done some kind of deal with the Nazis. They were to be exchanged for trucks and were due to be shipped out and transported to Switzerland. The female side of entire families would survive, from children to matriarchs. The news was good, but somehow surreal and beyond belief, that they would leave Hell unharmed. While I was eating, I chanced to look up, and staring down at me from her bunk-bed was a young woman with a high forehead and spectacles, who gazed my way with one of those long sad, serious stares that stay scorched on the memory. I looked up and smiled. She looked away, unsettled by my response. I gave her a little wave and looked away. According to the women who fed me, I was not the first to come through the door. Many had come that way to beg for food, and just as I was about to do, disappeared back from whence they came.

My stay in the women's barrack was necessarily short as an inspection was due, so I was out of there quickly. As I left, I looked up at the quiet girl and waved. She waved back. I was out into the bright sun, across the yard, quickly in under the trees. I couldn't resist it, I found a space in the long grass under a tree, out of sight I hoped, and had myself a little rest.

I woke with a start. It was dusk. I rose and ducked back through the railings into the grey, gritty world I had left hours before. No guards, no kapos, just ground strewn with bodies still unmoved and fly-infested. After the sweet smell of grass and celandine, the all-pervading stink of Belsen returned. I couldn't return to my barrack to be clubbed to death, I had to duck in on another group. Eventually, I found a half-empty hut with around a hundred or so prisoners. These men were from further east, but took me in. Their kapo had died from typhoid so they were left pretty much alone. Other kapos took turns to give them the 'once-over' but with the non-arrival of food or medicine, these inmates were quickly falling by the wayside. The bunk I took up was next to a couple of lads from Transylvania, both of whom were a little older than me and in slightly better shape. With one of them, George, a carpenter, I struck up a relationship instantly; the other, Gregor, was a bit remote but friendly. Together, the following day, we set about our single, designated task of removing the dead from the hut and the outside yards, to the large pits a few hundred metres off. It is true to say that hardship, pain and suffering are lessened in the sharing. Our exertions were half-hearted and pathetic, taking hours to drag a few bodies to the pits, but fear and habit drove us on. Often it was all too much and we would put down our burden and just sit staring vacantly at nothing at all until we got a kick from a passing kapo. A couple of times Schreiber passed while we were toiling. I would turn my head away and hope. I guess by now we were so wasted, we all looked pretty much alike, as do skeletons, in our striped-pyjama uniforms. Whatever, he didn't register.

George developed typhoid and was quickly gone. Gregor could not stop crying, and we dragged our friend to the edge of one of the pits and lowered him in, reciting all the prayers I could remember from the days of freedom. And a Goethe poem my mother loved:

Über allen Gipfeln ist Ruh,
In allen Wipfeln spürest du kaum einen Hauch;
Die Vöglein schweigen, schweigen im Walde,
Warte nur, warte nur, bald ruhest du auch.

(All over the mountain peaks peace reigns,
In the treetops, barely a breath of wind is to be felt;
The birds are silent, silent in the forest,
Wait, just wait, soon you too will be at rest.)

Gregor and I returned to the hut and continued our praying. The gentle Romanian carpenter was in our thoughts through the night. The following day we resumed our tasks, after we had drunk a little water that was left for us by the barrack door. Our drinking supply came infrequently and was quickly gone. It was on this day that I found myself in the pit with George, and in the dark I was hauled out. Finally, Gregor succumbed and I was alone again. These final hours passed in a haze. I watched as the camp was deserted by the guards. Those who could leave before the Allies arrived, did so. Some of those caught in the net donned prisoner clothing and tried to pass themselves off as us. A physical impossibility. Hungarian guards who had been shipped in were manning the gun emplacements around the camp.

The dying went on, the killing went on as anarchy chimed the death knell. I witnessed a man clubbed to death by kapos. His offence? Eating the liver of a fellow inmate. So it was. Opened up the body out of need. My brain and my body were no longer obeying me, they were obeying typhoid. I was down.

Liberation came to Belsen on 15 April 1945. The British entered the camp and were forced to make their way slowly, as corpses had to be cleared so that the trucks could enter. Prisoners stood and watched apathetically as the young Brits, stricken by what they had found, underwent a trauma from which they could not be spared. One by one these ordinary lads moved slowly through the camp in a mixture of shock and the deepest anger at what they discovered as they went. Some wept, others were simply stunned that their senses were showing them the unthinkable in a waking reality that they could see, touch, smell and, in the solid air, taste. The darkness of human depravity had been visited on their fellow beings. Some could not contain their revulsion and were violently sick. Someone was taking photographs of us. I raised myself onto one elbow from the dusty ground to watch the first soldiers go by, then collapsed and was out of it.

Faced with the enormous task of dealing with thousands of sick and starving inmates, the British got dug in and, with their usual cheerful efficiency, began to make a difference. Water was made available when fire brigades were detailed to lay hundreds of yards of hosepipe. There was a shortage of people to administer to the thousands but somehow, in those first hours, everyone living received fresh water. Makeshift latrines were hastily dug, made available for use and caringly split up into single-sex units, though nobody paid much attention to the allotted gender of a given box. Typhoid and all the other associated gastric disorders from which we suffered were no respecters of the moment. Many didn't make the latrines, and just let go where they were. The Tommies were completely shocked, but still let their humanity shine.

Typhoid victims were confined by the British to barrack blocks where we rode out the condition in comparative comfort, having a bunk bed each and the beginnings of constant medical attention, sorely needed. The repetitive nature of the condition's effects, as with dysentery, had us all constantly on the move, weakened and staggering. By degrees, medicine, food and liquids began to win the day with many of us. There was still life loss, much of it through trauma now that the threat had lifted. Thinking back over years of terror, now departed, for the physically weakened just proved too much and, mentally exhausted, some simply stopped living. Some were killed with kindness. Soldiers had unwisely given some types of food to the starving too soon. Early in the quarantine, before the young medics arrived from Britain, food had been left at the hut entrances. The soldiers expected the inmates to share. Those able to walk, ate; those held to their beds by weakness got nothing. Those who ate, ate too much of the wrong stuff and died. Some who had nothing to begin with were latterly nursed back to health, along with carefully controlled feeding. A deep irony. Picked up out of the dust and hospitalized, slowly my strength began to return. Able to stand and walk around, limited exercise became possible, if utterly exhausting. Resting up one evening after a bit of a walk, I stopped to lean against some hay bales to catch my breath. A familiar figure approached.

'I don't believe. It's Ernest Lowy!'

It was Mr Spiegel, a man I knew from Dunajszka Streda, who was a regular visitor to the Weiss household when we put up with them at the time of expulsion from Bratislava. He had been very helpful to us refugees.

'I am happy that you made it through, Ernest. Many haven't.'

He nodded across to a barrack block. Almost in passing: 'You know who just died over there? Someone we both know, I'm so sad, the older Weiss girl, Medy. Such a beautiful child, she became a beautiful young woman and now ...'

He talked on into my numbing shock as it overtook me and brought me to near-collapse. He talked on about the living and the dead as my mind conjured her face and our moments together. Spiegel said his goodbyes and moved on across the spaces between the barrack buildings. I was destroyed. If I had known, what could I have done? I slid to the ground against the hay bales and watched the day fade. As evening closed in, I made my way unsteadily to the barrack Mr Spiegel had pointed out. From the doorway, I looked in. The scene was familiar. Some recovered girls were standing or sitting together in quiet conversation, others supine, maybe dying on their pallets. Was she still there? Had she been taken away? I could not bring myself to enter. Time here would have changed her, and even in death, I realized I would not be able to tolerate the change in her. I had my memory, and I had this

204

dark despair at being so close and possibly able to help her before this moment of absolute disconnection. Crazy, unreasonable, but so is adoration.

The temporary isolation at the actual camp was to be over for me and a few others. I was to be properly hospitalized across at Hanover. A process of selection was obviously taking place. As personnel arrived from Britain and the Red Cross became present, along with military rabbis, groups and committees, army and political choices were being made. As supplies arrived, both food and medical, it became obvious that in dealing with tens of thousands of survivors, the more promising in terms of treatment were selected. Selection, still selection. I was lucky, starved, delirious at times, but not at death's door.

It was obvious that the Allies had been caught on the hop over the camps. The 'liberation' was not a planned moment, the frontline soldiers had stumbled on us. They had done their best to stem the tide of death there and then with what was available to them. They had seconded civilians from nearby. They had ordered some of the Germans troops into clearing up some of the mess; others were confined to barracks. Even inmates who were deemed capable had a hand in beginning to clear this ocean of filth.

I was not witness to this, being deep in delirium, but Kramer had been driven through the camp beside the British colonel in charge of the soldiers who had found us, when, with a megaphone to his lips, the Briton had informed the dead, the dying and the uninterested that they were now free and the war over. Kramer, the guards and the kapos remained installed temporarily. They were a depleted and cowed crew. The mad gangsters like Schreiber vanished. Kramer was too high-profile to disappear. Snagged on his seniority, he would in time meet his fate as a war criminal. Meantime he went about assuring the colonel there was food enough for three days, that the inmates were dangerous and politicized. He was pissing against the wind. The British found out all too quickly that the criminal and the mad lie until they die.

Across Germany, all kinds of prisoners were freed from all kinds of conditions. People on death marches were suddenly free to roam. Others being ferried across Germany in trains found themselves abandoned, and once out of the sealed box cars either took off into the countryside, or foraged around locally to return to their temporary base-camps on wheels. Non-Jews made up the majority of this vast army of alien internees, free to roam and inevitably terrorize local Germans, now brought low, but relatively well-stocked with the two objects of universal need, food and drink. The length and breadth of Germany (and greater Europe) was home to the stateless and the wandering. Most captive Jews were in the camps, and now subject to a hold-back policy brought on by disease on the one hand and a chilling indecision about our future on the other. Were we Hungarians, Romanians? What were we? Jews, yes, but of a given country. That made sense to the British, but what awaited us back 'home'? The arguments raged over our heads and out of our hands. Palestine came into the equation, as Palestine inevitably would. The destabilizing effect of hundreds and thousands of Jews descending on the fledgling community would blow the Middle East wide.

The resolution, where possible, would be repatriation for those who chose, and a dispersal to welcoming countries for those wishing to make a fresh start. Truly a nation without a home; though some did make it to Palestine, before the debacle of the refugee ships of sour recall.

It was the end of May by the time I had strengthened enough to be moved from the recovery unit to a collective quarantine, housed in a complex of buildings originally built for recuperating soldiers of the First World War, somewhere between Hanover and Celle. Eventual recovery would see me back at Belsen with the Hungarian contingent awaiting repatriation.

In the hospital, normal human life began to permeate my mass of daily emotional explosions of memory. As the pain lessened and my flesh began to develop under my skin, and I no longer retched after eating, I began to take in my surroundings. The endlessly long ward through which the sunlight of the warming year cast its strong beams, slowly asserted its reality on me. Ward One. From the Belsen dust where I had collapsed when the first troops moved in, unable to greet my liberators on my own two feet, to this place where for days on end I was still unable to properly stand for any length of time, or for that matter, sit. Each time I woke to the day, I did a double-take. The fresh linen, as white as white can be, clean-smelling; what is more, I was no longer taking in my own odours. I was a child again. So much so, that daily I received a kiss on the forehead from Sister Emma. She looked after Pinki, a young boy from Warsaw, and me as though we were the only two survivors from Belsen.

Sister Emma was tall, well-built, beautiful and German. A Wagnerian goddess who sat by our bedsides and spoon-fed her two Belsen charges until they were able to stand tall, walk properly and return her beautiful smile. One evening when I was able to sit up and take notice, Sister Emma and I sang lullabies for Pinki. The crowded ward fell silent as all listened to our efforts. I sang one in particular that had a melancholic feel; very Jewish. She looked at me and said tenderly:

'That tune was very sad. Sing something else, Ernest.'

It was one of my father's favourites, but for her, overnight, I revised the whole thing from minor to major. It worked.

At times, a Greek survivor in his middle years, wheelchair-bound and legless, made with us a threesome. He played a small octagonal accordion. Yet another George. This one had rich moustaches, twinkling eyes and a rich, ready laugh. Both he and I left the same day. I was at the nurses' station waiting to say my farewells and 'thank yous' to Sister Emma when George turned up. Emma appeared. She leaned down to give George a little kiss. In broken German he addressed the nurses:

'For all you have done for me, I thank you. For what you have done for those two Jewish boys, I bless you. Yet only a matter of weeks ago, Germany was wiping Jews off the map of history, kids included. Today, look at you all, fighting for their lives. This is one crazy world.'

We watched him wheel himself down the long corridor, at the end of which he passed through a door where he vanished into bright sunlight, a waiting military ambulance and repatriation. What George had said made Emma blush. Her farewell to me was very sweet:

'Ernest, it looks like you're going to make a good recovery. Eventually you will marry, have children. Grandchildren. In this way, Jewish people will recover and thrive.'

I could visualize George shaking his head to this. 'Crazy world'. What a crazy world. For me, I would never forget Emma's devotion, and I told her so. For the other German nurses also, my gratitude is enduring.

In the quarantine, every block housed different nationalities. In my block, it didn't take me long to tie in with my Belsen friends, those who had made it through. Any familiar face at that stage was a bosom buddy, but there were those who were brothers; Slomo Braun, Davide, Toby, Vaganfi, Joe and George. We had come so far and made it. Quarantine would be a cakewalk, and then, repatriation. A delight-to-come, laced with worrying mystery in that we just didn't know who among loved ones and friends had survived, and who had been lost. As our strength returned, we began to feel the desire to recover our lives. Then there was Susan, a pretty, cheeky Czech survivor who thought I was the tailor, and wanted to borrow the iron. Her infectious humour, along with that of her mother, touched many lives with laughter and was to colour the days on the journey to repatriation.

The post-quarantine period seemed to drag on but it enabled us all to regain our composure, our grip on reality. Fraternization was positively encouraged, with the occupying British joining in. Enjoying oneself socially was an awkward step forward. Done in groups, it proved easier. Being part of the real world again was really something to be celebrated. Yet something was different, an indefinable but very palpable atmosphere. We had lost our liberty in the death throes of an epoch that led inevitably to somebody like Hitler, and a social upheaval that shed conventions like scales. Where were we now? The Brits provided a cheerful edge to our continued incarceration, and their generosity in even little things proved their sincerity; they had our trust and respect. By comparison, we were the shy guys, though as our strength returned, we dared breathe the air and enjoy the day. Maybe it was the opportunity to enjoy the summer sun without fear, the rain without dread. Whatever it was, it felt new. Was this the air of freedom?

Our relative lack of fitness and bulk didn't help. The British military personnel looked superfit, like gods when they walked into Belsen. They didn't march, they walked. In the months of recovery everything was done for us, medically and humanly, though at first good intentions when providing sustenance, killed. As soon as the medics were in place, correct action on revival went into overdrive. At this point the vexed arguments over the Palestine Mandate and our destiny were absent from our quarantine and recovery. Raised voices in another room.

THE LAST DANCE OF A MASS-MURDERER

It was a Sunday afternoon. We had heard that a dance was going to be held in the Romanian block, that there would be a band. Although we had no intention of gatecrashing the affair, it would be a chance to see what was going on and hear dance music. We had a kilometre to walk and, for the first time, no escort or detail. We took our time, teasing each other about our choice of clothing and footwear, which of course was no choice at all, but what had been handed us, charitably, by the British. A raggle-taggle crew, but enjoying the day even if we slightly dreaded the exposure. From a distance we could hear the music, a mixture of Glenn Miller and pre-war dance favourites. We arrived at the block and the man at the door allowed us in just far enough to get a look at what went on. Six curious young men stood along a back wall, a little wide-eyed at the crowded enjoyment, the high level of talk mixed with laughter against the volume of the band playing loud and lively. There were flags and some bunting draped from the walls. The fraternization was working well, and though the principal interest seemed to be in the British Army female personnel, other women – some previous inmates, some German helpers and medics – had found their way into the building and on to the dance floor. Soldiers and civilians were mixing very well. We stood with silly smiles on our faces, absorbing the scene and going with the music.

We all saw him at the same time and looked each to the other, appalled. His partner was tall, in British medical corps uniform. Against her, holding her, waltzing with this fresh-faced, laughing girl was the monster of our nightmares; not fled, not dead, but alive and grinning as he tippy-toed his bulk around the dance floor in spruce flannel trousers, crisp neat shirt and smart polished shoes.

Slomo pushed himself off the wall with a look that spoke for us. Schreiber was a dead man. We quickly hauled Slomo out of the hall into the open air where we spent several minutes in a huddle, stopping our proud fighter from using his recovered strength to break the neck of the foul kapo.

'What then?' He demanded of us.

We would seek justice through the authorities. Across the way, having a smoke, leaning against a jeep, were two military policemen in their distinctive white helmets and snow-white gaiters. We ran towards them. Instinctively, their hands went to their holsters as we were regaling them in a mix of languages and gestures. In our excitement, we surrounded them. Patiently, they heard us out, established the complaint and went into action, following us back into the hall. Back inside, the place seemed loud and vibrant. If anything, there seemed to be even more people on the dance floor and it took us a few moments to spot him. Still with the tall English girl, he was quick-stepping. The pair danced past us, he employing the nasty little shuffle he did after a 'kill'.

Slomo groaned loudly and for a brief moment, Schreiber's cold eyes looked our way. My heart leapt involuntarily.

We identified Schreiber to the two MPs. One moved through the crowd, the puzzled attention of the dancers on him. Reaching the bandstand, he silenced the musicians. Everyone then looked toward the other MP who had made his way out on to the floor past standing couples and laid his hand on Schreiber's shoulder. The stocky little man swung round, not letting go the hand of his partner.

'Don't make a fuss. Come with us please.'

All eyes were now on the little group in the middle of the dance floor.

'What is he supposed to have done?' demanded the English girl who seemed now to be holding the hand of an errant child.

'War crimes, Sarge. Your mate here liked killing starving prisoners; weapon of choice, a baseball bat.'

Her face changed. She looked down at Schreiber who was protesting and arguing the toss. She let go of his hand and took a step back. Still looking at him, she asked the MP: 'Got proof?'

'Six angry survivors.'

She looked our way, then back at Schreiber who also stared our way. We were changed physically and our striped uniforms long since ash.

'I don't know these people.'

'They know you.'

The second MP joined them.

'Come along folks, these good people want to get on with their dance.'

The English girl pushed the protesting Schreiber away and, under escort, he left the dance floor. Before he and the MPs had reached the door, Slomo was on him. The military police intervened kindly, but forcefully, compelling the big guy away from the target of his hate.

'Don't worry chum, he'll get his. Any more from you and we'll have to nick you, and it's such a nice day. Comprendi?'

The other MP detailed us to turn up in numbers at the British High Commissioner's office the following morning, and to have a spokesman to give voice to our accusations. Schreiber was pushed roughly into the back of the jeep and driven off; we stood and watched as it disappeared down a tree-lined lane, kicking up dust in its wake. Turning back to the hall, triumphant, serious and deeply gratified, we determined to catch a bit more of the music. We resumed our backs-to-the-wall positions near the door. The effect of Schreiber's arrest had died away and dancing was on again. From the washroom, the female English sergeant emerged. Catching sight of us, she came over: 'God. I'm so sorry. I had no idea. He was so touching about his terrible time in the Warsaw ghetto and the camps ...'

Severally we assured her our offence was not with her. She smiled winningly and thanked us. This elegant army beauty turned on her heel and made her way back to a sizeable party of uniforms near the bandstand, who were agog to learn what the heck was happening. The band played on until the afternoon was spent.

The following morning 150 or so tense, excited, revived Belsen inmates thronged the office area where the British High Commissioner was temporarily housed. Choosing a spokesman was fairly easy. Pinter, the kapo from camp KZ Wustegiersdorf. He was one of those trusties who managed to walk a fine line between the power allotted him by the Nazis and the humanity residing in him persistently, in spite of everything. Little kindnesses all round, and for me salvation at one point. Pinter was from Budapest. He had known my father, which led to a certain resonance between us, though in any camp under the Nazis, no side could be shown or on the face of it, quarter given. But ...

A hungry day back in Wustegiersdorf. I was in the queue for milk soup, a dilute soya gruel that lacked milk in any quantity. It had heat. The queue seemed to be moving slowly, and against my hunger, the delay seemed endless. Finally, it was my turn. Tin vessel in hand, I held it out. The kapo-chef, Janek, was having a joke with another kapo and he only half-dipped his ladle into the soup, pouring the inadequate contents into my tin. I stood momentarily. He glanced up to gesture me on. I was being pushed in the back by those behind me, hungry and anxious for their moment with the ladle. Tears of anger mingled with the soup which quickly vanished, doing absolutely nothing to diminish the racking pain of starvation never baulked by such a weak opponent.

Desperation took over and I made up my mind to rejoin the queue, a rarely tried taboo. Would Janek recognize me? When thinned down, we all tended to look alike at first glance. It was a risk I was prepared to take. From the end of the queue, I took time to study him. Overweight for his height, he obviously was eating our food, or had access to food we could only imagine. Either way I hated this being who stood between me and my next plate of soup. He didn't seem to pay much attention to the food queue and was still enjoying a chat with the other kapo, whose sole task seemed to be to keep Janek company. The pulse in my neck started to hammer. I knew I was trembling and colouring up. Two back from the ladle, he glanced my way. I reached the ladle which Janek dipped in the soup. I held my breath. He raised it, then stopped.

'You. Stand to one side.'

He alerted the small group of kapos clustered at the end of the barrack with a short shrill whistle. They were beside him in seconds.

'Greedyguts here tried for extras.'

A public beating would be next. Starting with the groin, a general kick around would ensue, leaving me with a sporting chance of an agonized death. Some of the kapos were Polish Gentiles whose very toes were anti-Semitic. I was grabbed and dragged away from the queue, but, before a fist landed, Pinter had appeared and hauled me away from the group. The respect he commanded amongst these killers stayed their hands.

'Okay, okay, let me deal with this. The kid's alright, well-behaved. Best on my block. Leave him to me.'

213

Janek objected. He wanted me on the floor, dying. He yelped in Yiddish: 'You're dead, you little shit. Catch you later when your boyfriend's not looking.'

Pinter laughed.

'My eyes are everywhere, Janek. Think on.'

Janek's memory of me faded. The next day in the food queue, he barely acknowledged the face behind the proffered tin. It was the case that many of the Hungarian prisoners had Pinter to thank for their moments of comfort or survival.

It was natural then for him to bear witness on our behalf. Escorted by military policemen that morning, he disappeared inside the building. A kapo to neutralize a kapo. We were left outside, waiting if necessary, to be called.

Pinter was in the place a little over thirty minutes. He emerged with a grim smile on his face. The military police came with him and stood at the doorway. One of them called out to us.

'Alright lads. Back to your quarters. Your mate Schreiber has been charged with war crimes. You'll know the outcome in due course.'

A loud murmur of approval rose as the soldier's words were translated by Pinter. As we walked away, he added: 'They found the baseball bat under his bed; worse, one of the SS had him on camera. He's going to hang.'

And so he did, along with some Nazi brass including Kramer and a few more insane kapos. We were all invited to the executions as they took place in Belsen, the scene of their crimes. Of my friends, Slomo, Toby and Vaganyfi went. They returned, quiet, calm and unsmiling. Slomo spoke after a lengthy silence in the barrack:

'Ernest, lad, you should have gone. It would have laid some ghosts to rest.'

To watch a couple dozen Nazis and kapos choking their last at the end of a rope I knew would neither save nor cleanse my soul. I didn't know what would, but somehow I knew it would take more than the removal of these 'vessels' of evil to rid the planet of the evil itself which, though badly wounded, had the capacity to revive and enslave another collective consciousness, any time soon.

Schreiber had gone, but Schreiber's kind live on. I looked at my friends, knowing them as loyal each to the other.

'Put it down to my weak constitution,' I said.

Slomo smiled to himself and lit a cigarette.

16 The Long Way Home

The photograph of George VI and the large Union Jack pinned to the wall had such an effect on me when I sat in the office of the British major in charge of repatriation at Belsen. No tension here about life or death because of misdemeanour or a wrong word. But the man was puzzled. Why did I want to go to Bratislava? It was occupied by the Russians who weren't 'all that keen' about Jewish people, and who were 'inclined to be socially repressive anyway'. I explained that I wanted to discover how many of my family had survived. At this he nodded and signed the necessary, as did I. I was on my way to repatriation. It meant the parting of the ways with Joe, who had opted for Sweden. What do you say to someone on whom your life has depended, whose life you have saved? A brother in all but blood. At the station we sat in silence, drinking coffee from a flask, until it was time for his train. Then we cried like a couple of girls until the train doors were slammed shut and steam swallowed his wave.

I had heard nothing of my family's fate since my father waved to me as he left the police station in Budapest all those months ago. A year in which my life had been catapulted forward into a maelstrom of experiences that no being should undergo; and now I was to walk away from it all and return to God-knew-what, let alone where. There was train transport to Bratislava. There were people there that I used to know. I grew up there, I knew its streets and, best of all, from there it would be simple to get to Budapest and my parents. So clear in the plan, so different come the day.

Susan, the young Czech from the quarantine period, had mentioned this train. At the scheduled time of departure, I turned up with a rucksack with some rough clothing acquired and provisions hoarded over time. On the train (an open goods, forty to a truck) I made myself as comfortable as possible. There was an air of excitement as the journey across Germany to the border began. The Brits had provided an army unit to accompany us as far as Prague. At the first station I needed a drink and found a standpipe on the platform. I was bending over to take some water, when I received a light kick in the pants. Not taking my mouth away from the tap, I looked round to see a laughing Susan.

'I thought I recognized you.'

I smiled back. I'd missed seeing them at the departure. I had been busy with farewells and promises. It had been a hell of a wrench to say goodbye to my friends – in spite of all and because of all. But it was done. Done with hugs, tears and hope in the heart that our paths would again cross. All headed for the unknown in a partial daze that hadn't lifted, which for some never would.

'Come and join Mother and me in our luxurious compartment.'

'Better than mine?'

'Bound to be. We're on our way to Zneim, not common old Prague.'

So I joined them. Their fellow passengers squeezed up to make room for one more. Mother and daughter were both needed for their high spirits and excitability, for the journey turned out to be a grim experience as the goods train threaded its way through war-torn Germany. All villages and towns through which we passed, or stopped at, were in ruins. Shell after shell of broken-tooth buildings, greyer than grey, even in sunshine. Debris on the line frequently interrupted the journey. Passing through ruined areas, children frequently stood near the track in little groups, pairs and singles, to wave at the train as kids will always do. Nobody in our truck waved back, except Susan, her mother and me. The kids' faces dropped at the lack of response, but cheered a little at apparently the only three people in thirty trucks responding. A voice called from the end of our truck.

'Why you wave at those German children, after what has happened? For shame.'

I replied: 'Because they *are* children. None of them has "guilty" tattooed on the forehead.'

Susan's mother chipped in: 'All our tomorrows reside in the young. We make a little start here. Yes?'

From that moment on, Susan's mother made a point of waving to the kids we passed. At Bayreuth, approaching the Czech border, the train made a stop and we were led to believe it would be a while before it made a move. As I stretched my legs on the platform, I bumped into a group of young people headed for Budapest. It turned out that these Gentile youngsters had been holed up in a work camp. Now liberated, they were making their way home. Chat led to an invite. A beer? I hadn't had a decent beer since Budapest. Of course a beer. Susan would like one also. On my way to fetch her and take her to the station restaurant, I watched in horror as the train moved out of the station. Stranded in Bayreuth. With my meagre possessions on the train with the two women, I stood alone and unbelieving.

Down the platform stood a very tall American military policeman, a sergeant. I spilled out my tale of woe. Not only was this man endowed with classic good looks, he spoke fluent German. Later, he let on he was Jewish.

'You sure you were in Belsen? You don't look that skinny to me.'

I became very serious with him.

'I assure you sir, I was. The British fattened us up during quarantine.'

'Okay, just kidding, buddy. You're with me.'

He grabbed my arm and together we marched into the ticket office where he demanded of the surprised clerk information about how far down the line my train might be. He explained how I had missed the train, how it was crucial to meet it. Looking at me, this small thin, neatly uniformed German suddenly spat venom. Jumping from his chair, he pointed the finger: 'Stealing fruit from the gardens near the station, that's what your sort do. We see you from the train, can't help yourselves. You're not immune from prosecution.'

His voice contained the anguish of bitterness and hate. I felt uncomfortable. The large American seemed to lose his temper. He pushed the clerk back into his chair with one hand, with the other, drew his gun, and placed it to his bald head. It was a very tense moment, but I noticed a twinkle in the Yank's eye and the merest hint of a smile when he glanced my way. He had total power. The little man groaned quietly into the silence. The American loosened his grip on him. The German jumped to fawning attention. The MP's eyes burned into his.

'The war's over, yes?'

'Yes.'

'You know who started it, yes?'

'Yes.'

'Then you'll know who lost it.'

'Yes.'

'Then keep your big mouth shut. This boy has no fruit. Turn out your pockets, son. Show the little motherfucker.'

No fruit hidden.

'Now you kraut sonofabitch. Find me that train!'

I couldn't have done any of that. My will had been sapped by years of submission to a cultural perception for survival's sake, and which, in the latter days, had all but killed me. The perception had to go, I had to stand in this century and be a man of this century. A Jew of my time, like this American soldier, not a Jew of a subservient past.

Again my arm was grabbed and I nearly broke into a run trying to keep up with the American's stride, taking me into an area of war-damaged Bayreuth where there seemed to be nothing but American personnel. He stopped by a truck whose black driver was happy to chase the train, offering me chewing gum, not kosher, but very sweet, as he shook my hand and helped me into the truck. The three of us sat in the cab for a 'hell-and-back' drive along rough country roads, chasing the train and catching up at a halt forty-five minutes later. In mangled English, I thanked them both. The sergeant responded in faultless German. As their truck pulled away, he leaned out the cab and tossed me a couple of packs of Philip Morris. The truck sounded its horn a few rhythmic times, then was gone.

I walked across to our train. Susan and her mother reached down from their wagon and helped me back in. Susan giggled: 'What's so wrong with us that you go in a taxi? Is our luxury carriage not good enough?'

Susan's mother: 'We thought you'd gone for good.'

Despite the promise of an escort all the way to Prague, the British left us at Pilsen, with no explanation. Nevertheless, we said goodbye to our protectors and liberators with deep thanks for all that had been done for us by them.

The atmosphere at Pilsen changed. The station was swarming with battle-weary Russians, some of whom slept on the hard, concrete platform with nothing much to cushion their heads. Others were awake and eyed us menacingly. Fortunately, the British stayed with us until the new train we had changed to finally pulled out of the station. Compartments and wood benches. The old feel, it was luxury, it was normal. It was 'stretch-out-and-enjoy' time, which we did. Then, of a sudden, it was Prague. Susan, her mother, Ruth and myself stood ready to say our goodbyes. There was going to be a delay in my train. Theirs was not yet in sight. We talked.

Ruth: 'We're all out of food. God knows what we'll eat in the next few days; still, something will turn up, it always does.'

I had my hands in my pockets. My fingers played with the two packs of cigarettes. Me: 'I have an idea. Ruth, you'll be alright by yourself for ten minutes. Susan, let's go find the market. It's bound to be near the station.'

The two women looked puzzled. Cigarettes were good barter. Money right now had little meaning. I was relatively well-off. Susan and I traded at barrows, street corners, shops and restaurants, coming back to the station laden with our acquisitions.

'For one cigarette, a cabbage?'

Ruth found this hard to believe. We had four cabbages and any amount of fruit and vegetables, all for cigarettes. Such coinage.

Laden down with their supplies, Ruth and Susan bade me a tear-filled farewell before joining their train to Zneim. We vowed to keep in touch, but somehow, in the mad swirl of the early post-war months and years, it didn't happen. Very much alone, I reboarded the train to go deeper into Czechoslovakia. After a while, the train pulled into a small country station where the Czech army had us out on to the platform for a 'head-count'. As our names were being called, I noticed a well-built man in Czech uniform coming my way. He had thick wavy hair, was waving his cap over the heads of the crowd to catch my eye. In German he shouted: 'Ernest. Ernest Lowy. Don't you recognise me? Feldko?'

I took an astonished step back. Feldko was a distant cousin on my father's side. Not since childhood had I seen him, yet he knew me, and I him. Now? Here? His hug was furious, almost desperate. As he released me, I noticed the badge of the Soviets in his lapel, and the pistol in his waistband. I was impressed.

'I've been fighting with the Red Army,' he said proudly in German for all to gather.

He continued: 'You're headed for Bratislava? It says so in the papers I saw in the station office. I wondered if it was you. I looked for you in this crowd. You've changed, but the family thing. Soon had you picked out. Your name been called yet?'

I shook my head.

'When it is, come and join me in the train, we'll travel together to Bratislava, and together, we'll search out our families.'

I had a travelling companion. One who had history and doubtless a few tales to tell.

It was good to talk of family and past times. The frown never left his face as I unloaded my memories of my captivity upon him. He had heard stories, and had witnessed much himself, but the death camps were a revelation. His face hardened and his eyes became cold as he realized that some, if not all our dear ones had been murdered during the Eichmann period of eliminations. We spoke animatedly in a mix of German and Czech. I spoke with concern about the Russians.

'Don't worry, little cousin,' his arm went round my shoulder, 'I'll look after you now.'

I was grateful for his company and protection. The train moved further into Soviet-occupied territory. The journey was slow, sometimes deliberately delayed. It had to make an overnight stop at Nove Zamky, a few hours from Bratislava. Gone midnight. People in the train were trying to sleep as best they could, huddled in corners, stretched, or seated on benches. I was curled up with my head on my rucksack; next to me, a snoring Feldko. A dig in the ribs woke me. Feldko was awake and alert. From other carriages, we heard screaming and shouting. Outside was starless, there was very little light by which to see. The carriage was suddenly alive with panic as intruders with flashlights grabbed possessions. They were forcing their way through windows and doors, swinging in like apes. They were not only taking possessions, they were also taking people. The screams of young girls became deafening as, by torchlight, they were dragged to the carriage door. Fighting had broken out all round us.

'Red Army renegades.' Feldko muttered this into my ear. Camp survival instincts took over. I stowed my rucksack behind me. Feldko covered me with his body and called out in Russian.

'Leave us alone. We have all been fighting for the Red Army together, dammit. We're on *your* side, comrade bastards.'

With that he fired a few rounds from his pistol, which had the desired effect. One of the raiders laughed hysterically. The shadows left in a hurry and, in their wake, a silence broken only by groans and whimpers. In the darkness, we could not tell the damage overall, but come the dawn, it became apparent that belongings had gone. People had gone. Mothers had lost daughters in the melee. A woman muttered caustically: 'So that is what is meant by solidarity of the working classes. Keep it.'

Feldko responded half-heartedly: 'Still they did win the war at Stalingrad.'

She looked at him long and hard. 'Phooey. Stalin. Same beast, different garb.'

Feldko tried again. 'You're Jewish, I'm Jewish. I'm not a Nazi.'

The woman fixed her gaze on him: 'Not yet you're not. Give it time. You have a uniform and a gun. I am a woman, I have neither. You are told to shoot, you shoot. You are told to kill, you kill. Me, I wait on rape, starvation and death; who knows, maybe all three. And you're not a Nazi, big deal!'

Feldko stared back, then a smile gradually crossed his face and he gave the greying woman a kiss on the cheek.

'You're safe from me, Mother.'

She harrumphed, the women she was with teased her and the edge was taken off the moment. Outside the train, the relatives of the abducted were pleading with uniforms, who seemed impervious to the pleas, as they tried to get them back on the train. Most refused, so that when the train moved off, we left a sizeable number of irate Czechs and Hungarians arguing it out with Russian and Czech soldiers. Where the abducted went, who knew? At best, labour camps in the east. The young girls' destinies remained a horrible thought in most of our minds.

Three quiet hours later, our train pulled in to Bratislava. Feldko and I hadn't slept since the raid. We were tired and edgy, with only one thought; get news of our families. We alighted to a reception committee of Jewish officials who welcomed us and directed us to the old quarter. One of this group I knew. Older than I recalled, and in a flash suit, but it was still Frommer. The 'get-up' wasn't him. He was trying too hard. He didn't know me straight off, but stared the stare of the realizing moment.

'I know you.'

'Ernest Lowy?'

Big gesture from Frommer.

'Dear God, how wonderful! Ernest!'

The hug was for everyone to see. A friend of Frommer. I introduced him to my uniformed relative.

'Feldko. My cousin and guardian angel.'

'Glad to know you Feldko. You're a guardian angel and I am a *macher*.'

A *macher* – a fixer – doesn't call himself so, that is left to others. Big mistake. Feldko's eyes danced with merriment.

'Like the suit.'

'You do? Good threads, good threads. I'll give you the man's name. Now, I look after both of you.'

He gave my back a friendly slap. I couldn't wait, I needed to know.

'Frommer. Do you know what has happened to my family.'

He responded: 'Wonderful news. Your mother and two of your sisters are known to be alive and living in Budapest.'

He stopped there.

'The others?'

He fiddled with his gaudy tie. I needed to hear, but I heard as if at a distance, while he imparted the sad news. Brothers Karl and Max were still missing. Worse, my father, my dear brother Alex (Munky), Else's husband Bernat, my sister Hedwig, her husband and their small child, gone. Brother Karl's wife, my beautiful Kato with her 10-day-old baby boy, had perished in Auschwitz.

Frommer and Feldko found me a bench on which I could sit and weep for my loved ones. Frommer had to deal with the incoming crowd due repatriation, so had to leave our side. I had his card, this friend I hadn't seen since childhood, this caring, born-again *macher*, this fixer of problems. I thanked him and we left. Feldko came with me to my old family home in the Schanzstrasse, a five-minute walk from the station. We went there istead of the Jewish reception centre, later for that. To my earlier suprise, I had learned that among the strangers occupying rooms in the house, a couple of our cousins, Mady and Trudy Donat, were to be found. They had recently been released from the camps and now occupied space in the house. I could return, in part at least, to a beloved place; for a spell.

Though the house had been stripped bare earlier, sparse furniture had been found and the sisters were making comfortable use of their section. After the initial rejoicing at meeting up, Feldko went off to try to find a bottle of wine. He had vodka to exchange and, as we had been invited for a share of their food, he wanted to supply the table. When he had gone out, Mady began to break the bad news to me:

'Ernest, I have news of your family ...'

My eyes filled as I put my finger to her lips.

'Mady. I already know.'

Later, with some food and wine in us, Feldko and I left our gear at our cousins' flat and went to the Jewish centre to register. A big building in the old Jewish quarter, it had a wide, imposing entrance along with a stone facade displaying ornate carvings. Inside, from behind a row of tables, volunteers wrote down our details and added our names to the survivor lists, which were being circulated to other centres. Naturally, the other conduits of information were the synagogues around the city. We mixed a little and finding ourselves still hungry, had a couple of bowls of soup that were on the go, taking time out to trade names and places with others as anxious as ourselves for news of those dear to them. We felt pretty full by the time we got back to the apartment on the Schanzstrasse, but made space for the soup Trudy and Mady had cooked for their new charges.

The future lay in Budapest with my mother and two sisters. The next morning I sent her word to our old address, hoping that she would be there. The message never reached her, so when I turned up at the front door, she collapsed into my arms sobbing. The moment was too much and she fainted. She was still waiting for any snippet of information concern-

225

ing Karl, Max and Fritz. My return had broken an unbearable tension. Slowly over the months to come, links would be made, people would turn up at the door. As usual, with the help of others, I had endured and survived the long way home. But for me, was it home?

17 Beyond Survival, What?

From mid-1945 into 1946, everything was flux and confusion. Everything was a question, was *in* question. Simple survival, gaining work, all difficult due to the precariousness of any European economy, let alone those of us inside the Soviet bloc, causing money to be an unstable value, so much so that barter was often more reliable. A thriving black market existed everywhere, and a lot of early post-war fortunes were made, even where the socialist flags fluttered. I began to seriously embrace socialism as an ideal, ignoring, or by turns excusing the repressive nature of communism in day-to-day life; putting it down as a necessity due to the chaotic state of affairs brought on by the war. The fact that communism was undermining religious belief by enforcing secular values, worse by banning public worship, muddied the waters of everyone's certainty. With my anger at God and the faith for allowing the Holocaust through divine neglect dominating my thoughts, that reality didn't dawn on me for quite some time.

Budapest was a wreck. Many grand buildings were destroyed. There was enough of the old place left to gladden the heart, but like Bratislava, the repair and replacement would take time and devotion. With the communists in charge, alongside a need to house the homeless and the poor, the blueprint for the future would have to include building upward. In time, concrete would blight sections of Buda and Pest; for now, children played their dangerous war games in the ruins.

One paralysing question was answered when Karl returned from a Hungarian labour camp. He was very thin and limp with lassitude. With total devotion, Therezia, my mother, along with Else and Lillie, nursed him back to health. Where I could, I helped. Often, he and I would talk late. One of the things that cropped up was his desire to leave Hungary. After the forced labour camp and what the Hungarian nationalists had done to Munky, he saw little point in staying, hoping against hope that the anti-Semitism that existed as an enduring mental complaint in the brain of the European, would somehow, like a dream, vanish. There were also the ghosts of his darling Kato and their infant child. Whatever was going to exorcise the demon, it was not showing its face. What the Nazis had done could not easily be undone within us. We were vulnerable to ourselves and simply not equipped to take on a resurgence of public anti-Semitism. As the condition stood, it was fairly dormant. The odd graveyard was subject to attack. Graffiti, as always, found fresh expression. For the remainder, most people were okay, even friendly. But there existed, as there always had, an aloofness, a shyness towards us that we helped to cause by our singular belief, our customs and our dress. At this point in history we were deeply damaged and mentally scarred, consequently very, very sensitive to social nuance, and for us, at that time, it wasn't good in eastern Europe.

Karl and I talked of Father, how he had perished in Buchenwald, and how when Bernat, his son-in-law, Else's husband, the handsome rescuer from Dunajszka Streda, had the chance to escape, he would not leave his Leopold, in spite of Father begging him to survive. According to the contact who told my mother the story, Bernat said he would not be able to face Else and the family after leaving Leopold to perish alone in Buchenwald. So, together, they went to their deaths. We talked of Hedwig, how she was sent from Gyor near Papa to Auschwitz, along with her husband and his entire family. Hedwig's little 3-year-old girl, naturally, was with them. I went in the springtime and those rail wagons were oppressive. They went midsummer. All that time sealed into those boxcars, they must have baked and sweated before their exhausted arrival at the place of death. Three or four days without water. Almost the whole population of little Gyor was wiped out in Auschwitz, like so many communities across Europe.

We tried to speak of Kato and the child, but Karl found this beyond his tolerance, that he had survived and, cruelly, his beautiful wife and child were lost to him. Yet Else, Lillie and my mother had been saved. Else was protected by Lillie's husband, Andre, who had the ear of the influential Swedish activist, Raoul Wallenberg, and instead of being deported, she was returned to Budapest. Although Bernat was lost to her, she was reunited with her son. Wallenberg furnished her with Swedish national papers which allowed her and her son to stay in Budapest. Andre, though unpopular with my father, truly was a *macher*, and a good one. Lillie, the pretty one, the rebel, knew her man. She fought opinion against him, and with him was instrumental in doing good around the community.

We talked of Munky. My childhood was wrapped up in my closeness to Alex. He was the spiritual one, the one to whom faith was not a problem. A natural at the synagogue. His wry ironic wit playing against my slapstick made us a pair. Come Sunday, we used to stroll across the elegant chain bridge connecting Buda and Pest, make our way to the majestic Elizabeth bridge, then to a Konditorei, where the thrill was to take in the smell and taste of fresh baking. This is a particular memory, the kind where the sun always shines. Memory persists, even including what we spent; twenty-four *filler* on a custard-cream bun. Beside the Danube with my brother.

In the late summer of 1944, Munky had been taken by a gang of Hungarian fascists to a small place called Fertorakos, near the town of Sporon, in north-west Hungary. There, with other young Jewish men, he was made to dig his own grave before they shot him in the back of the head. My young *tzaddik*. In these late days, the warmth of our formative years, the excitement and the fun, even the danger shared, return me to a world so different and remote from Glasgow in the twenty-first century.

Frank Matushka was an old friend from pre-war. He and his wife survived the days of persecution and the bombs so that, as the dust began to settle, we were able to revive our relationship. This led to a business idea. With barely any means we gained a foothold and set up making fountain pens. It paid the rent and, as time went by, a bit more. Nationalization became a policy and brought about the closure of our little enterprise. I returned to light engineering and, in spite of the closure of our partnership, life chances seemed a little better. I earned enough to afford a second-hand green motorbike that had caught my fancy. It replaced an earlier model that had taken me to see Greta again. Motorbikes were a necessity in a world where cars were a luxury and public transport unreliable.

Early 1946. I answered the door to a stranger who asked me if I had a brother called Max. I nodded and began a question, but the stranger interrupted me to tell me Max had been a prisoner of war and, now released, was on his way home. In a matter of weeks, he was on the doorstep and in the arms of my mother. In the last days of the war, Max, who had been a communist sympathiser for a while, took a chance and escaped behind the Russian lines. Once he had made known his political beliefs, Max was received with open arms and seconded to Moscow where he undertook indoctrination at a school used to re-educate and extend horizons through Marxist-Leninist ideology. Now a fully-fledged party member, he was home.

In terms of miraculous adventure, it was Fritz and his young wife Datya who had the escape that was marvellous. He had met Datya Pollak during the war. Her family was deported, but she and Fritz went into hiding in Budapest, then in the last weeks of her pregnancy, they decided Budapest was getting too dangerous. They decided to risk everything, slip out of Hungary on forged papers and try to make their way to Palestine. Wearing peasant clothing, they trekked through occupied territory until they reached

Romania where they became separated when they had to dodge border guards. Datya was tough and strong-willed. She moved through Romania and entered Turkey. Near Adana, in open countryside, she gave birth to her daughter, gave herself a day to recover, then moved on to Constantinople and finally by boat to Palestine. She couldn't know that Fritz had also made it to Constantinople. His boat to Palestine hit a mine. Rescued from the water, he eventually tracked Datya down in Tel-Aviv, where father met daughter for the first time.

Fritz and Datya made a brave move, a clean break with the past at the very height of personal threat, to walk into the bright sunlight of a new day, one with dangers for sure, but the oppressive weight of the European storm clouds left behind. To secure their future, they had to struggle along with the new citizens of Palestine to transform it under David Ben-Gurion into Israel. To achieve this, the struggle for independence, a brief war took place to secure the state and unfasten the grip of the British. In 1948, Israel became a state, and ever since, Israelis have had to fight to maintain their hold on the territory, surrounded as they are by people religiously and historically committed to their removal; in some extreme cases, their annihilation. The area of land became internationally recognized, and people like Fritz and Datya made the place vital and become fertile. A new world. Back in Budapest we trod the old path as a community within a community, trying to return to pre-war rhythms of life, though I knew Fritz was on the right track. Even if it wasn't Israel, it had to be a breakthrough, not a sinking back into the 'us-and-them' world.

After their war of independence, from Israel, Fritz sent us a letter:

> Should you try once again to integrate, to adapt to Hungarian society? The answer is no. It's the old story. It works for a while, then you are back in trouble again. Why impose yourself on a society which has repeatedly

shown dislike and resentment towards you? Why condemn yourself to [being] a forever-harassed minority? Is there any point carrying on praying, lamenting for redemption, pretending nothing has happened? You don't have to be persecuted any longer. Come to Israel.

I felt I could contribute to a new start in Hungary by embracing the socialist ideal. To that effect, I put my back wholeheartedly into the secular world. My work-life, away from the independent workshop, was one of engagement, not only light engineering, but the social life surrounding it. I tried to avoid the world of the synagogue, but, in Jewish culture this was still an impossibility in Budapest. Because of the ban on religion in public, for example, brother Max took the precaution of hiding the Sabbath candlesticks, only to bring them out on a Friday. I had to fault the logic. A visit come Friday would be typical of a real snoop. Max was a living contradiction, carrying the card but maintaining the tradition. In spite of my protests to myself, I couldn't sign up and join the Party like my brother. Like him though, I found it impossible to sever the link with tradition.

Then there was my voice. I had to work, I needed to sing. Karl was friendly with the leading cantor of Budapest, Bernard Linecky, a big handsome man from Odessa with an enormous voice.

Karl and Linecky arranged for me to join the choir of Dohany synagogue (impossible to refuse), which was the second largest Jewish choir in Europe. There I met Kato Phluger. An opera singer of note, married to the famous Gentile conductor of the Gewandhaus Orchestra in Leipzig, Gerhardt Phluger. When the Nazis seized power, she had left him so as not to put his career in jeopardy. Kato turned out to be a brilliant teacher. She took me on as a pupil, started my voice production, and after a little time, I began working in synagogues, sometimes officiating at the high festivals in the smaller *shuls* outside Budapest. I was on my way to discovering my vocational reality.

Occupational conflict naturally occurred, and the plant manager advised me more than once to 'leave the religious business alone'. Due to this I was repeatedly passed over for promotion, and eventually, as the 1940s ended, I turned my back on communism, kept my socialism and devoted my time to the faith. I started attending the college in Budapest where cantors and rabbis were trained.

Harking back for a moment to that period between repatriation and beginning to settle back into Budapest's way of life. All, everyone had lost. It was a time of ghosts, a time of people walking through the ruins of Europe looking for the lost ones, being the lost ones. It was a time of leaving captivity fed and cured, to find on arriving back at the place of origin that it was neither organized nor officially caring enough to feed and clothe the returnee. Many European towns and cities showed indifference, sometimes hostility, to their returning citizens. Where there was a Jewish community still available and connected, things were better for the returning men, women and children; so lost, so deeply traumatized.

In Berlin, Dresden and the many cities, towns and villages across Germany, the once-proud populations dragged themselves around pitifully for a time before rethought and rebirth; something new and more lasting, more credible to themselves and their neighbours. Though anti-Semitism had not yet vanished off the scene, in West Germany in particular, grief and guilt changed everything within a generation to an atmosphere of respect for humanity at large. Germany had been split by war into two territories, two mindsets: a split where, on one side, the democratic West held sway under the watchful eye of the Allies, while the East lay under the military and political influence of the Soviet Union. Our minders also.

In Hungary, early post-war, social gatherings were occasions where one would be staring into the face of a stranger, half-hoping that they would be a lost relative, friend, neighbour even; someone, anyone who would provide a vital link to a yesterday that was rapidly retreating in the face of immediate need. There was also the ever-present fear that Europe would soon be on fire again as America and Russia eyed each other across the ruins, their mutual 'paranoia' affecting everyone. Social fragmentation touched absolutely everyone in the Jewish community. It was profound, it was terrible. Those who had smelled the perfumes of collective death were in deep shock. The trauma expressed itself in a variety of ways. A person, for example, could develop a normal public face as they recovered, yet remain, underneath, deeply disturbed, a cauldron of developing neuroses that would break the surface to stun loved ones in a totally destructive way. Finding friendship where trust could develop, let alone love, was a great rarity among those of us used to betrayal for survival's sake. Taking the Nazis out of the equation had not made much of a dent in the effect they had caused. There was armour-plate around our souls, along with the habit of holding everyone except immediate family at arm's length. It was an emotional permafrost that would take a lot of warm weather to melt.

I was comparatively lucky, in that my mother, along with my surviving brothers and sisters, offered each other, and me, a cushion of compassion and mutual affection against the losses we all shared. Beyond the family there lay a landscape of lost faces, close and more distant relatives, friends, people known. The winds of regret and loss blew steadily through the gaps they had left. For some the loss of even one person, it has to be said, along with everything else happening around them, was destabilizing enough to prevent them putting the pieces of their lives back together. Marta's brother Albert for example ...

18 Waiting for Marta

I looked at my watch. Gone three. She was late. Clouds had darkened the day and an icy wind was warning of winter, drawing the falling leaves into dancing eddies around my feet. To me they looked like small brown mice chasing each other in never-ending circles. I smiled at the idea as I pulled my coat collar up against the sharp sting of the drizzle. My chin went down into my scarf, my face began to glow in response to the needling coldness of the October rain.

Of all the possibilities that should have crossed my mind, only one skewered my brain and squeezed my heart into submission: rejection. I was 21, what did I know beyond my intoxication, a mind-numbing, all-consuming passion that danced in heavy boots on the thinnest of ice? I knew that I had to make up for lost time. My time, my puberty and youth, spent in the company of dying prisoners, my young being abused by the demons of hell, my mind bent out of shape. A malevolence directed to me and at me, personally and collectively. Now I was free, lost time had become wasted time. I paced worriedly, turning over the truth I had realized from day one, that Marta didn't feel for me as I felt for her. Perhaps for her, things had gone far enough, and she didn't want to see me any more; by not turning up she was dodging embarrassment. I needed a 'Her'. She didn't need a 'Me'.

It was 3:30. Never before had she been a second late. It was more likely to be me. Her, always 3:00, never 3:30. Our meeting place was always in front of the Deak church at the heart of the city. We both lived fairly close by, and it made sense to meet up at a half-way point where, across from the church, was a coffee house, scene of many close conversations in which Marta and I solved the problems of the planet. The pair of us paraded our socialism with earnest looks, raised excited tones and carefree laughter. We were on first-name terms with the owners of the coffee house, Franco and Antonia. Franco made brilliant ice cream which we never resisted. Somehow when we walked into that bright café, the drabness of recovering Budapest vanished. Our place.

I crossed the street and entered 'our place'. I felt very cold. My coat was covered in a fine film of tiny droplets from the drizzle. I took it off and hung it up, with a couple of other coats near the door. The warmth of the coffee house met my face, the reassuring smell of roasted coffee met my nose; everything felt lighter and better. I took a seat by the window and looked for Marta. Franco called from behind the counter:

'Espresso, Ernesto?'

I gave him a faint smile and nodded. A few moments later he brought it across.

'No Marta today?'

'She's running late.'

'Makes a change. Give her a call. You can use my phone.'

'The family doesn't have one in the apartment. There's one in the hall but I don't know the number. I'll hang on here for a while.'

Franco put the coffee down and gave me a friendly wink before easing his way across to another table where he paused smiling, to take an order.

Outside, it was getting darker. The light in the café made it hard to see out, but my eyes did not stray from the window. From behind me, in the reflection, I saw Franco return behind the counter and busy himself with pouring coffee. Antonia came out from the kitchen and placed some cakes into a glass showcase. She looked over my way, said something to Franco, who shrugged. She returned to the kitchen. I forced my eyes to look beyond the reflected brightness within, to the dark of the street outside. No sign of Marta.

My thoughts strayed to the day we met. A Communist Party meeting some months before. The expectant buzz of the audience, the speakers on the stage about to give forth. All became distanced, sidelined when Marta appeared in the doorway. Medy. Whenever I saw a girl who looked like Medy, a shock would run through my system, only to be met by the memory that darling Medy met her end in Belsen, beyond my reach but not beyond my love.

Medy of Dunajska Strada, the small border village that had taken in all we startled and scared refugees, giving us shelter when we were expelled from Bratislava, pre-war. Marta had the same hair, the same inner calm that made both their faces radiant with spiritual peacefulness. Shock upon shock, this vision came and sat next to me, meeting my eyes evenly with a slight smile and a little nod. I was lost. She turned to face the platform, then turned to speak to the people on her other side, people she knew and had joined. They laughed and talked. The main speaker for the evening had yet to arrive, so the buzz in the hall continued. I was fixated. Staring at her profile, then at the back of her head, drew a puzzled response from her companions. She turned to face me. I blushed to her questioning smile.

'Forgive me, but you remind me so much of a friend. It was like seeing a ghost, so much are you like her.'

Marta smiled a gorgeous, dimpled smile.

'She might be offended by the comparison.'

'She died in Belsen.'

Her expression changed to concern.

'I'm so sorry. I lost my father, so I know what is happening to you. Even now, I think that I see him on street corners, in shops, wherever. It's that we *need* to see them once more.'

Her eyes filled and I loved her beyond redemption. She continued: 'Are you sure she has gone?'

'People I knew were with her. I was at Belsen also. So close. Just two days ago, I met her brother Ernesto, my name also, and in tears he broke the news to me; it flooded out. I could-n't tell him that I knew. We were outside the synagogue on Kasinsky Street. We went in and prayed for her soul.'

'So many lost. And your family?'

I told her. We discussed the dead and the missing, the years of trial. Her friends joined in, and soon the talk spread to involve several people around us, all recounting loss and bereavement, all exhibiting the need to get things out into the open, to get it said.

From the stage, a woman announced the arrival of the speaker. We stood and applauded. The hall lights were dimmed. Just two bright lights shone; one on the red flag, the other on the speaker's podium. At the end of the meeting, everyone stood again and sang '*The Internationale*'. All sang, all sang loudly. With feeling.

Outside the hall, I stood with Marta's little group. They invited me to join them for dinner, but I had a singing commitment, so with several kinds of regret, had to turn down such promising company. I turned to walk away when Marta caught my arm.

'You know there's a gathering of returners organized by the Party. It's in a couple of weeks. Twenty-fifth at the synagogue just along the street from here. They are letting us use the hall, which is very nice of them. See you there?'

She released her grip.

'Wild horses will not keep me away.'

My smile must have been a mile wide.

'That's a "yes" then?'

'That's a "yes" then.'

The little group of friends watched me to the corner. We parted, waving. Sunshine had returned to my soul.

'More coffee, Ernesto?'

Franco was standing over me with a concerned look. I dragged my gaze away from the window. Outside, the street-lights had come on.

He moved away to get my espresso and my eyes returned

9. Working at a lathe for a light engineering company, Budapest.

10. Kathy and I on our wedding day, 1965. Standing (left to right): my nephew Leonard Lowy, Kathy's father Alexander Hermann, my brother Charles Lowy, his wife Magda Lowy, Kathy and I, my brother-in-law Stephen Ballas, Kathy's uncle Zigi Honti. Seated: Zigi's wife, Kathy's aunt Roszi, Kathy's mother Elizabeth, Kathy's grandmother Ester Honti, my sister Elsa Ballas.

11. A snapshot taken on the set of *The Lost Tribe*. My co-actor is Alan Shinwell.

12. An interfaith meeting in Wales with Sir Harry Secombe, his musical director Ronnie Cass and other members of the group.

13. As a member of the Jewish Male Voice Choir, front row, fourth from right.

14. Working with youngsters at the East Glasgow Youth Theatre.

15. Officiating as a visiting cantor at Garnethill Synagogue, Glasgow.

16. With my wife Kathy. This has always been a favourite photograph of our daughter Judy.

17. With Provost Liz Cameron, receiving the Humanitarian Services Award, 2004.

18. My portrait, as painted by David Reid, which hangs in the entrance hall of the Giffnock and Newlands Synagogue. I have the greatest admiration for David for doing such a wonderful job.

19. Standing outside the Giffnock and Newlands Synagogue.

to the darkness of the street outside, to the normality of it all. Marta and I had sat here and talked and talked. Franco returned with the coffee.

'Looks like she's not coming Ernest. Why don't you go round? You never know.'

I did. She'd grown tired of this tedious bore. My low self-esteem sired by what had befallen me in the last years allowed for no alternative to her rejection of me. The unrequited martyr felled by one cruel blow from the divine Marta. I nodded in pretend agreement with Franco, but quietly agreed with myself to return home, tail between my legs, not to the bosom of my family, but the quietness of my room. I looked out from the café window. No Marta. Franco went back behind the counter and my mind drifted to that night in the synagogue when the hall was full of people staring at each other in the hopes that among the milling crowd might just be a loved one, a friend, a familiar face from down the street of memories.

I had turned up early. It was heart-warming when the flash of recognition brought people together, and these moments were usually instantaneous as a person was framed in the doorway. A shriek, a cry, a call would come from those within, and the hugs and tears would proceed apace. Apart from maybe one or two, most of my close family and extended family were accounted for. My moment came when Marta arrived. With her in the doorway was a handsome young man. They stopped to talk to several people. I took the time to adore her from afar and feel jealousy over this young companion. She had spotted me: 'Ernest. Ernest! Over here.'

My legs turned to rubber, but I made it. She introduced me to the couple she was speaking to, then the young companion: 'Ernest, this is my brother Albert. Albert, this is Ernest Lowy, I mentioned him to you. He survived Auschwitz and Belsen, remember?'

My relief, I hoped, was not too obvious. I extended my hand and shook his, limply proffered and slightly damp. Our eyes met. It was immediately apparent that Albert was not comfortable with people. Looking into his eyes was looking through into eternal darkness; a being in retreat.

'Albert's returning to university soon,' Marta offered.

'What are you studying?' I asked.

'Medicine.' He replied from somewhere within.

During the course of the evening our eyes met occasionally, and there were moments when Albert was fully with us. At such moments, his pale eyes seemed to go through me and his conversation would keep pace, but competitively. Then there were those moments when his remoteness seemed plain rude. I just felt ill at ease with him. Marta had noticed this and later, when we were alone, she tried to explain.

'Albert finds it difficult in company. Doesn't like to talk much.'

'Why not?'

'He used to be a chatterbox, very outgoing. He adored Papa and when Papa was taken to Buchenwald and we weren't, he became depressed and remote. He's a lot better than he used to be.'

'You were all so lucky.'

'Albert feels guilt. What can I say?'

I knew, I could sympathize. My father had been such a huge influence on us all. I had had moments that were purely mine with Leopold and I treasured them. Best of all, the religious legacy had seen me through the trials of Auschwitz, and, in spite of my denials of God, the undertow of belief continued to nag away at my professed atheism. In spite of all, I had even started singing again in the synagogue choir. The communist chorister could sympathize.

In the weeks and months through the summer, Marta and I became very close, but she saw our relationship as platonic. I on the other hand was on fire. She had become the sole object of all my desires, my road to fulfilment. I saw Albert in passing as I became welcome in the family home, but we never became close, always formal, more often than not, remote. Marta put it down to his being deep in his studies. Attendance at university meant he was away from the family

240

for long periods. When he did return home, he would spend much of his time locked away in his room.

Marta's mother, Anna, was a true matriarch, running the household in a very traditional way. The apartment was dark and heavily decorated in turn-of-the-century fashion, with a few concessions to Art Deco. There was little of religion in the place, though dates and days were observed. Marta's father was a socialist who had readily embraced communism, his atheism a bit of a 'top skin', as with most Jews in the Party. In his place, his widow maintained his will, his momentum and his desire for his children. She watched me like a hawk. As for Albert, her devotion was total, and around her, he seemed to brighten.

I returned to the presence of the café. My coffee cup drained, the day outside had surrendered to the streetlights. I could hardly see across the street to the church, for the bright lights of the café almost completely obliterated the outside dimness. I left the window table, and by the door, put my coat on. Waving to a slightly concerned Franco, I made my way out into the windy wet dark. Depression, like the night, enveloped me. Collar up, I leaned into the wind and headed for home. As I rounded the corner, I could see a figure in the porch. As I got closer, I recognized the little 10-year-old lad who lived in the same block of apartments as Marta and her family. My dread began to rise.

'You must come quick,' he instructed. 'Something terrible has happened.'

'What?' I demanded, as he dragged me from the porch and into the street.

No answer came as we panted our way along the wet pavements. My imagination went into overdrive. Something had happened to my beloved. The girl of my dreams had met with a terrible accident. My brain was numb with worry.

Marta's family lived on the top floor of an enormous four-storey building on Vorosmarty Street. I knew the place from way back when Munky and I had been 'voluntary' firemen during the war. Built around an open courtyard, the stone staircase spiralled up and around each floor overlooking a cobbled courtyard, with only an iron banister between the stair and ominous walkway flagstones below. It was frightening to look down from on high. Finally, we reached the top floor. Breathing hard and gasping, the boy pointed me to the open door to Marta's flat as though I were a stranger. I gave him a parting nod and entered to the sound of muffled sobs from within. I feared the worst. The apartment was full of weeping people; relatives, neighbours, in the hallway, in each room it seemed. Marta was nowhere to be seen, my panic was complete. A large woman in her forties came across the crowded hallway. Putting her hand on my shoulder, she quietly asked: 'Are you Ernest Lowy?'

I nodded. She took a breath:

'It's Albert.'

Momentarily, I was relieved. Marta was safe. The woman began to sob quietly: 'He's taken his own life.'

She turned her head away and down, moving it from side to side in sad denial of such enormity.

Stunned by the news, I dream-walked in the woman's wake to a closed door. She knocked and turned to me:

'Since it happened Marta has locked herself in that room and refuses to speak to anyone except you. Marta. Marta, Ernest is here. Marta!'

The door opened a little and I slipped through. I nodded to the woman and the curious few who had followed us down the hallway.

I closed the door behind me. Marta stood in the middle of the room, her expressive face pale with shocked sorrow, her hair drawn back tight. She almost collapsed into my arms, weeping. She talked into my shoulder a stream of agonized words of regret. Her muffled voice raised and lowered as she let go of her grief. Eventually, she came to the end of crying, for a while at least: 'Ernest, I'm so sorry. I didn't mean for that to happen.'

'You have to let go. Marta, never hold back sorrow.'

She stood back from me, looking around the room as if to get her bearings, then fixed on my face.

She seemed smaller, hunched, her femininity somehow neutralized. She seemed unable to move, so I reached out to her and drew her to me. We stood for a few minutes in an embrace, where no words were spoken, no weeping done, just a few minutes for intelligence to take a hold, and destabilizing unreason to be laid to rest. From outside, voices and the odd sobs.

Eventually we found ourselves sitting side by side on the bed, staring absently into the room. I turned to her: 'How did he die?'

'He threw himself into the courtyard, from up here. Dear God. How could he?'

'Was he alone before he fell?'

'We were here, talking. He was in one of his remote moments. Mumma just said it would be nice to see him smile, and he snapped. It was like a dam breaking. All the feelings he must have bottled up over time. Ernest, you know how you and I talked and talked about the bad times? Albert couldn't. Mumma tried, I tried, but he couldn't face the circumstances of Daddy's death in Buchenwald.'

'Was there something else to add to his troubles? Were his studies proving a problem?'

'No. He loved university. He never had problems. Oh Ernest, the terrible things he said about us, you and me. Then he turned on Mumma, accused her of dominating his life, of betraying Daddy, how I don't know. And why wasn't she sent to Buchenwald? He had a massive tantrum. Finally he stormed out of the apartment, banging the door hard. He was shouting on the landing; then nothing until the screaming started downstairs.'

Silence in the room. We sat there holding hands in the semi-dark. Finally, a gentle knock came on the door. I rose to answer. Opening, I came face-to-face with the woman who had sought me out.

'Is Marta up to talking to the police now? They've called

again. Waiting in the lounge.' She looked past me into the room. 'The doctor is still with your mother, Marta. I know he wants to speak to you as well.'

Marta rose from the bed, wiping her eyes with the back of her hand.

'Thank you Lottie. I'll be with you in a moment.'

Lottie moved off, leaving the door open. Curious eyes peered in, then followed us as we moved through to her mother's room, which was in semi-darkness except for a bedside light which gave it a warm orange glow. The doctor rose as we came in. Marta's mother lay sedated, staring vacantly upward.

'Marta. I have to go soon. Is there someone who can stay with her?'

'Of course.'

The apartment was full of women, close friends and neighbours, all of whom would not question the need to be with Anna throughout her period of mourning.

On Vorosmarty Street, evening prayers were held to allow friends and neighbours to share in the grief. Marta and some relatives attended, but Mother Anna was prostrate. Close family had come from all over the city, and turns were taken to stay at her bedside. For the funeral she rose, and, like a ghost, haunted the proceedings. A wet October morning. The wind blew great gusts of leaves around the crematorium as Marta and her mother stood beside each other to accept the condolences of all those attending. When it came to my turn to stand in front of Anna, for the first time in our relationship, she reached out and drew me to her.

'Ernest, you have been so kind and strong to my Marta through this. You must forgive my misery. Accept my thanks.'

I murmured something that sounded apposite, but I was out of my depth. All I could show her was a grateful little smile through my tears. Her husband was taken by the Nazis, her son, by the Nazis taken at one remove by a wound driven deep into the young Albert's heart at such an impressionable time in his growing. It had festered, it had grown, it had taken him away from youth's laughter and kept him away from the present; much of the time to dwell with the dead in Buchenwald. He had perhaps finally found his true present in the defining moment of his death. Who knows?

I spent a lot of time with Marta in the ensuing weeks and months. Our friendship, through Albert's death, had become stronger, but at no time did I feel from her the love that I so desperately craved. She knew it, I knew it.

One afternoon in early spring, in Franco and Antonia's café, 'our place', we were sitting at the window table enjoying the bright sunlight. In its warm rays we lingered over our third coffee. As usual the chat drifted into politics. Marta was fired up.

'... with the British going, Ben-Gurion is going to declare independence. The UN backs us. Ernest, wake up! It has begun.'

'Another war has begun. The whole of the Middle East will be on fire.'

'Why?'

'The Arabs are not going to accept a divided Palestine. Abdullah will want the West Bank as an annex, not specifically for Palestinian Arabs, more as part of a long-term strategy.'

'In that lies our salvation. Arabs cannot agree on a future. Their tribal differences keep them in a permanent conflict. It's their tragedy and our opportunity.'

'The thought of all the immigrants from eastern Europe coming their way will hold them together sufficiently to produce ferment and conflict. They'll gang up, they've said as much. And what's with all this 'our' suddenly?

'Ernest, I can't keep it back ... it's not settled yet, but Mumma and I could be emigrating to Israel, and soon.'

My face must have been a picture. My loved one was about to exchange me for the insecurity of shifting the soil of a new state, along with a life of ducking bullets.

'Don't look so crestfallen, *silly*, be happy for me. Think

about it Ernest, what has Hungary got to offer but bitter memories, and ...' she lowered her voice and looked around, '... oppression bringing on fear and persecution. See it coming.'

I was silent. I looked at her with new eyes. She was, if nothing else, her father's daughter, a card-carrying Communist; she had almost got me to sign on the line. Here she was voicing the fear all true socialists were fearing.

'Does the Party know?'

'Not yet. And don't you say anything.'

'I'm not a gossip,' I retorted.

'May you be forgiven,' she grinned. 'You *are* pleased for us, aren't you? Ernest, you are, aren't you?'

My stomach was in knots and my heart was in freefall.

'Who is your sponsor, your connection there?'

'Aunty Sarah.'

'The spinster.'

'Yes, so? Ernest, you're upset by this.'

I called for more coffee.

'You want ice-cream?'

'Yes. Thanks. Don't change the subject.'

I called again:

'Franco, ice cream also. You want the truth?'

'Of course I want the truth. Our friendship rests on it.'

I looked into her eyes, searching for a glimmer of what I knew was not there. 'I am deeply in love with you. I'm losing you, and you are going headlong into a conflict that could see Israel in flames.'

'Ernest, we've discussed this love thing. I think you see in me, Medy. You're trying to exorcize her ghost with me. I would never quite fit your dream. You need someone unlike her ...'

I cursed my big mouth for mentioning Medy that night. I was covering my embarrassment when caught staring. Marta had a point and she knew it. My intellect understood; my infatuation, however, could not stand it.

'... as for Israel in flames, I don't think so. Maybe a skirmish, but Arab unity won't hold when the deals start; and they will. Ben-Gurion's not a starry eyed optimist. Neither am I.'

'Your mother is okay with all this?'

'She's got the cases packed in her mind and the flat emptied, with household items and furniture scattered round the neighbourhood. Ernest, she and I have a marvellous chance to lay the ghosts of the past, to leave sadness behind. Though we love our community, the shadow of death hangs over everything here. It is too dark. We both need light.'

'True light comes from God and is within you.'

'You're just like Poppa. You talk socialism, wear the materialist mask, but when the chips are down, you have God up your sleeve and lay him on the table like a trump card. God has nothing to do with any of this.'

'So God is not allowed to be a socialist?'

'If a deity has any sense other than a sense of self, a socialist that deity would be.'

In spite of my disappointment, I laughed. The coffee and ice cream arrived with Antonia who did as she always did with me, ruffled my hair and winked at Marta, as if some secret was being celebrated in that affectionate action. I returned to serious. I resented the excitement, I resented losing her.

'Do you think if Albert had had a faith, he might still be here?'

'Maybe, Ernest. But he believed, like Daddy, that one had to stand clear of worship to properly understand creation and existence. Unlike Poppa, creation and human existence appalled and overwhelmed him. He wanted to preserve life, while around him people wasted life like spendthrifts. The baser instincts seemed to proliferate and swamp the good in humanity. He screamed all this at us in the last minutes of his life.'

Just the two of them now, and no faith beyond a political ideal. What was Jewish about their lives took the form of partial observance and the social network. The little family was thoroughly integrated, intimate in every way except that,

247

I felt from my side, without the core of Jewishness, the love of the Torah and the worship of God, a Jew was unable to stand alone in a hostile world. It was this element in my thinking that Marta had seen. How I was trying to espouse socialism, an essentially humanist position, while not letting go of what I was beginning to see as central to my being. She knew that our relationship depended on a mutual tolerance that with closer ties would at a point in the future, because of belief, become intolerance, to be pushed into a corner and made to shout 'Uncle!' So did I.

It was to be our last rendezvous at the café. After Marta had left Hungary, I stayed loyal to the place though, even in company, I never felt quite the same about going there. Then Franco and Antonia sold up and took off to northern Italy where they had family. The new owners catered for the new young, the teenagers, and consequently were in permanent conflict with the new generation of bossy party officials and governmental 'jobsworths'.

I saw Marta and Anna off at the station, as did half the neighbourhood. There were tears and hugs and general agreement that the move would be for the best, a new start. Marta at no point ever suggested I join them, and besides, I had my paths to tread in Budapest. I felt a little that I was losing Medy all over again. This was fancy, part of my romance from my den of dreams, not the real Marta, not the new Israeli woman prepared to face heat and hate to lay the foundations of Zion.

After leaving the station, I stopped by at a *konditorei* and picked up a couple of cream buns. It was late May, the sun was out and heating up the morning. Over in Israel, things were hotting up also, with seemingly the whole Arab world, and a fair number of others, reacting furiously to the arrogance of the Israelis declaring a state to exist with borders and aspirations, ambitions to turn rock and sand into a fertile demi-paradise. Me, I retraced the steps Munky and I used to take some Sundays to the chain bridge that separates Buda from Pest. I leaned against a parapet and ate our custard-cream

248

buns, one each, and I listened to the echo from my childhood of my brother Alex being very wise and funny as only he seemed able. For a moment I heard us, then some real flesh-and-blood kids cycled by and our ghosts faded. I was once again alone in my city.

1961

An overcrowded bus rattling through Tel-Aviv with me and at least a dozen others strap-hanging, getting tossed about as it made its rumbling way through the city in the heat. Someone was being pressed hard against my back. Turning round I came face-to-face with Marta, who took several seconds to register who I was.

'Ernest?'

I smiled.

'Yep. Ernest on your bus in Tel Aviv.'

Her face became wreathed in the dimpled smile I remembered so well. Behind the smile, I sensed embarrassment, though why? Maybe her age, she had broadened. Maybe just the sudden surprise of the past turning up on a hot afternoon in the middle of a life that had bleached it out.

'Why are you here?'

'Trying to make up my mind about settling here. A little engineering, some cantorial work.'

'Are you married?'

I noticed the ring on her finger.

'I see that you are. Well done. No, I'm still playing the field.'

She gave a tight little smile. Her eyes began to avoid mine.

'I'm on my way to pick up the kids from nursery. Two girls, would you believe.'

'And Anna?'

She looked down and her face clouded with sorrow.

'Mumma died last year.'

'I'm so sorry. I admired her. She recovered so well, twice

over in her life.'

'It wore her down. She should have had more years.'

'You have her strength.'

'And her weaknesses. Ernest, my stop is next. It was wonderful to see you. We're emigrating to Australia in two weeks' time.

She was closing us down, finally.

'My husband is Australian. He wants to get back to his roots. He's not Jewish and we both feel that in the interests of the kids ...'

'You would be safer there.'

'Not only that. I don't like the religious edge everything is getting here. Religion and politics don't sleep well together, didn't we once agree?'

She moved toward the bus door, squeezing past me as the vehicle slowed.

'Thank you, Ernest.'

'What for?'

'Being you. See you around ...'

The bus stopped and with others she got off. Still the object of my deep affection, she paused, looked up, gave me a little wave and was gone into the afternoon crowd. She had escaped; I had had the 'brush-off'. Yet again there was no invitation to her future.

The encounter made me feel strange and the feeling lingered for days, reviving all sorts of recollections. Her parting smile, bittersweet, from the road, seemed to call out a message I couldn't read. The bus had pulled away, our mutual waving was a very final curtain.

19 Bella and Ore

In those early years, family tragedy and renaissance were everywhere. Marta and her mother truly lost Albert at the time Albert's father was taken away. The full effect occurred a few years later, but Albert never recovered from the loss of his father. For me, I cannot speak for those of my family who survived the Holocaust, but my father's loss somehow ties in with the overall loss of innocence we experienced at that time. He was faithful to our beliefs, he was genuinely orthodox, a dreamer of great dreams, funny, paradoxically shy; tough on us at times. Ambitious, but only so far for himself. He was ambitious for his family; he wanted the boys to shine, preferably as cantors, and the girls, in the tradition of the time, to marry well. We only provided him with minor frustrations. All in all, he was proud of us, perhaps ashamed that he could not shield us from the tide of Nazism, but deeply aware that by his lights he did the right thing by not running.

How could any of us really know how *bad* bad was? The well-connected in Germany knew, and left. The military machine grew and grew, but somehow we again didn't realize until too late, that the 'machine' would want to cross borders with us as one of its prime targets. In the main, those who didn't leave at best offered only passive resistance, except Warsaw and the odd Jewish members of political resistances. Being civilized people, most Jews expected civilized methods such as censure and criticism, influence in the community, ecumenical contacts, to work long-term, which they didn't, couldn't. The prevailing mental climate was coming from a malign source which had no moral boundaries, could persuade Christians of its righteous respect and of its love for

Jesus, just so long as it dragged along the protestant and catholic orthodoxies. Ultimately, like some pantomime villain, it revealed itself as pagan, a species of pagan that would repel most pagans, but pagan all the same. It was essentially criminal. It respected force, for it sensed that, ultimately, force would destroy it. It fed on the weak, the gentle, those prepared to appease. Those who individually opposed, it would collectively turn on and destroy. It was sly and crafty, double-dealing and paranoid; it was, in the final analysis, a hysterical coward. Big as it became, it had a small, weak soul, the antithesis of what it believed itself to be. Uncle Ore and Aunty Bella knew this.

WINTER 1944

In the dark, just the warm red glow from the bowl of Ore's pipe. Its smoke hovered, a chest-high blue haze. He moved out of the shadows and crossed to the window overlooking the street. Moonlight streamed in. He stared down five storeys. From a shadowy corner of the small living room: 'Any sign of them?'

He turned his head toward the voice.

'Just the lookout on the corner. They won't be back until morning.'

Bella shifted in the shadows and came across the room, linked her arm into her brother's and looked down to the empty, ill-lit street.

'I was getting stiff sitting there. Peter should get some decent-sized furniture.'

The furniture didn't suit their size. Not little creatures, the Janitor's penthouse flat was a poky refuge for the siblings, jangled, out of sorts, on the run, hiding out in the dark. Not them at all. Peter the janitor was downstairs scouting out where danger lurked. Bella and Ore needed to escape from the apartment block, which, until a few hours before, had been their Budapest home where they had stayed since the mass ejection from Czechoslovakia six years back. The day before, the Hungarian Arrowcross militia had chosen their block as the target for the day, had arrived and rounded up all the Jews found on the premises. Ore and Bella had refused to go, had made a show of resistance to people whom they knew personally, could call by name and bring on an embarrassed state of affairs. A conflict that only local overlords could resolve.

The atmosphere of pogrom was like a penetrating smell that never really went away, but rose and fell to the tides of fortune. Right now, in the death throes of fascism, the atmosphere reeked. The couple's old friends and acquaintances outside the Jewish community had grown aloof, latterly hostile, had even vanished from their lives into the grey of the crowd, or were to be found hiding inside an Arrowcross uniform.

After the Battle of the Bulge, the Allies were wiping the floor with the remnants of the German forces on all fronts, with Hitler in their sights. The Hungarian Arrowcross knew its days to be numbered. As individuals they would, when the time came, melt back into the population from which they were recruited. A rag-tag bunch kitted out Nazi-style, and given carte-blanche by Hitler, via their leader Ferenc Szalasi, to massacre as many Jews as they could lay hands on. To protect the susceptibilities of the population, these massacres were planned to take place out of the public eye, though it did the public heart good to see the Jews 'railroaded out of town'. They could be dead elsewhere, it didn't matter. It was, after all, an international Jewish conspiracy that was raining bombs on them from Russian planes. An established fact; the propaganda had told them so.

Although committed Zionists, Ore and Bella held strong socialist beliefs and their network of connections across the city, in all communities, was a wide one. An athlete, a swimmer and wrestler of note, the large frame of Ore Schonfeld was known and respected across the city. Among Jews, he attracted admiration for his abilities. All this had

253

given him the edge in yesterday's confrontation, when over twenty Jewish men and boys were rounded up. From the balcony of his apartment, two floors below where he now stood, he had traded insults with the Hungarian greenshirts. His eyes had met those of his old friend, Leopold Lowy. He must have been visiting someone, for he lived a few blocks away. There he was with the others, being pushed out through the front doors of the apartments. Their gaze stretched like taut wire, finally snapping when Leopold was momentarily dragged sideways. Ore went on calling out each fascist by name; locals who were now given to dragging and pulling polite, conservatively dressed Jewish men and boys through a baying mob; neighbours who had traded, met daily, laughed with, quipped about the vicissitudes of life, the weather, the kids. Driven mad by fright from scarcity of food and the bombing, these same people were relentless in their spitting and screaming. The militia had its catch. They called to Ore that they would be back for him.

That was yesterday. Now it was close to dawn and the wait had been interminable. Just what could he and Bella do against armed, determined men remained unanswered. He could fight, he could kill, but it was unlikely they could escape. Peter, the janitor, hurried into the room, the sudden rush of air disturbing the serene hang of pipe smoke. Peter had found adventure in these last days. Driven by decency, this Hungarian Christian was helping out. He had been approached by the Arrowcross often enough to betray the Jews in his block and, despite pressure, had never done so. Their neighbours had done the job instead. Outraged, Peter had thrown in his hand with whatever resistance he could find. He knew the risk but hated the years of collaboration with the Nazi regime where family, friend, neighbour and group fed on betrayal as a staple diet; years where trust had disappeared and eyes rarely met. He beckoned: 'Come now. I think we can make the street. After that, who knows? Maybe we can make the ghetto. It's early enough to get a clear run.'

Shining a powerful torch, Peter led the way down the stair-
cases, past doors shut tight. Some residents would be sleeping, some gone with their captors not to return. The
remainder would be prowling their apartments waiting for
the entertainment to resume; good to see those filthy Zionists
brought low and dragged off by the bonny boys who only
recently were clerks and porters, now full of Magyar pride in
their uniforms and upright bearing.

As the trio reached the ground floor, they saw a figure
standing at the glass doors beyond the foyer. Peter flicked off
the torch, but not before the figure reacted by rattling the
locked doors, then putting his face to the glass, cupping his
hands around his temples in the attempt to see more clearly.
Ore and Bella stayed silent as Peter went forward and showed
himself to the uniform at the door.

The figure acknowledged the moment and turned away, his
frame in silhouette against the street light opposite, rifle over the
shoulder, hunched slightly to light a cigarette. A couple passed
by and stopped to exchange greetings with the militiaman.
Inside, the trio slipped across the foyer to a side door. Peter led
the way. Stairs, very steep and narrow with a stout bannister
rail. Bella made her way slowly down, helped by Peter from
below. They giggled quietly at the absurd care Bella was taking
not to fall. Peter whispered up: 'Ore, secure the door.'

When they were all safely in the cellar, Peter switched on
the light. They stood expectantly in the pale light, surrounded
by mops, buckets and janitor paraphernalia.

'Welcome to my den.'

Ore had to bend slightly in this low-ceilinged hideaway.
He wasn't overly tall, but in the confined space his height and
girth were accentuated. Bella was no shrimp and Peter a little
above average height; the three of them filled the tiny space.
Bella remarked drily: 'No place to hold a dance.'

The men laughed quietly. Peter lit a gas ring and brewed
coffee. They would wait a while to allay the suspicions of the
sentry outside; alerted by the torchlight, he could still be sniff-
ing about. The coffee tasted odd against the mixed smells of

disinfectant, oil, paint and putty that permeated the cellar, but as welcome as it was strong.

Coffee done, Ore's pipe knocked out and Bella scarfed-up against the cold, Peter donned his fur cap and switched off the cellar light. Opening the street door, he climbed the half-dozen stone steps to reach the side alley. Brother and sister followed, closing the cellar door behind them. They stood momentarily in the alley. Ore to Peter: 'That's far enough, Peter. You go back now with our thanks.'

'Oh no. I'm coming too.'

Bella chipped in: 'Peter. Enough. Stay. Be safe.'

He shook his head. 'My boats are burned. They want me as much as they do you. Yesterday, as they left, I got the pointed finger. Besides, I'm sick of being polite to dregs in uniform. We all go.'

The back alley gleamed damp and insipid from a single wall lamp and the first pale fingers of daylight. Peter beckoned Ore and Bella along the alley towards the street ahead. From behind: 'Stop!'

With their backs to the voice, they froze.

'Turn around.'

They turned. A tall youth in Arrowcross uniform stepped up to them unclasping his gun from its holster. The uniform was too small for him and it gave the menace a comic touch. With trouser cuffs at the ankles and sleeves above the wrists, his courage seemed a tender thing.

'You Jews are under arrest. Come with me.'

Ore looked at Peter. Peter stepped forward and the lad retreated slightly: 'Three against one boy.'

The lad aimed his gun. Ore calmly stepped forward, reached out, took the gun, and applied a 'sleeper' to the lad's throat. He slipped into unconsciousness. Ore released him and he slumped to the ground. Quickly, quietly, they left the alley. In the growing light, the bomb-damaged city began to take shape and stir to the day. Wearing no star, the fugitives passed almost unnoticed by those hunched against the cold, work-bound or heading for a bread queue. Early trams clattered by, the odd horse-drawn cart rumbled by on the cobbles. In the abnormal, the normal insisted on its daily role. A patrol went by and a doorway became a hiding place. After thirty minutes, Bella began to slow and they all knew that if confronted, no running would be possible. Because of this, she rewarded the two men with little blessings and 'thank-yous'. A cold morning sun had begun to shine round ruined corners, slanting low and fierce to the eyes as they came close to the ghetto. Just a few hundred metres. From somewhere above, a voice: '*Halt!* Jews. Stay put.'

A shot. Again they froze. The voice had come from behind the blinding sunlight. The arresting patrol had lookouts posted on a rooftop, and now five armed Arrowcross stood in a line across their path, their bodies in haloed silhouette.

'Hands behind your heads!'

The three captives obeyed. The patrol leader broke ranks and came insolently close to their faces.

'You are to come with us. Our orders are to detain all Jews.'

Bella pointed to Peter: 'He's not a Jew. He was directing us. We're lost.'

The leader slowly turned to face her. He sent the back of his hand across her face which made her stagger backward a few steps.

'Speak when you're spoken to, bitch.'

Ore stepped forward, his eyes darkened with direct anger. Four rifles behind the leader clicked menacingly. Bella in tears of pain nursed her bruised face, but fixed her gaze on the patrol leader. He broke the stare and spoke to Peter: 'Your papers, mister "he's not a Jew".'

Peter handed them over and they were pocketed.

'No papers, eh? You sure look Jewish to me pal; you're with Jews,' he leaned forward; 'you even smell like one. Now if you will all kindly step this way.'

The morning sun dimmed away behind developing cloud. In the chill air, the coming of snow could be felt. Ore placed his arm around Bella who wept silently. Their thin ray of hope had dwindled to nothing and the darkening of the day cast its shadow over them. Peter walked, escorted, slightly ahead. They were led down a side street to a waiting wagon. Peter turned, smiled at them, and shrugged as he stepped in to the van. Ore and Bella followed on.

The holding room was of medium size, had a centre table, four or five chairs, a long wall-side bench, a high window and a couple of green shaded lights dangling from the ceiling. On the walls, the usual wartime propaganda posters extolling the effort and damning the 'Nigger–Jew Conspiracy', along with the 'Soviets equals Jews' libel. There were photographs of Szalasi and Hitler.

The room was holding upwards of fifty men, all Jewish. Many stood. Conversation was muted but constant. Most in the room were soberly dressed. Being a well-known face, Ore was greeted, sometimes embraced, by those who recognized him. Being a Zionist made him slightly dangerous. For some in the community he was a role model, for others a point of blame for their misfortunes; a fighter who had brought down fascist wrath on the whole community, a species of blaming common in a climate of terror. Ore stared at the twin banners that hung side-by-side down one wall: a carefully embroidered arrow cross coupled with the swastika. He shook his head balefully, edging his way across the crowded room to the window. On tiptoe, he gained a glimpse of the street. Morning Budapest was crowded and active, but almost silent in the thick snow that had begun to fall since he, Bella and Peter were separated. He had demanded to know where Bella was being taken. His captors had looked at him for a moment before deciding to reply. Humour with a callous edge: 'Not Belsen just yet, big man. The girls are off to a nice holiday centre across the Danube. Trains out are in short supply with all those Jew bombs falling. Don't worry son, it's all girls together there. We respect women.'

They laughed at the edge of their joke, knowing Ore would be suspecting the worst. His frustration was complete, he could no longer defend his little sister. She had been in his charge since the death of their father. His mother had plunged into helpless grief when Jacob Schonfeld succumbed to lung cancer. After two years of parental neglect, their mother passed on to join Jacob. Ore, a teenager, had a little girl on his hands and he had to make his way. No academic, but very active and sociable, he made out well and later became a trader in leather goods. Athletic, he was a little over medium height but powerful and thick-set, giving him the impression of height. As a swimmer and wrestler he became well-known and popular in the Jewish community and beyond, attracting the admiration and envy that goes with physical achievement. As they grew up, both he and Bella became active Zionists, which added to their reputation; gave them edge at a time when such things mattered only in living rooms, political halls and over dinner tables.

Looking out from the holding room at the snow-filled streets and the activities of a population every bit as much under the cosh as he felt himself to be, with death round every corner and air raids taking lumps out of them, he felt deep compassion for all at this turning point in history. Propaganda had laid the blame squarely on the Jews for all of it – and propaganda was easy to believe. He shrugged ruefully and came down from tiptoe. As he turned back to the crowded room, he caught a glimpse of a couple of orthodox men sitting on the bench, deep in prayer. Through the beard of the younger he recognized a face he hadn't seen for a while. Before going across, he waited for the praying to cease. A sudden shaft of sunlight finally interrupted the proceedings. The two men paused to look up at the sudden brightness in the room. Eyes met.

'Ore Schonfeld.'

'Hello, Mishka.'

The little boy whom Bella had given the 'run-around'. Grown up now and serious, behind beard and spectacles, he seemed still her 'little puppy'. He stood and they embraced emotionally. He stood back, took off his spectacles to wipe his eyes.

'Bella. How is she? Is she safe?'

'We were both captured this morning, on the streets.'

'It may be okay. This war can't go on much longer. They're on their last legs.'

Ore nodded but gave Mishka a penetrating look.

'Don't drop your guard, lad. They're like a scorpion in a ring of fire. Trouble is, we're right in there with them. The stinging has become wild and reckless. It will sting itself to death, eventually. Meantime, dodge or die.'

'God will provide, Ore.'

Mishka's pale, earnest face looked across in that glazed way believers have when the odds are stacked against the faith into which their being is immersed. Ore gave him a hug. What good trying to break his dream so deep into this nightmare. Mishka's companion, an old rabbi, was poring over his scripture. He looked up: 'In nemesis, in extremity, walks the coming Messiah.'

All his life, Ore had heard such words. No religious academic, he bit his tongue when the belief's authority asserted itself, but all his life the evidence had been stacking up, that no Messiah was walking his way to them through smoke and flame. He wasn't about to show his face for Ore, Bella, the old rabbi or anyone else. He smiled at Mishka and sat down on the bench beside the old man.

'For my sister, a prayer, rabbi.'

The old man reached up and placed his hand on Ore's shoulder.

'We are with God. At no time is there separation. We'll pray.'

The room had become silent. All faces turned to the three men on the bench at prayer under a poster exalting the grandeur of the Third Reich.

With the prayers barely away from their lips, the door to the holding room swung wide. Armed Arrowcross militiamen stood in the doorway. They pointed their guns into the room, calling out a number of people, including Mishka and the old rabbi who was slow to move; slow enough to draw a militiaman into the room. Ore's hand twitched. The Arrowcross reached out for the old man and dragged him to his feet. Ore tried to intercept: 'Go easy. He's frail.'

The militiaman looked up from his task. Another boy in uniform, with his hair slicked down into a flat shiny mass divided by a centre-parting, his cheap cologne mingled with sweat which radiated from him as he came close. Recognition passed between himself and Ore. Ore had taught this kid to swim.

'Back.'

The lad gestured to Ore with his gun. Mishka and the rabbi were making their difficult way to the door, following the group already leaving. The boy hurried after them. He and Mishka both looked back at the man from their past, large, alone and helpless to prevent their shared future. With a slam, the door to the holding room was shut again.

Those remaining in the room all found somewhere to sit. Silence reigned. Ore found his way to the bench near the window, sat quietly for a while, then slowly, ritualistically, he took out his tobacco pouch, filled his pipe, and lit it. He took in the smoke and very gently released it, where it curled its snaky blue way into the fug of the holding room. He was grateful that the Arrowcross were crassly amateur in their searching him. Peasants in uniform. Had they been German, the search would have been more thorough. A prisoner with tobacco and matches, what next? He smiled grimly. That passive acceptance shown by Mishka and everyone else, he'd seen it so much in the last twenty years; sit idly by, pray a little, wait on God. He and Bella would have starved a dozen times over with that kind of passivity. He had learned to battle for a crust, knew what his life was worth. You had to make out to survive, you had to. You don't learn to bake bread in a seminar.

His thoughts turned to the men who were taken off yesterday from his apartment block. How tamely they had left. No fight, no flight, just acceptance. Head in hands, Ore's fingers sought out the deep dented scar at the centre of his forehead. He thought over the old formula, the one common to Jewish history: poverty leads to unrest, revives superstition, feuds and hatreds. Jews are blamed if they are around, pogroms ensue; time to go. Historically, they were shown the door after being beaten and raped, but these fascists, of whatever stripe, were bent on mass-murder and the Nazis on a programme of annihilation. His men, the men of his race, his community had gone down to the courtyard with those Arrowcross popinjays. Alfred, Ben, Leopold. Leo Lowy who had given him his business break in the leather game as a young man. Leopold, the religious dreamer and his wonderful children who loved him and Bella as family. His thoughts doubled back to a day out with some of the Lowy children. Must have been in the early 1930s.

It had been a run in the sun, a dance in the flowers, a stroll over the hills; a time of laughter and warmth. In the train home, he had been telling them tall stories. They loved the one about 'The Fool and the Forest Demon'. Lillie and Else had cuddled up to him, Munky and Ernest sat opposite. Munky loved the style of Ore's tales and was poised on the edge of his seat. Ernest lounged temporarily; at that age, restless, given to squirming about and making mischief. The huddle was wreathed in pipe smoke. They were headed back to Bratislava from Pesinok. Evening light was closing in on the group. Every now and then, the low sun cast long beams across the fields and danced around the carriage.

'Want to know how I got my dent?'

Of course they did. The dent in the forehead had been a talking point as long as any of them could remember. The adults knew, just as they knew about Bella's beau, a doctor who had to go to jail for a mercy killing. From the kids they kept such shockers. Ernest read about the doctor in a report that he read at a news-stand; now they all knew. This one however had been kept tight secret until now.

'True or false?' He grinned.

'True', they chorused.

He drew deeply on his smoke and bit by bit released it in

thin curly blue streams.

'Papa does that with his smoke,' Ernest volunteered.

Ore gave Ernest one of his mischievous looks: 'Does he have a dent in his forehead as well, Ernesti?'

Lillie and Else told Ernest to shut up and let Uncle Ore tell his tale. He looked at the four expectant faces, smiled kindly and began: 'February 1928. The coldest winter in our history. Every inch of Slovakia was buried deep in snow and ice. As you know, I travel in leather goods. I have to sell to live and that winter was leaving me short of money. So, against my better judgement, I took a trip on the train through the snow to pick up some orders and call in a few payments at a small place out of Bratislava. Getting there was okay and once there I was able to make my calls, in spite of the weather. My sample cases were a problem. By the time I needed to return to the station, all transport, cab, horse, everything was snowed in. All day, it hadn't stopped.'

Ore looked at the children's intent little faces and stifled a ripple of laughter, which threatened to break open into a wide smile. Why break the spell?

'So, I had to trudge through the snow in the evening light, those bags of mine dragging me down. I stopped at the confectioner for Bella's sweets. When I got to the station, the lights were on, everything was covered in deep snow, the place seemed deserted. The plough had been through and for the moment the line was clear. So I went further. I went to the platform for the Bratislava train and walked in the narrow path cleared towards the waiting room where light could be seen. No immediate sign of porters or Kovacs the stationmaster, just me and some character ahead of me. In the shadows, tall, a little bent. The daylight had all but died but the snow gleamed, and with the station lights, I could see well enough. As I approached him, the figure slipped through the waiting-room door. He didn't hold it for me, so I had to struggle against a heavy spring holding it to. It kept trying to shut as I forced my way in.'

'By the time I made it through the door, the man from the

platform had taken himself off to a shadowy corner of the room and had lit himself a cigarette. The heat from the stove was stifling, but very welcome. The smell of damp and bodies was a bit much, but my pipe would take care of that. As I brushed off the snow I greeted everyone there. The man ignored me, but the four peasant girls round the stove had quit their chattering to watch my struggles with the door. One of them smiled at me. Pretty girls. Then they went back to their gossip. Against the dull light and the drabness of the waiting room, in their *babushkas* they were a delight of colour. The man in the corner caught my attention because he was keeping to the shadows. Ragged, furtive, avoiding my eyes. Agitated. Before long, Kovacs, the stationmaster appeared. I knew him well. I came this way half-a-dozen times in a year; I'd even met his wife. Jolly woman. His news wasn't good. No trains till late, maybe not at all. We'd have to hang around. He would come back from time to time to let us know if things were improving. He took off, as did the four girls, after a discussion about what to do with the time. That left me with our friend in the corner.'

The young Lowys held their breath, sensing menace in the moment.

'The fire in the stove had begun to die down and I could feel a heavy draught from the door. The smell in the room didn't lift. Maybe it was the room, maybe him, who knew? I stretched out on a bench, wrapped my coat round me tight and placed one of the bags under my head and shoulders. Putting my hat to one side, I tried settling back. My wallet was uncomfortable, so I moved it from pocket to pocket. He in the corner was staring at me, maybe not me, maybe the wallet. Either way it didn't feel good but I tried to rest anyway and naturally, after a while, my eyes drooped. But suddenly, I was really awake. He had raised himself. On the bench beside him, a small axe.'

The children were pop-eyed. Else whispered: 'What did you do, Uncle Ore?'

'Nothing. One of the peasant girls came back into the

waiting room. The man pocketed the axe and was out the door and into the night.'

The four young faces round him relaxed a little.

'A bit later Kovacs came back in. The ploughs had cleared enough track and there was likely to be a Bratislava train around ten. Two hours. Tall and skinny, Kovacs, good man.'

Ernest was concerned: 'What did you do about the man with the axe?'

'No proof of intent, Ernesti. Apart from the look he gave me when he went out.'

'And the axe?'

'Bought it that day? Needed it for his work? The other three peasant girls came back one by one, and everyone settled down for the wait. There was some wood for the stove but not enough and the place began to cool; finally it was too cold to be comfortable. As nine-thirty dragged round, I stirred my stumps and made my way down the platform to Kovacs' office. He was at his desk and beckoned me into the warmed office. We exchanged pleasantries, as you do, and he poured me a vodka which was very acceptable. A maybe about the train, but he told me of a Jewish guesthouse that had recently opened up in the town. As we talked, the phone rang. A train in half an hour, certain, enough track was clear. We shared another vodka until he had to prepare for the train coming. I made my way along the platform, the bit they'd cleared. Where snow lay, it was thick, and its crystals gleamed and glistened under the short line of platform lights. The brightness of the snow stretched a fair way beyond the glow of the lights before it gave way to the dark. A clock tower bell chimed out ten, a thin muffled sound I remember. No train yet. Away down the platform beyond the lights, someone had appeared and stood motionless.'

'The man in the waiting room,' volunteered Munky.

'The man in the waiting room, Munky. When he finally moved closer to the light, I could see that it was him. We were alone. I figured that if I needed to, I could get back quickly enough to the waiting room, but the train arrived and saved me making that choice. It drew into the station moving to a slow, muffled puff. When it stopped, to be certain of safety, I settled for a middle carriage. I hauled my bags onto the train and followed them in. To my surprise, I had the carriage to myself. No company. Get off again and find some? I decided to stay put, after all I'm big and ugly enough to defend myself. Anyway, it could all have been fantasy on my part. I had a seat on a train that was going home. Enough. I loosened my clothes, lit my pipe. The carriage had some heat, which was pleasing.'

'The train took its time getting to the next station. Through the carriage window, all I could see was a dim outline of things through a thick fog which had ice crystals floating in it. As the train pulled slowly away, the link door at the end of the carriage opened and ...'

'... in came the man with the axe,' gasped Else, stirring herself from cuddling Ore.

'In he came. I thought at first as the door opened it might be the ticket collector, but no. Our friend, axe in hand. Should I pull the communication cord? Now this is self-pride, I didn't. I didn't want to show panic. He came right up close to where I was now standing. "Put your money on the seat," he said. "No," I said. "Do it," he said, "or you're a dead man." He had that kind of voice that comes from poverty and cheap drink. I stared back at him and shook my head; he could see I had no intention of handing anything to him. He gave me a hard grin, his mouth had a few teeth gone, then he went for me with the axe. I deflected the first blow with my forearm and was on my feet instantly. The movement of the train had me staggering slightly. He was wild but canny and the second strike caught my forehead. Everything went into red shadow and we were on the carriage floor, locked. My fighting skills came to my aid and I had him in a wrestling hold. Blood was in my eyes, on my face, down my neck. I struck him very hard and wrenched his neck. The last thing I recall was seeing the axe go spinning and sliding down the carriage.'

The children were silent, looking at Uncle Ore. Total awe. Nobody moved.

'Two days later, I came to in a Bratislava hospital with a number of policemen sitting by my bed.'

His young listeners relaxed a little.

'It turned out to be just the one policeman, but my vision was screwed. I couldn't get my eyes to adjust. But I was not dead; I was weak, on my back, but still here. The one policeman severally told me that the robber had died by my hand. There was a case to answer.'

Pausing, Ore let his fingers run across the dent. He frowned a little.

'It was weeks before I had anything like clear vision, and during the court case I had a blackout. Bad. But my name was cleared. Maybe the blackout helped, I don't know.'

'What was the verdict Uncle Ore?' Ernest wanted to know.

'Self-defence. "Ore Schonfeld, the court is satisfied you acted in self-defence," to quote the judge.'

'Nobody messes with Uncle Ore.' Munky settled back in his seat. The young Lowys gave a little cheer.

'Nobody messes with Uncle Ore'. He stared round the holding room. The remaining detainees sat silent, disconsolate. Where there was conversation, it was brief, clipped and quiet. Ore knocked out the ash from his pipe, and stowed it away. Noises from outside set his heart into rapid motion. The door swung open, and the lad with the slicked-down hair entered behind two older Arrowcross, neither of whom Ore recognized. The larger of the two spoke: 'All out. Come on, move!'

Everyone stood and filed out quietly, almost apologetically, except Ore who walked out glaring at everything in particular. The larger Arrowcross spoke again, his accent was from the south. He also had a Croatian look to him: 'Young Karel here says you're a champion swimmer.'

Ore nodded, looking long and hard at his ex-pupil whose eyes darted away from the big man's relentless stare.

'Well, Mr Schonfeld sir,' he continued, 'maybe we'll get a chance to see you in action.'

267

Ore was on to this. Bodies had been seen floating in the Danube. Forced in to swim would give him a chance, in spite of the severe weather. No. They would shoot him along with the rest and dump his corpse in the river. These actions gave the game away. This was endgame, and the scorpion was stinging randomly, wildly, before the ring of fire consumed it.

With the other prisoners, he moved down a dim-lit corridor past an office of unoccupied desks, their tops covered with papers and files. A man stood at a filing cabinet and glanced up at them as they made their way past his window. A civilian woman stood to one side in the corridor, to let the group pass. She stared upward briefly at Ore who somehow appeared alone.

Through a door and out into the intense cold of the yard. It bit through clothing, bringing on violent shivering. Ore's boots were stout, thank God, so that the snow on the ground gave him no trouble. The group stood huddled against the sharp wind that whisked powdered snow off walls and low roofs and whipped it into their faces. It was dusk. The last light shone peach over the housetops. A van pulled into the yard. They were all herded, with the help of rifle butts, into the vehicle. Some sat, some stood. Apart from the boy, Karel, these Arrowcross were strangers and the threat had taken on an impersonal feel, all the more chilling to the soul. The result was going to be the same, but somehow known faces gave the whole experience a measure of credibility. Even with Karel present, this was starkly incredible. It woke Ore to the craziness of what they were all 'conspiring' to do. Actors in a surreal drama. Everyone knew that the Allies had the Axis powers at bay. At bay and wounded, able only to lash out and thrash about, drowning slowly in their hatred and panic. To assuage the terror, what better way than to torture, shoot or drown the cause of their plight. Jews, Jews, all the way. The nemesis for fascists came courtesy of international Zionism; only fitting therefore that the local yids should partake of the bitter cup. In the rage of this kind of despair, killing Jews felt good.

Ore had explored the insane logic, up, down, inside-out over the years and had just arrived at more questions. The murk that floated around in the minds of gentile peasants, the superstition and simple lack of true knowledge to counter misinformation from those who ruled their destiny, created the European pogrom. The perfect distillation had been Adolf Hitler, one of their own, fired up by myth, music and hokum. He had too easily foisted delusive fantasy into the *Realpolitik*. As falsehood cannot endure, his paste diamonds turned to pulp in front of the world and the world felt the heat of a being's wrath in the guilt and shame of being found out. The proletarian Prometheus hadn't delivered.

In the van, Ore's fellow passengers had their eyes down. Any fight or curiosity seemed to have vanished, their body language expressed resignation. What point, apparently, in screaming for one's life; who would hear? God knew. God waited on their humble give-it-all-up presence in his kingdom. A checkmate. Ore was sure of one thing. None of this was of God's making; God had nothing to do with any of this. The wagon rolled along the riverside, past the chain bridge. They were heading out of town, the road eventually taking them away from the river. Ore began to think that maybe a watery end was not to be, but further on, beyond the city limits; the van turned off the main road, and rumbled down a track, past a farm set in virgin whiteness, to a jetty beside the river.

'Now or never,' thought Ore, 'but what? How?'

The vehicle made its way along the narrow jetty and everyone was ordered off. In front of them was the inky blackness of the Danube. Behind them and the truck, at the end of the jetty, an expanse of whitened countryside. The extension of the white glow into the darkness reminded him of the night of the axe. The indentation in his forehead throbbed with his agitation.

'How? When? Got to do it.'

Four Arrowcross, counting the driver. Their torches flashed instruction to the huddled men who scrambled off the truck to stand inches deep in the snow in front of its blazing headlights. Hardly a word was said. No shouts, no pleading, all compliant in the terror of the moment. Ore felt his heart thunder; mercifully no blackout symptoms had shown. Indeed, he felt as if he were the only one awake in this dream-scape. He looked for light in the eyes of his fellow captives as torchlight flashed across their faces. No fire, just ice. How could he know this, how dare he know this; what remained behind the eyes or in the breast of any one of these doomed beings?

'All of you. In a line,' came the order. Obediently a line developed. Ore thought about jumping off the jetty into the water. He realized that he would not last minutes. Second thought, run into the night. Better. Bullets would follow though. The truck. Steal the truck. Its engine was idling, the driver out of the cab preparing to kill. Somebody at last started a tantrum. On his knees screaming and crying to be given mercy. The torches turned on a terrified young man. Ore crept quietly into shadow and took a quick step to a point behind the truck lights. A shot – and from the young man the plead-ing was over. The torches followed the corpse into the water.

'*Stay still, all of you! Turn! Face the river!*'

Ore was in the truck. The engine roared. The gears crashed and he was reversing hard along the jetty. Shots followed the truck, taking out a light and shattering the windscreen. He caught sight of running figures and he prayed that some of those unfortunates would take their chances as he did. The night was vast, cold and dangerous. For the moment he was free and headed away from Budapest to a village where once it was safe to be. He would gamble on his friends being there and the Allies getting through some time soon.

BUDAPEST, JANUARY 1945

A large brown bakelite radio was playing music from Voice of America. The Hungarian translator was explaining Ore's adventures to the Russian major who was sitting behind the desk at the captured Arrowcross HQ in Budapest. The smile was a mile wide at the little tale of the escape from the jetty that night beside the Danube. He asked: 'What then?'

'I went to my friends' village, but they had gone. I went to the outskirts of Gyomro and dumped the truck. I found a large barn to sleep in. Found an old overcoat that didn't fit me, but it was a blanket. Couldn't sleep, so before dawn, I walked into Gyomro and hid myself in an old outhouse.'

'How long did you stay there?'

'Couple of days, then grabbed a bike and took myself back here. Finally, you took the city. Here I am.'

The Russian major sat back and nodded his approval. Through the translator: 'Go get yourself a beer. Come back in a few hours and we'll probably have your papers, now we have the details. Good luck.'

'Thank you.'

The announcer on VOA talked in English. Ore's ears took in 'Duke Ellington' as he stood. As he left, the familiar notes of 'Caravan' serenaded Ore's secret joy at the prospect of a day without fear. The Arrowcross emblems and Nazi propaganda had all but vanished, just like the militia, which had melted away like morning frost to become mechanics, plough-boys, bakers and clerks, offering the new regime their co-operative credentials, for the time being. Ore smiled as he walked down the corridor, thinking, 'Whatever happened to all those feathered hats and armbands? In a drawer, on top of a cupboard? In the wife's wardrobe?' He passed the same woman who had stared his way when he and the others were taken out to be murdered. She gave him a warm smile and disappeared into an office. Just before reaching daylight, at the doorway he found Peter the Janitor leaning against the wall, waiting. He too had come here to retrieve his identity. Ore put his arm round the Hungarian's shoulder and together they walked out into the daylight to get that beer.

LATE SUMMER 1945

An explosion of laughter blew into the kitchen from the dining room. Bella turned from the task of preparing coffee to give me a conspiratorial smile. I was helping her with the trays. I had doted on Bella from our very first meeting years before when, as small children, we were introduced to her and Uncle Ore by my father, who clearly had embraced them as 'family'. We quickly followed on. Father for once, turned a blind-eye to Ore's secular stance and Ore, likewise, Father's orthodoxy. When they shared a pipe, the house became enveloped in fragrant tobacco smoke. The memory of my father must have clouded my face, for Bella looked concerned: 'You feeling alright, Ernest?'

'Thinking back, Bella.'

She put her hand to the back of my neck and drew me to her.

'Step by step, angel.'

Another burst of laughter came from the next room. Bella lifted her tray: 'Another joke from Ore.'

I smiled: 'He shouldn't laugh at his own jokes.'

She responded: 'Why not? You do.'

I lifted my tray of cups. Bella paused at the kitchen door: 'What d'you think, Ernest. Are they a match?'

'Who match? What match?'

'Ore and Welma, stupid.'

I teased: 'I'm to know?'

'Don't be dense. You have eyes.'

I warned her that her tray was tilting.

'Well Ernest, I'm waiting for an answer.'

'From what I can see Bella, we may have a little more work to do.'

'No, Ernest. The one with the work to do will be Ore.'

When it came to women, Ore was painfully shy. In his life there had been the odd liaison which faded into nothing. Through his adult life he had remained almost aloof, untouched by the feminine world, except when Bella brought this into their shared life, which they both knew had become habit and had gone on too long. The time-lock had been broken, partly by the war, and also by the release from prison of her beloved Geza, the doctor who had killed out of kindness. Ore was alone in a 'limbo' which found him at times more than a little lost and subject to depression, along with the odd head-wound blackout. Bella and her friends felt Welma to be the answer. She had survived the camps along with Bella and a few other girls who had looked out for each other in the last days of the war. Now under the vagaries of Russian influence, they looked set to keep a good thing going.

Widowed in the Holocaust, Welma was the right age and the right kind for Ore; a little younger, and a lot wiser. She'd handled the loss of her husband, Belsen and Terezin, her own agonies and the agonies of others; so blackouts and depression would be a pushover.

Bella and I eased our way back into the warm atmosphere of the dining room. Geza, Bella's husband (at last, at last) had acquired a case of good Hungarian wine. The little dinner party had gone well on this and Bella's great cooking. The atmosphere was cosy and blush-warm. Bella announced: 'Coffee for those who need a change from Bull's Blood.'

Ore looked up from his intense conversation with Welma and Geza: 'A choice. Geza's wine or Bella's coffee and sweets? I cannot choose. I must reluctantly settle for both.'

He lit his freshly filled pipe and poured himself a full glass, offering the bottle around. Geza added to his glass, Welma waved the offer away, smiling. She watched Ore intently; and he offered her a shy glance or two. He almost batted his eyelashes. His swarthy face reflected the confusion that comes when one realizes that one is under affectionate scrutiny. He lifted his glass to Geza.

'It is good to see that austere times cannot separate a doctor from good wine.'

'Jail did. *Salut.*'

'*Salut.* You got nothing there?'

'Gut-rot vodka, high-days and holidays or in exchange for cigarettes.'

When we had put out the cups, Bella and I rejoined the table. Welma poured the men their coffees.

They nodded their thanks.

'Did you get much bother from the other prisoners?'

'No. I was too useful. Most of them saw the point of mercy killing anyway.'

'Ironic how you kill out of compassion and get jail. I killed in a fight and got off.'

Bella scolded: 'It was self-defence, Ore. You were cleared.'

'Maybe I get to pay with blackouts.'

Welma studied the dent in his forehead, which in mild agitation he caressed. She was concerned.

'Are the blackouts frequent?'

'They occur under pressure. I can go months.'

She nodded: 'And the man who attacked you. How did he die?'

'Of a broken neck.'

For a moment there was silence in the room. Bella looked at me: 'Time for a song, young man.'

'What would you like?'

'The one you sang that first day we came to the house in Bratislava.'

'*Kappear Chatoenu.*'

Bella looked around the table at the faces of those she loved, whose history was eloquent with shared pain: 'Yes, Ernest. Sing, 'Forgive us our sins.'

I let my voice lift into the room. No longer the boy soprano, a tenor now, but still able to change expressions and wet the eyes. I rejoiced at the effect. Geza held Bella's hand. Ore smiled at Welma, and I was taken back to another room in another brighter time. Bella was younger, just as pretty, a tad smaller but with a physical generosity that made the heart sing then as now. A little lad then, and now, still too young. Then as now, just the smell from her was a delight. As a child I was ever-close to catch the warmth and gentle odours that came from her that would lull my senses. Just occasionally now, in the odd embrace, my childhood would be revived.

The last note of the song hung momentarily in the smoke from Ore's pipe. All eyes were damp. These graduates of the Shoah, its survivors in a grey aftermath, were allowing emotion to wash the grime from their being. Now, as then, Bella hugged me, my reward, the delight of her holding me and breathing her once more into my being.

A few months later, Ore and Welma married under the *chuppa*, glass under foot, with blessings from all present. I had sung. Everyone had cheered, cried then danced. At the top table, the little dinner party of three months earlier was gathered again. Geza stood and offered a toast to the couple and their future. The guests, all standing, replied with a loud '*Mazeltov*'. Demands for a speech. Ore stood to cheers, his face radiant, his form erect and proud. For a moment he looked down as Welma looked up. Their mutual smile was angelic. He looked out at the pleased faces of his friends and relatives:

'Thank you. All of you. Welma thanks you. My sister Bella is the matchmaker here; so we know who to blame. My little sister who seems to have become big sister. I was her carer when she was small; now she is my carer and under her influence, I find Welma. Six months back, I had my head in my hands, I was that grubby little speck on the face of the universe. "What now? Poor me." Everything was dark; you all know what I am saying, you know. No more war to divert my attention from the fact I was reaching middle age alone. Now, drunk on the affection of this beautiful lady, I am married, you are witnesses. And we, dear friends, are off to Palestine. A little place called Petach Tikva.'

Sweet surprise. The ripple of response from the guests went round the small local hall. Some called '*mazeltov!*', some looked to each other for opinion. The decision was made during a walk in the park. Ore had told Welma of his admiration for the fledgling state, owned up to his beloved socialism and found to his delight that his new soulmate was cheering him on.

'She wants me to roll up my sleeves, dig some ground, help

grow lemons. I love Budapest, of Bratislava my memories are likewise, but I have no love for the disease that struck them down. I hope, as you must do, that they recover and the disease disappears forever. For us ...,' he looked at Welma,'... we are done here. Now for the sunshine and bright ideals. Thank you for the solidarity in the darkest days; thank God we have each other. Thank you for honouring us with your presence. I drink to you, all.'

In tears, he sat to our cheering.

Ore had five happy years with his beautiful Welma at home in the sunshine of the little town in their new country, where Zion was a coming reality and the State of Israel was born amid huge opposition and weapons-backed hostility. Increasing numbers of blackouts and dizzy spells left him senseless for hours at a time. From the final attack he didn't wake, the assailant's ghost finally claimed him. Welma and Israel had to move on without a good, good man; a *Mensch*, our beloved Uncle Ore.

PART V
FLUX

The years 1945–55 were very much catching-up years, a restless time both in terms of settling back into what we were able to accept as normality within the Soviet bloc, and making sense of what we could learn of the world as it developed beyond Stalin and his string of successors. Hungarians attempted the usual political compromises, had leaders who were compliant to the Russian command over all our destinies.

Across the planet, things were turning around. Under the umbrella of nuclear terror, the two dominant political ideologies played their dangerous mind games, played off states and leaders, interfered with human destinies, killed and maimed in the cause of the greater good – world peace. For some, this meant global expansion of capital, the opening of markets along with consolidation of trading partners internationally, for others it was ideology. For everyone, oil. No matter which side of the Iron Curtain, both forces were at work, though the stresses differed depending where you found yourself. There was more stone-faced dullness, however, in our neck of the woods. It was due mainly to a terrible insecurity, bureaucratic inefficiency and overall lack of know-how in coping with the future. I was subjected to this when our little workshop had to close. The engineering job that I took in its place was adequate, but personal fulfilment was not there, and the place was run, not for efficient production, but for bureaucratic posturing and personal aggrandisement for the party faithful. Repeated across the Soviet bloc, one can only imagine how truly slack the system was. The events of the 1980s and 1990s could be seen developing in that state-run workshop.

Because of my religious studies and singing activities, I was passed over for promotion, and less skilled people were elevated. My enchantment with the Party died as I tried to function within it. As the Shoah faded a little, my social and my increasingly active love life began to develop. My singing activities kept me in close to the faith which had begun to reassert itself. My socialism stayed real, but the authoritarian pseudo-socialism of mid-twentieth-century life was leaving me cold. The elements of socialism were misinterpreted and cynically employed to culturally engineer the coming generation, who, to their eternal credit, were giving it the thumbs down, wholesale.

Whole populations under communism had to watch as the western world forged ahead into massive affluence and cultural diversity. Yes, the Russians kept pace with the West militarily, but socially, those in power knew only oppression as a controlling tool. To liberate the human mind meant giving it choice, and the human mind might not have chosen the status quo. America had its problems, but a gradual process of mental and social liberation was taking place there. At times painful, at times absurd, the West, with its dominant culture, enjoyed relative democratic freedom as it realized itself. In Hungary we watched. In that ten-year period, we lived, worked, moved on, stayed put and felt, by degrees, the vice about us tighten. As usual, we Jews felt the bite keenly. Social unrest always leads to the minority feeling the boot of both the oppressor and the oppressed.

We in Hungary felt with the death of Stalin in 1953, and the overtures the new men were making to America, that a thaw was taking place in what had become known as the Cold War. However, Nikita Krushchev had all the states in the Soviet bloc sign up to the Warsaw Pact, a like-for-like response to the North Atlantic Treaty Organization. It was crucial to the Soviets that subject states toe the line. This did not square with the growing self-image of countries like ourselves, and there was a steadily developing resistance to the pressure that Russia was placing on Hungary. As a nation, we reacted, resisted to such a degree, that in a huge 'police operation', the Russians invaded in 1956, replacing our leaders with puppet yes-men.

20 Helen

'Soviet troops are here for the purpose of restoring law and order, and at the request of the Hungarian government. We cannot permit UN observers to enter Hungary, since the situation is purely an internal affair of the Hungarian state.' This from the new Hungarian government to the UN Security Council, 12 November 1956.

Uncle Cohn had run out of food. He'd called on the Shabbat. He was trapped inside his house, like thousands of others, pinned down, while the bullets flew between the freedom fighters of Budapest and the Russian troops who had been sent in from across the border 'to restore law and order'. As usual, the people at large had to make the best of it; join the fight, duck for cover, stay in, run for it. Die. In the heat of battle, force is relentless, unavoidable. Uncle Cohn couldn't do much of anything from his parlour; old, slow of movement, joining the morning bread queue was high-risk for the young and agile, let alone this frail old boy. Following a family emergency meeting, and having the short straw in my grasp, I set off for Uncle Cohn's house across the city, a lovingly prepared and tight-packed food parcel under my arm. I left, giving them all a solemn promise to be back soon and to take care, take care, take especial care. Still the little boy. Thirty-one, a graduate of the universities of Auschwitz and Belsen and still to them the little lad, the boy soprano who had wrung their hearts in the 1930s. But it felt good to be coddled a little, especially as we knew death intimately, and death was enjoying a fresh spell of luck.

The family get-together was Friday, Saturday when we got Cohn's call. It was Sunday morning early when I set out.

Dark, cold and rainy. The wind blew the rain in sheets along the street as I left the house. Through the night, the noise coming from the areas of fighting was intense and forbidding. We had lived with its volume. Curiosity has always been my downfall. Against all sensible urging from within, I had to have a nosey; so I did and sneaked straight into trouble. Grabbed from a doorway by two freedom fighters, one of whom I recognized from childhood, I was cajoled, forced, part-dragged protesting to a building on the Madach Place. Under the eaves of a fine, ornate building, an armed group was holding its position under sporadic heavy fire from the Russians.

The garret was too small a space for the six men and one woman, all bristling with weaponry. The air was thick and a blue haze of fragrant French tobacco hung sweetly on my nostrils. I was gestured into a corner and told to stay put; I would be useful later. Someone passed me a bottle of vodka. I crouched down beside a low table where a radio was playing. Voice of America, pop music, loud. It wasn't properly tuned so sounded phased and tinny. I took a swig from the vodka bottle, its rough warmth immediately put me in touch with the atmosphere of the garret. A cigarette was offered me. I accepted politely, trying a smile.

'Someone fix that radio.' The voice came from a rough-looking guy at the window, his face and rifle trained on the street below. The face I knew came over and re-tuned the waveband.

'Are you okay, Alex?'

Herschel. Finally I had remembered his name.

'I'm Ernest. Alex was my brother.'

'You were like two peas back there. You still play on the wing?'

'Not in a while. Alex died at the hands of the Arrowcross.'

He made the face we had all learned to make since the end of the war. A habit we Jews needed to develop when hearing of yet more loss, the horrific becoming commonplace through endless repetition. It was meant, it was usual, it would never

282

be threadbare, but it was an effort to muster something new to the eyes.

Herschel Klein had German–Jewish parents; a little aristocracy in our neighbourhood. He had early flirted with communism, and his socialist leanings had brought him here unscathed and seemingly the full-blooded Hungarian socialist patriot.

'Did your family survive?'

'My parents are in the US. We lost my sister.'

I expressed my sorrow at his loss. I remembered her smile.

'Look Herschel, I'm on my way with food to a hungry relative. He's old and infirm. The fighting is keeping him a prisoner in his own house.'

'I sympathize. You can be on your way as soon as your errand is complete. Desperate times, desperate measures.'

A rush of bullets rattled against the area around the windows. Some found their way into the room and buried themselves into whatever they hit. One had glanced off the barrel of the rough-guy's rifle and scored its way along his right cheek. He swore roundly and was quickly covered in blood. He let off a few angry shots at the street before coming back into the room to grab an old towel which he held to his face. Someone lit him a Gitane which he drew on hard. He held the smoke in while giving me the once-over. He then released smoke as he asked, 'Has he been told what to do?'

'Not yet.' Herschel spoke a little nervously, I guessed, to the leader.

'Can he do it, you reckon?'

'Good runner on the pitch.'

'Not the same. Not the same.'

I was angry at these two, speaking of me in my presence.

'I survived Auschwitz, the Long March and Belsen.'

The rough man held the towel to his face. His dark eyes blazed with deep passion which momentarily twinkled and a half-held smile moved his mouth.

'That was a few years ago, laddie, who knows, peace time might have softened you up.'

They'd won; I was now anxious to prove myself to these suicidal lunatics, who had my admiration, and my time. I took a deep swig from the vodka bottle.

'What's required?'

'We've lost contact with more of our group who are supposed to be down there by the city-hall gates, but it's gone quiet. We need to know if they're okay and what they can tell us about Russian numbers. Your job, laddo, is to find out what's going on and come back and tell us.'

'Is that all? May I have another swig of that vodka?'

'Sure, help yourself, we've got crates of the stuff downstairs. Pour some on this towel will you?'

With Uncle Cohn's parcel and a half-empty vodka bottle tucked under my shirt and zipped in under my bomber jacket, I later followed Herschel down the ornate staircase of this grand old building to the double doors to the street. Two armed men at the door stood back at Herschel's nod.

'Hurry back, Ernest.'

He carefully opened one of the two large doors and peered out at the street. He held me back at arm's length. Then suddenly, '*Go!*'

I started away. He called out to me, bringing on the laughter of the two men with him, 'Don't get shot dead or it will be the worse for you.'

The Russian fire had been unremitting and came from several points, but mainly from the two streets this building cornered. From the looks on the faces of those holed up there behind me, fixed sharply in my recall, they knew it was just a matter of time before they would be evicted by a tank shell, but maybe, just maybe, the boys at city-hall gates had an answer. Back there in the last hours, from a well-tuned radio, the Voice of America serenaded them with 'Heartbreak Hotel', 'Long Tall Sally', and 'My Blue Heaven'. Heart pounding, Uncle Cohn's food parcel under my jacket, safe, if a little bent, under a hail of bullets I crouch-ran across the main road. Getting to the other side, I flattened myself against the town-hall wall. From where I was pinned, I could see faces at the garret window, one of them frantically waving me forward, so I thought. If I wasn't so scared, I'd have given him the single finger, American-style. As I reached the gates, from a doorway a large heavy-set Russian officer reached out and grabbed me, hauling me into the porch of a tall apartment building; maybe the frantic wave had meant this. Terror of death changed to terror of the living. With big paw-like hands, he shook me until my teeth rattled and Uncle Cohn's food parcel dropped to the floor along with the vodka bottle which didn't smash, though the parcel broke open, scattering its contents at our feet.

'They're for a starving relative.' I spoke in German as there was more chance of him understanding this than Hungarian. He nodded gravely as he checked me top-to-toe for a weapon.

'You're damned lucky we haven't got more time for you. I'm confiscating the vodka.'

He spoke in hesitant German, but I got the message.

He watched gravely as I gathered up the family gift from the black-and-white tiled floor. He then pushed me past a group of soldiers at the ready, along a hallway and out into a yard where eight or nine Hungarian lads and girls were lying face-down, then pushed me through a gate into a back alley. I was dispensable. He shook his head and said something about 'Yiddish loony', but I didn't care, I was out of it, my killer curiosity had nearly proved so, but I was clear.

Not so clear. It was now late into the afternoon. Time had been concertinaed, though each event remained its own little island within the flurry and the fighting. In deserted streets there was no one to ask safe directions. Gunfire could be heard in every direction, plus more powerful stuff; maybe tanks, maybe bazookas. That apocalyptic dread, the waking dream that had haunted me since childhood had once again taken centre-stage. It came as little surprise then that the theatre should make an appearance.

Alone and fed up, worried over my family, knowing they would be worried over me, I had my head down. I became lost in a city I thought I knew. These streets, known by style, unfamiliar in location. Seemingly from nowhere, a big, heavy figure of a man lumbering forward, distressed and out of breath. I didn't need to take a second look. This was Bessenyei Ferenc, one of Hungary's most celebrated actors. He paused in front of me and spoke not to me, but at me.

'There are rotten Russians absolutely everywhere,' he panted. 'Can't go anywhere without being shot at. All I want is to get home, but oh no, like an idiot I am forced to run round and round in circles since this morning. Not a chance, not a chance. Look at me, I am on the verge of collapse.'

Still gasping for breath, he lumbered on past me before I had a chance to sympathize or to tell him I was in the same boat. However, the waking dream had afforded me a brush with fame on an empty Budapest street; another little island in the madness.

After making it safely through a few streets, I finally stumbled out into the familiar and was face-to-face with the Dohany synagogue. I worked my way round the magnificent exterior, trying every door and knocking on every window, but wisely perhaps, the place was shut; so I made my way into the Jewish quarter. I ran the length of Wesselenyi Street. On my way an elderly woman leaning out of her window, shouted down to me.

'Don't go near the Palace picture house, you'll be killed.'

No sooner had she pulled her head back in behind a closing window than the bullets began to fly. I wasn't the target, but the stuff was coming in all directions. I ducked, and continued running. I turned a corner into a sudden eruption of Russian heavy weaponry. A building behind me took a direct hit, its rococo fascia crumbling into a deep scar and smashed windows. I found temporary shelter in an elegant doorway close by Kertesz Street and had to crouch in a corner, the gunfire much more intense than previously. It was getting darker, the day's rain clouds continued to scud restlessly in the fading light.

A whining bullet ricocheted its way to the floor in front of me where it spent the rest of its force, spinning at my feet as I held my breath and prayed a little. In the half-light, I noticed a figure limping along my side of the street, and making for my little shelter. A girl in a light-blue tracksuit struggled into the doorway and fell against me, her right foot soaked in blood from a bullet wound. Fighting back tears, she grabbed my hands and gripping them tight, groaned and tried to crouch down. I helped her.

'What on earth are you doing out in this?'

She winced back.

'I could ask you the same. I was looking for my father. He's with the resistance at the Palace ... hold me ... thanks. Name's Helen. You?'

'Ernest. I'm taking food to a hungry relative. Your foot needs immediate attention. We have to get help.'

'I should not have left the last doorway. I just knew I was going to be hit. Yet I went.'

She was crying with the pain, darkness had fallen, and the shooting was less frequent. First course of action, ring the doorbell. With not much hope of a response, I pressed the bell a few times. Almost afraid to hope, eventually we heard some movement behind the large solid door. To our great relief, it opened a little. His name, we later learned, was Varga. Being the house warden and quite frail, it had taken the ageing gentleman a while to get to the door. What did we want? I pointed to Helen's foot.

'My friend needs help now.'

Varga was understandably agitated.

'Follow me.'

We moved through the house by torchlight. Every so often, Varga turned round to see if we were okay. We reached his apartment at the far end of the ground floor. He lit the gaslight, which revealed a nineteenth-century parlour in all its heavy dark wood and damask.

She had my full attention. In the glow of the gaslight, dark hair haloed, her full blue eyes had left tear-streaks down the lower half of a truly beautiful face, pale, tired, expressing pain. But those tears had only managed to cloud a presence that came from an inner peacefulness untouched by the madness outside and beyond. Varga had vanished into another room. Helen and I stood in the middle of his parlour taking each other in, unable to move, unable to speak. Varga quickly reappeared with a basin of steaming water that smelled of some kind of disinfectant. Cloth over his arm, tall, gaunt, slightly bowed with a kindly air, he gave the appearance of a headwaiter at some pre-war restaurant.

With my help, Mr Varga gently removed Helen's socks and tracksuit bottoms. With the blood gently flannelled away, a swelling on her foot showed the bullet's outline lodged just under the skin along from the small toe in the edge of the sole. The shock was beginning to show. She leaned back on Varga's sofa shivering, with the tears reappearing in her eyes. The corners of her mouth quivered. Even in the urgency of the moment, our eyes held. I was entranced by this injured angel. Varga took the bloody bowl back through to his kitchen. I broke our stare, I couldn't help myself; her legs, like the rest of her, were beautiful. I part-pretended to be concerned about her foot, as I truly was, but she saw through this and struggled out a smile.

'You like my legs?'

I coloured up.

'I like your legs.'

She smiled through a wince.

'I like your eyes.'

Varga returned with the bowl refilled, this time with ice-cold water to help numb Helen's foot. He got her to place her foot in the bowl as he unwrapped a Gillette blade.

'Don't be afraid my dear, I was a medical orderly in the Great War, I know what to do here. Young man, you must hold her leg, or she will flinch and I need you to hold it and the foot, to prevent too much movement ... clear?'

I nodded. He told Helen to lift her leg from the bowl, he wiped the foot dry, gestured me forward. I crouched beside the sofa and took hold of her leg. The contact was electric. My body came alive with the feel of her, the fine porcelain look, the texture of her skin. It was too much.

'You'll need to hold me tighter than that when he starts.'

I blushed again. Varga rubbed alcohol along the wound. She looked to me as if to say 'help' as he made a quick-sure incision in her skin, three, four centimetres maybe, out from which popped the bullet which fell harmless to the floor. Though she had tensed, Helen had not flinched, but I had created finger marks around her lower calf and ankle. We all sighed with relief as the bullet hit the floor.

'You can let go now Ernest.'

I released her reluctantly. Our smile was mutual.

'Ouch.'

Varga was dabbing the open cut with alcohol before expertly dressing the wound and applying the bandage.

Over a glass of wine a little later, Helen and I toasted Mr Varga, who smiled modestly when he was hailed as a wonderful human being.

'We must leave soon.' Helen shocked us.

'No, you must rest that foot', Varga was adamant. 'Besides, I don't want to lose my patient to the Russians so soon. There is an empty apartment in the basement, a little cold, but I will lend you an oil fire.'

We sat side-by-side on the edge of a creakily sprung bed, topped by an ancient mattress that smelled and felt damp. Varga afforded us a blanket each, and these we had wrapped around our shoulders. Through a window looking out on to the steps from basement to street, a waxing moon gave us light.

'Strange how his generosity didn't extend to food.' Helen snuggled closer. 'That stove is going to take all night to warm this room. Ernest, I'm ravenous. Let's risk the street.'

'Walk round the room.'

She tried and didn't make halfway.

'You must rest up until the morning.'

'Okay, but only if you ask Varga for some food; and see if my tracksuit bottoms are dry.'

'They won't be. Have my blanket.'

Here, my conscience took a holiday. Uncle Cohn's food parcel started to press against my chest like a living thing; maybe it was my heartbeat. Ernest the rat, Ernest the seducer, Ernest, Helen's knight in dubious armour.

'There is food. I have food. You asked what I was doing out in the middle of a battle. I'm taking food across the city to an old relative. I should be there now but I was stupid. I wanted to see what was going on.'

She snuggled closer.

'We can't eat his food. Can we?'

'We can if I double back in the morning and get fresh. Already this food has seen too much action. It should go.'

Her smile was conspiratorial.

'Should I worry? This will be Jewish food, yes? Kosher, yes?'

She had me worried.

'I'm Christian. Will I die after eating it?'

'Worse. You'll go mad.'

Laughing, we spread the food across the mattress and ate equal shares, smiling like idiots, my eyes straying from her face to her legs, now displaying coyly from under my blanket. Her hand reached out in the semi-dark and brushed tenderly my face. My whole being became warm, my heartbeat rose. A deep sense of privilege met my lust in a confused whirlpool.

In a moment, the feast had disappeared. The last pickle shared our tooth-marks until it too vanished into memory, just as the Russian tank lumbered down the road outside. Helen looked up and toward the window: 'Nikita's calling card. I hope Pa's okay.'

'Helen, the resistance can't hold out forever, even on home ground.'

'I know. War on civilians, this century's contribution to human history.'

'D'you still carry the card?'

'Torn up.'

She said this in part-anger, part-guilt: 'My socialism is my heartbeat, and this is breaking my heart. It is a betrayal. I had so much hope when Rakosi was booted out.'

'I fear the future is not good for Nagy. For him, prison or death.'

She pursed her lips.

'We get ourselves a halfway decent leader, one who maybe the world can respect, and the little fat man sits on him. I hate the Russians; they never have understood socialism. They only respect tyrants and bureaucrats. Born slaves. An ideal is lost on them.'

Her beautiful eyes shone with passionate anger in the moon's pale light.

'While good socialists have to duck and run,' I observed.

'Or stand and fight. How come you didn't go to Israel when the war ended?'

'I did briefly. Somehow, though, I was stuck with Budapest. I love this place, in spite of all. During the war years, my faith drained away and the communist ideal appeared to be a secular faith with tangible ends.'

'Like any belief in the hands of the wrong people, it becomes a spectre, a shadow of the real thing. So you returned to Judaism.'

'Redoubled.'

She looked me in the eyes.

'God's going to get us out of here in one piece in the morning.' The effect of her ironic remark lingered.

'He's got us this far.' I ventured.

She touched my face, leaned across the tiny distance between us and brushed my lips with hers.

'Until the morning, I guess we're on our own time.'

A second tank rumbled and rattled past the window. The house shook to its vibration. Lips lingered. My thoughts raced; she was much younger than me, yet in her generation, mature, free of the constraints handed down to me, forward and open, not yet fenced in by the world's madnesses, not yet completely disillusioned. I wanted to be 20 again, 30 was too old. In the ten years lay a thousand. I felt ancient but my passion for her was growing as was an ambition to know her beyond this accidental night. On that rough old bed, those beautiful legs wound round me and those beautiful eyes drowned me in her soul as the blankets, from time to time, found their way to the floor.

Dawn discovered us awake and dressed. The sweet dream had been broken into at times during the hours of darkness by the crackle of small-arms fire. Varga was also awake and handed Helen her dry tracksuit bottom. Together as a couple, we said our goodbyes and profuse 'thank yous' to Mr Varga, who stood alone in the doorway watching us down a silent street to the main thoroughfare, Kiraly Street, where gunfire was sporadic, forbidding. But we needed to go that way. Helen hobbled a bit, complaining that with the bandage inside the shoe it was hard to walk, and painful. Progress was slow. We turned into Kiraly and came up against a small group of people all waiting for a lull in the fighting. It came, and all of us made a dash for the other side of the street. A mortar shell suddenly whistled by and exploded in the street a little way ahead of us. It scattered the crowd, and when I reached the opposite pavement, Helen had gone from my sight. More shells landed, creating panic and sending masonry flying through the air. I ran for shelter behind the synagogue. In a later lull I went looking for her. She was gone, the small crowd, gone. I stood in the settling dust of my dream, caught up in a huge knot of despair. I looked to the sky from whence came no inspiration.

I returned home, and my reappearance was greeted with much delight. Fresh food was prepared for Uncle Cohn and delivered directly by me with, this time, no detours. The old fellow fell on the food parcel with relish and gratitude. For him, for days, it had been bread, water and blackcurrant juice, so the sight of salt beef, rye bread, pickles, fruit, coffee and chocolate delighted Cohn to tearful thanks and a loving hug for me. I didn't let on that he could have had the food twenty-four hours sooner but for the deliverer wandering about an urban war zone.

1958

Visegrad is a beautiful town edging the Danube. A holiday, just for me, to look at new sights, rest up, eat a little, drink some and just be. A cab from the station to the hotel, bags unpacked, a shower with knocking pipes and a gigantic metal head yielding a warm trickle. Still, the view from my room to the river was more than pleasing. I took an afternoon stroll. The riverside walk was enchanting, with children having the run of the banks and splashing around the water's edge. I began to feel the mild frustration that comes from being still young, still single, but wanting something of what was happening around me. A partnership, children, a black dog shaking off river water on passers-by, even. The late afternoon heat was a little oppressive. Down to shirtsleeves, I made my way back.

On the way, in the same tree-lined street as my hotel, was a guesthouse with a volleyball court. A game was in progress. I paused to watch. Two couples were deep in their cheerful competition. My heart leapt. Helen. Her back to me, her rich voice calling and laughing.

The night in Budapest thundered back. The world was suddenly blotted out, my brain became chaotic. I stood alone and, slowly, the world returned. The warm afternoon light bathed and blessed the beautiful Helen, in a heaven-sent glow. It had been love at first sight in that dark doorway in November 1956, and here was the woman who had been the injured girl, the angelic 20-year-old student, whose strength surprised me and impressed Varga when he removed that impudent bullet.

It wasn't until 'game over', and I walked toward the little group busy towelling their faces, that she noticed me:

'Ernest.'

She dropped the towel and rushed to me the last few steps between us. A long embrace, a kiss to both cheeks and in her husky voice, lower than I recalled: 'I can't believe it's you.'

She released me and swung round to face her interested group.

'Everyone, meet Ernest Lowy, my shining knight of 1956. He saved my foot, maybe my life.'

An interrupting voice: 'I thought that was me.'

A young man stepped forward and took my hand. Helen showed little embarrassment.

'Ernest. This is Leci, my husband. This is Hanna my sister, and her friend from England, William.'

I mumbled something through my shock, exchanged pleasantries through a voice strangled with emotional pain while Helen went ahead and explained the reason for her excitement. I smiled on through this agony. Married, how could she? How dare she without consulting me first about how I might feel? She didn't come looking. She must have known I'd be looking for her. This lack of reason blocked my attention, but I picked up enough to know I'd been invited to meet up with them later. I suggested the bar at my hotel. It was agreed.

Leci led the party into the bar, his hand outstretched to grab mine and give it a good shake, slightly over-hearty in his manner. Small in stature, slender and very boyish, he didn't look at all the orthopaedic surgeon, but it had been he who had taken over and repaired my injured darling. His reward? Her. My inner-self ruefully shook its head and waded around in the shallows of irony and self-deception, still sifting the wreckage of denial.

'... when the explosions started, I ran back to the pavement. I fell against my foot which buckled under me. I tried to hobble back to Mr Varga's house, but blood was flowing out through the bandage from the bullet wound. I fell a second time, and passed out. Next thing I knew, I was in the sidecar of a motorbike pulling up at Leci's hospital and then bundled into a ward to be treated by this man.'

Helen's voice was a joy to hear. It seemed deeper than before. Sexy, ever that.

'A terrible fortnight,' Leci reflected, 'I was in at the deep-end as a junior doctor. The time since then has felt like a vacation by comparison.'

Hanna leant across the table to take some matches from William and lit a cigarette. She smiled at Leci, and spoke to me: 'We think he kept her in longer than necessary. Waited on her hand-and-foot, so to speak.'

The evening dragged on cheerfully. I was lost and Helen realized this, her concerned look came my way more than once as the amiable chatter took us away from one another more certainly than death. A few glasses of good wine and we were all firm friends. I couldn't tell from the way he was whether Helen had told Leci the whole story. Emotionally I felt he should know, be made aware of my importance to her, not just some passing acquaintance. The adolescent in me wanted to bend the conversation so that I could make this known or at least acknowledged, but the man in his thirties knew a lost cause when he felt one. So why do damage for the sake of it?

They took their leave late with kisses all round and hugs from the men. Helen held me tight.

'You have our address in Budapest. Please call.'

She drew back and said quietly as the others made for the door: 'I like your eyes.'

'Yours too, but I *adore* your legs.'

We laughed. As she reached the door she turned, gave me a lingering look, and was gone. We both knew we would never again see each other. I left Visegrad the following morning.

21 Platforms and Farewells

October 1956 saw the uprising against the Russians and the consequent military suppression of an entire population. Many made the border to get the hell out for good. Shortly after my beautiful adventure with Helen, and a little after the Russians had put paid to resistance, I crashed on my motorbike, hurting my ankle. The bike survived but I had a limp for a while. Budapest was in bits yet again; bullets, shells and mortars had scarred the city. It was scattered debris that brought me off the bike on my way to work.

One evening, I was late back from work. My mother was home, the smell of her cooking brought on the realization how little I had eaten during the day. I kissed Therezia and sat at my place, the food was there instantly.

'No Max?'

'No. He's out playing with his communists.'

No approval from my mother on that front.

'Your friend's here.'

I looked around. 'Friend? What friend?'

'The country girl.'

'Her name is Yetta, Mother. You've known it for six years. She in the back room?'

She folded her arms. 'I fed her. You were late. She's upstairs, probably asleep in your bed. Why can't you find a girlfriend who lives a little closer?'

She didn't know about Gizella. Gizella, a divorced flame who, ten years older, was showing me life. Yetta didn't know about her either. The daughter of a well-known and respected rabbi, Yetta lived a half-day train ride away. I hadn't been expecting her. Therezia had not liked Yetta from day one.

With huge eyes, pretty lips, dark hair and a ready laugh, she was very direct, sometimes carelessly rude, although always managing to be friendly. There was an edge to her conversation that didn't sit well with her elders. In that, she was typical of the new young. I found myself between the generations, belonging to neither camp and often winding up the referee in tussles that were to do with outlook and attitude.

Yetta and my mother rubbed each other up the wrong way. I had met her at a Budapest theatre in 1950, and our relationship had bumped along to the present. Though we shared a lot of interests, which kept us very close, the question of marriage never really came up. Two bosses under one roof didn't appeal to either of us. I once joked, 'I will never marry you. After a fortnight, you'll be calling me a fool.'

She replied with a sweet smile: 'Wrong. A week.'

With Therezia playing policeman, and her ongoing disapproval filling the house with sulphur, that night I slept on the sofa, well away from the country girl.

The following morning found us walking the rubble-strewn streets in the uneasy quiet of a wary, damaged Budapest. What Yetta had to tell me was not for my mother's ears. Her brother and sister had joined a group of young people who had decided to make a break for freedom. Would I come along? She was genuinely fond of me, but I think that she knew, for me, this was more than just the challenge of making it across the border. Family bonding was very tight. Therezia would be virtually on her own and this created conflict in me. Not to mention my affection for Gizella.

My brother Karl had been the first to leave Budapest. He went in 1948 after an offer to become cantor at Queen's Park in Glasgow, Scotland. Remarried, he also underwent a name change to become Charles. In the early 1950s, Lillie followed suit, and with Andre went to live in Munich where they made a good life for themselves. Half-heartedly, I agreed to go along with Yetta and the gang. After a train ride to a point near the Austrian border, we split up into twos and threes. I was moving too slowly, my damaged ankle causing pain and limiting mobility severely. Yetta cursed my motorbike but loyally stayed by my side. A patrol caught us and we were kept at a police station under Russian guard overnight. Though very gruff, the Russians seemed almost friendly. We were fed, and locked up together. We guessed that the others must have made it into Austria.

'Tomorrow, they will release us. We'll try again.'

Yetta's enthusiasm was undiminished. I had second, third, thoughts.

'I can't.'

'What?'

'My ankle is hurting too much.'

She laughed at this: 'What are you saying? We've made it this far, it's just a few more kilometres.'

I avoided her challenging stare. Quickly, I added, 'I can't leave my mother. Who will look after her?'

'Max? Else? Suddenly, it's your mother. That didn't matter until now. Come on Ernest, I understand about Therezia, but you can get her out later. What about us? You and me?'

What about us? She had nailed the problem. Had my love been total, Krushchev himself with a sub-machine gun would not have stopped me making the border with her. As it was, I sat shame-faced and guilty in one corner of the holding room while Yetta stormed across to the other side, and sat, arms folded, by the door, where she waited out the night with a grim expression, barely blinking.

After we were released the following morning, we found Yetta's brother and sister drinking coffee at a café in the small border village. We sat in silence. The day was cold, and snow looked likely, but Yetta was determined.

'We go again today.'

Her brother and sister were used to obeying her. Though we all found her sharp approach hard to take, she had a fix on truths about us that we found uncomfortable, as she levered us into position to follow instruction.

'Ernest?'

'Sorry, Yetta, no. I can't.'

'Can't or won't?'

'Whatever.'

'It's not your ankle. Or your mother. Whatever or *whoever* it is, stay if you want. We're going.'

They moved out, leaving me to stare at my coffee cup and later to wait the best part of the day at the small station to catch a connection to Budapest. They, in the meantime, put some distance between themselves and the village; then, in deep country, dodged the patrols and jumped the border. They got as far as New York, a pond where the Yetta fish could swim easily. Back in Budapest, my first port of call was Gizella's apartment.

Our relationship had lasted four years. It wasn't going anywhere, but it pleased us. Though Christian, she had been disturbed by the rash of anti-Semitism reoccurring in Hungary, so was always glad to see me turn up at her door in one piece. I found in her a maturity and worldly wisdom lacking in many of the younger women, and though a social-ist, she had never swallowed any party dictum whole-heart-edly. In her company I could escape the conflicts that raged around and inside me, and relax on neutral ground. That night, Gizella and Beethoven assuaged the pain of my guilt and my ankle. I could put revolution and escape on to the back-burner for a day or two.

The social convulsions went on, and we bobbed along trying not to drown in the sea of confusion and change. Communism, Canute-like, resisted the tide of liberation, both mental and social, finding itself up to its nose in rising waters as it gurgled its last gasps of authoritarian Marxist-Leninism. It had fulfilled a purpose, had its place in history, its contribu-tion hard to exaggerate. But it had been hijacked by members of a dying breed of tyrants that the twentieth century could no longer tolerate. The process of overthrowing their twenty-first century, slightly diluted counterparts still goes on. People-power has been realized and successfully applied without the polluting interference of a Stalin or a Hitler, and, where ambitious, crooked men and women hold temporary sway, they are more quickly found out and exposed. Millions are still at risk or dying, but the century knows it cannot endure unless universal franchise is achieved.

Religion became more important than politics to me as I could contribute to the one but not the other. With such good voice training from Kato Phluger and others, I was indeed singing for my supper. The only remaining conflict was whether to go towards opera or combine cantorial activity with rabbinical studies. Meantime we all kept our heads down and tried to maintain normality. One thing was very clear, though; I should have tried to cross the border with Yetta, my alibis being my mother and secretly, Gizella. The truth was I had, to some extent, become my father in his hanging on, waiting for change. I loved Budapest; damaged as she was, there was still much of beauty to admire. In spite of periodic eruptions of anti-Semitism, I had managed to perform the mental gymnastics necessary to make a bubble of self-delusion and carry on as though I were immune. My relationship with Gizella helped. However, the bubble inevitably burst, compelling me to leave Hungary at any price.

In 1957, my sister Else remarried and was able to move to Glasgow. Soon after, my mother obtained a tourist visa to visit her, and never returned. Max was out of it with his political life, and I wouldn't see him for weeks on end. The family had gone, effectively. Apart from Max, I was by myself. I had a wide circle of friends and colleagues in and out of the Jewish community and would have stayed to develop my life, but for two close calls.

The first brought back the days of bullying in Bratislava, when Munky and I were young lads. Winter 1956. There had been a football match at the Nep stadium in Budapest. The winning team was MTK, a team traditionally supported by Jews. Walking home from the stadium, I was made aware of a group of men behind me. The catcalls started:

'Stinking Jews.'

'No wonder you support MTK, you're all fucking cheats together.'

I stepped up my pace, but one of them ran up behind me and grabbed my hat. I reached out for it and he held it just out of my grasp for a few moments, then finally chucked it into the gutter on the opposite side of the street where passing cars splashed water in its direction.

'Fetch boy, on you go.'

Suddenly I was back at a match with Munky or just walking home from school. Alarm bells were ringing loudly in my soul. This was going to be a repeat. Fascism lay dormant in the hearts and minds of ill-educated and gross people, readily awakened by the educated, then cynically used as a political tool. I was not going out as a Jewish statistic in another pogrom or worse, a revival of the Shoah. I consequently started a five-year battle with bureaucrats to secure a visa, a persistent quest to obtain the necessary papers to leave the country.

The second incident happened in January 1961 and was, if anything, worse than the bullyboys in that it was sneaky, underhand and quite, quite unexpected. I had been on holiday in the beautiful mountains around Mecsek where I had met a delightful Christian girl from Budapest, Magda; a porcelain-skinned blonde full of laughter and pleasure with life at large. We decided to return to Budapest together. The train was full, and though we were able to find her a seat by the window, I had to stand beside the door. Wearing my *yarmulke*, it was pretty evident it was a Jew who had taken to leaning heavily against the door of the crowded carriage, a door which swung unexpectedly open. I grabbed out at a handle which saved me. There were shocked exclamations and expressions of concern as I hauled myself back in. I reached out once more to shut the carriage door which clicked reliably shut. I checked it when shut. It wasn't about to open unless by hand. The two men opposite looked uncomfortable as our eyes met. The one nearer the door made some remark about my being lucky there and the young lady should be relieved not to lose me. My immediate recollection was of the powerful drag of the air-stream as the train sped through the countryside with me dangling as the door swung wildly. A low trick covered by embarrassed smiles.

Word came from Charles (Karl) that Mother was ailing. She had been moved to London from Glasgow to be with him at his new Hampstead post. I won my little battle with bureaucracy – though it felt like a minor miracle. I was allowed a tourist passport valid for two months. 1961 and summer was on its way.

JUNE 1961

Sunday morning. After a good deal of farewell toasting and a sleepless night, I waited, packed and restless, for the cab to take me to the station. It was fifteen minutes late. I had to make the 9:05, no choice. With eyes that had been staring into the darkness, and had seen the daylight begin hours before, I peered out, looking for the car which finally turned into the street and pulled up at the door. I had given up trying to sleep at five, was packed by six and ready to go. This damned cabbie was going to make me late, God forbid, miss the train and wreck my life. While I had been waiting for the taxi, I had noticed a young couple in a doorway opposite my apartment, deep in a kiss, his hand in her blouse, her unattended bag at her feet, both of them oblivious to the glances of passers-by. With the apartment locked, I hurried into the street to throw myself into the cab. Down and slightly breathless, I looked out the cab window to the couple. The kiss continued unabated. My last view of the neighbourhood was this intense moment of sweetness.

'9:05 you say. Big maybe.'

The large frame of the cabbie leaned round slightly my way, as he swung the vehicle into light morning traffic.

'Clutch is slipping. My partner does nights. Not only was he late getting the car to me this morning, he's ridden the clutch into the ground at last. He's been told, but what can you do? I'm going to have to have it fixed. I can't run this all day. I'll need to get someone out on a Sunday, that'll cost. And on my working day. Pray we get there in time.'

I growled back: 'No, you pray. If we don't make it, I'll have your badge.'

He was easy: 'Don't worry, we'll get there. Vienna train, eh? Going for long?'

'A while.'

'If I were you, I'd keep going. What's to come back for?'

I reflected: 'I've got memories, good and bad.'

He laughed: 'Good I could carry around in a thimble. Forget '56, forget the Russians. November 1944. The building I lived in was surrounded by Arrowcross looking for Jews to kill. My lucky day. Nobody in that building knew that I had two Jewish grandmothers, otherwise ...'

He ran his finger side to side under his chin.

'And these were my fellow countrymen. Insolent. They're still the same. They worship killers and tyrants promiscuously like whores. And they destroy clutches. All you have to do with a clutch is nurse it through medium revs when moving off, then let it go evenly. You don't sit there powering it up at bite, then have your foot on it all day. I've watched him do it.'

By this time my nerve ends were jumping. Slowly, slowly to the station. Not his fault, but I wanted to strangle him. Somehow when we arrived there was time to spare. Our eyes met properly when I paid him off and his eyes danced merrily as he wished me well:

'Remember what I said. Go anywhere else. Just keep going. Enjoy the future. No extra charge for the good advice.'

It was perhaps obvious to him that I had no intention to return. A new fare jumped into the cab and he was off with a wave. Max met me and took my case. He walked me quickly into the station hall where my waiting train had its engine rumbling, the smell of diesel fumes intercepting the deep sense of time and place which threatened to overtake me as I walked toward the self-same platform at Keleti station from which the Germans and Hungarian army herded us on to the cattle trucks, destination Auschwitz. This day, faces I knew

303

were waiting for me. I looked at Max who grinned broadly: 'We had such a good time last night, it seemed a shame to end the party. So ...'

I looked around this happy group. Some were from the café crowd, one or two from the choir, a nice young trainee rabbi and his girlfriend. And my close pals. They came bearing gifts, some brought food and drink for the journey. I was shocked and delighted by it all. Tears began to form. A tap on the shoulder. Gizella. Her embrace was warm and all-enveloping. She thrust a large parcel into my hands. It smelled appetising.

'Schnitzel, darling. Fresh-made at dawn for my angel.'

If she as much as hinted that she wanted me to stay, at that moment I would have stopped everything there and then. She was, to me, Budapest: 'Come home when you are ready, my darling.'

She released me and Max grabbed me in a bear hug.

'Who is she, dark horse?'

'Mind your own business.'

He laughed gently into my ear, then suddenly I was on the train and they, the other side of the glass, on the platform. I was alone in my compartment, looking out on the boisterous group cheering me on. Not one person in our 'goodbyes' had offered a hint of reproach that I was leaving, though I'm certain they knew this time it would be for good; the presents, the tears and cheers had finality. A conspiracy of knowing and knowing not. With the compartment window down, I maintained some kind of conversation until the whistle blew and the train began to move. My last view as the platform curved was of Max waving, and Gizella blowing me a kiss.

The train heaved and rolled as it slowly made its way out from the station and crossed lines to its eventual track. Alone in the compartment and therefore not drawn away from it, I watched the city unfold in bright sunshine. Moving slowly, the train glided past apartment blocks, past working yards Sunday-quiet, past some rough housing due for the wrecking ball and the newer, ugly, tall constructions going up to house those without a roof; or with a roof deemed by Kardar not fit for a citizen of the communist model, in the new Hungary. It was this from which I was recoiling, not the housing of the masses, though my eyes were offended by what seemed to be termite hills rather than places of social development. The offence lay in the attempt to make us all, Jews and Gentiles alike, into parrots repeating a secular doctrine, where uniformity of thought closed the doors on variety and difference. We were all meant to live in peace inside a social philosophy so deeply flawed, so open to contradiction within itself, and massive corruption. The communist ideal percolated through Lenin from Marx, had been twisted this way and that by those anxious to placate a killer tyrant. Stalin had died, and with him had gone that 'golden age' of the Soviets. Though cracks had appeared well before he finally went, under people like Bulganin and latterly Krushchev, the cracks had become fissures and, were it not for the nuclear threat, the ridiculous behaviour of Kruschev would be laughed off the world's stage. He held Hungary's leadership, like every other state under the Soviet umbrella, by the gonads. Time for me to go.

The train quickened its pace, as did my apprehension. I was cutting myself off from my friends, though the family had largely gone elsewhere, as the writing had been on the wall a while. 'But face it, Ernest, you are Leopold's son; you still feel like hanging around in spite of the regime. Why?' Suddenly the train was alongside the Danube and I began to fill up. My tears flowed freely for all I had left behind: my dear, dear friends, the beautiful city that somehow rose above the machinations of those who would bruise and despoil. Budapest, Gizella. I wiped my eyes and reached into my case for a book. The rhythm of the train wheels against the track as it speeded up fell into a faster tempo. It wasn't long before my sleepless night turned the printed page into a grey mass, and my eyes drooped.

I woke with a start. The train was hammering through farmland. My eyes felt gritty. Checking my watch, my Gizella watch, a birthday gift. It told me eleven thirty. I had slept soundly, but it would be a while to Vienna, and we had yet to cross the border. God willing, my guilty look would be seen as crafty young Jew out for a good time, not making a break for long-term freedom, my face being a road map to my character.

Gyor. A medium-sized place. I looked out; a fair number of people got on and off. Nobody wanted my carriage. I continued to lean from the window as the train left, until the air pressure caused by the movement made me draw in my head. I turned to face the empty compartment, thinking to try another, less dry book. Before reaching for my case, I thought to shut the carriage window as the speeding train was making something of a racket. Before I could turn, something large and hard hit me in the back of the head sending me buckled to the floor, clutching the area of pain that had sent my eyes into a darkness of deep red. Blood seeped through my fingers. On my knees, I felt immobilized for some moments. Eventually I made it back to my seat, still trying to regain my composure and work out what the hell had hit me from out of nowhere. I staunched the bleeding with a couple of handkerchiefs and my white scarf, regrettably. How had I been hit? I stretched out on the compartment bench seat, and moving my feet, something clattered to the floor. A sharp stone, golf-ball sized. A missile thrown up from the track, maybe, maybe some boy's lucky hurl from the bridge or embankment. It felt like a reproach. 'The very stones cry out.'

I stared blankly out at the passing scenery. My focus was attracted for no real reason to the passing telegraph poles which the brain could conjure into movement, the train to stillness. The distraction from the throbbing ache was only partial. However I explained this event even to myself, it had the elements of a 'tall story'. Try telling it to a border guard – and I was about to. The train had begun to slow down as we approached the Austrian border. It was a short while after stopping at Fertozenmiklos before the Hungarian border guard opened the compartment sliding door with a violent shove. Bang. They were here. Two of them, with special border-guard frowns.

'Papers. Nice smell. On your own?'

'Yes.'

The one not making demands saw the bloodstains.

'What happened to you?'

I held out the stone.

'It came through the open window and hit the back of my head.'

They looked at each other in response to the idiot's tale, their faces mutually impenetrable masks. My papers were in their hands. Were they going to question the notion of tourist, and suspect an escaper? I felt panic. The first guard broke the silence.

'No one attacked you?'

'Not in the way you mean. Honestly, it came through the window.'

'How come the window had been open?'

'I was leaning out at Gyor, having a look round.'

'Happened a while ago. How come they didn't get you between the eyes, if you were leaning out?'

Panic was turning to annoyance.

'The train was on its way. I'd come away from the window.'

'And your back was to it. What *is* that smell. Is it schnitzel?'

They both lingered over the papers. I sensed their mockery, but my future dangled in their hands. I fingered the stone, looked down at it and said; 'My being Jewish, you'll understand that I hope this will be the last knock-back I'll be getting from my beloved Hungary before crossing the border. Would you like some schnitzel?'

I'd said too much in the worry of the moment, but they laughed an indulgent border-guard laugh, handed me back my papers and took their leave, munching some of Gizella's schnitzel. A parting comment from the second guard.

'Get that head seen to Mr Lowy. Be careful, you're leaving the frying pan for the fire. Being Jewish, you'll get my drift.'

In a moment, they were gone. It was the normal delay at a

border stop. I got down from the train needing a drink. At the kiosk, in the queue, a hand on my shoulder.

'Step away from the queue please.'

I did. Two uniformed Austrian border guards. My heart leapt.

'Your papers.'

'They're in my jacket. On the train.'

'Come with us.'

I followed them into a station office.

'Sit down.'

I sat.

'No papers.'

'They're on the train. They've been seen and okayed.'

'By?'

'The Hungarian border guard.'

'Those illiterates. You could be showing them food coupons. How come you speak such good German? What happened to your head?'

'Please. I need to get back on the train. It will leave without me.'

The two Austrians smiled indulgently.

'It doesn't go without our say so. Answer the questions, then you can get back on the train.'

A mixture of fear, anger and loathing at the teasing humiliation I was being subjected to by all these border uniforms caused my body to shake. They continued their questioning.

'So the stone flew through the window and hit you on the back of the head. You sure you haven't been fighting? Then again, Jews are pacifists. Must be a message from the Almighty. I'd watch myself if I were you.'

All present in the small office, the two guards, a couple of clerks and a station official were enjoying the momentary return of my torment, my anxiety. It is strange how a smirk can ruin a face; the room had become a giant smirk, a self-contented wallow in a shared emotion that another 'Joe the Jew' was getting his deserts, although their hands were tied to go further and return to the halcyon days of terror and death.

This, officially, was as far as pushing the innocent could go. But it was something.

'We'll escort you on to the train, check your papers and you'll be free to wander the hills and roam the riversides.'

'In Vienna, there are even a few of your sort left to compare your experiences; but you'd know that, you're all related aren't you?'

We were through the door, across the platform and on to the train in moments, the stares of my fellow passengers following on, my embarrassment burned away by the deep loathing and contempt I felt for these victims of their own folly. When we reached the compartment: 'Nice smell in here. Schnitzell. Your papers are in order, Mr Lowy from Budapest. Don't separate yourself from them again. They are your lifeline. You never know, somebody might fancy passing himself off as an Hungarian Jew.'

His colleague chimed in: 'Not all Austrians hate Jews, remember that. The graveyards are full of neutrals.'

The two Austrians left the compartment laughing to themselves. I was left alone with all my limbs intact, my organs unsullied, my mental scars jangled but not re-opened, my soul was not bleeding. I had become toughened. I ate regularly. Their mistake.

The paper-checking went on down the carriages, while the diesel rumbled quietly away to itself. I had lowered the window and, like a curious boy, I watched events taking place along the platform. Suddenly, among the various groups and couples stepping at a quickened pace, a young woman, child in tow, was being escorted by a couple of rail officials to the platform. One gave her a final short push which she resisted bodily, giving them the darkest of looks as, turning, they briskly walked back, leaving her to fulminate and preen, to coddle the toddler and choose a compartment.

Mine.

I was relieved to see her get on further down. It was a long train, plenty of space. I relaxed until the moment my compartment door slid open. Her presence filled the doorway and flooded into the space between us. I recoiled mentally.

'Can you help?' She smiled across the space.

'Sure.' My reluctance came out as hesitancy.

She levered the half-sleeping toddler from her shoulder.

'Take Andriska and put him down there, I won't be able to. I'm getting cramp in my shoulder. Poor lamb needs to sleep. Careful with him, keep that blanket tight.'

Andriska was duly lowered sweetly, thumb in mouth; he grouched, rolled to one side and fell away to dreamland. I turned to help lift the cases onto the racks above the seats.

'I'm Magda.'

Another Magda, another blonde. This one a Magda of the incredibly short skirt, perfect legs, revealed underwear, tousled hair, pretty face, breasts that would, in time, hang low and make her middle-age appearance top-heavy and vulgar. But for now, however, she was a demanding, physical argument that would raise the heartbeat of most men and the competitive ire of most women. In some circles, a shocker. There was even an endearing touch to her appeal, provided by delicate, dark-framed glasses perched precariously on the end of a pretty nose. The ensemble was stunning, but she was in my space, I wanted alone. The train moved, we settled back opposite one another; the child stirred with the roll of the train and edged back into a peaceful slumber. Magda smiled sweetly and, in a quiet, slightly hoarse voice, began a conversation that would continue on and off until we reached Vienna.

'Those Hungarian bastards kept us waiting at the border for twenty-four hours. For nothing. Alleged irregularities with our papers. What do they mean? They never said. We had to spend the night on a hard bench. We've hardly eaten. If it wasn't for a nice German couple we wouldn't have had anything to drink either. Do you like Coca-cola? They gave me stacks. What's your name?'

'Lowy. Ernest Lowy.'

'From?'

'Budapest.'

'Nice to meet you, Ernest Lowy from Budapest. If you'll excuse me, I'm going to try for a little sleep.'

I hoped my relief was not obvious.

'By all means go ahead.'

As she raised herself onto the bench seat to curl up, my view along her lovely stockingless legs to her black-laced crotch was perfect as was the smooth line of her inner thighs. She was fully aware of the effect that she had on the helpless male eye and demurely made a token and hopeless attempt to 'cover-up'. She smiled across to me, winked, then closed her eyes. The train rolled on, her breathing slowed and her glasses threatened to fall to the carriage floor. I rescued them. She stirred and, with one eye opened, took them from me with murmured thanks, and slipped back into gentle sleep. For a while I read, then my eyes went. I remember thinking, looking out on the changing terrain, that Vienna wasn't far off. Sleep the rest then.

I woke. The train had stopped at Weiner Neustadt. Magda was standing over Andriska. She was giving him a little baby talk, and he was still murmur-sleepy. She showed no signs of leaving; I was to have this situation the rest of the way. She turned.

'Ah, you're awake, Ernest Lowy from Budapest. Train hasn't moved for twenty minutes. Just Baden to go though.'

Andriska stared across at me with baleful eyes. I smiled; he continued the unblinking thumb-sucking treatment on the strange dark man in the black clothes and the white shirt with bloodstains on the collar.

'This train's far too hot, don't you think?'

I had to disagree with her.

'Would you mind the window open just a little? Your schnitzell is a bit strong.'

I nodded an 'okay'. She moved her beautiful frame, just for me. I smelled perfume as she slipped past. Was she coming for me, or was this any man, anytime? She returned from the window and sat beside me, up close.

'Ernest, you're Jewish, yes?'

'Yes.'

Her voice became confiding, husky.

'I married Jewish, but I haven't taken the faith. Just as well. I've left him in Budapest. He had an affair with my best friend. While I was pregnant. We managed to patch that up for Andriska, but then he started with the insults. You know it's over when the insults start. Next stop, the violence. Well I wasn't going to hang around for bruises and broken bones.'

'I don't blame you.'

Her perfume was powerful. Her whole presence was overwhelming. Mentally, I was leaning to one side to escape; physically my entire side was subjected to soft force. Against my wishes, my groin was on the move.

'My mother's fault. She said marry Jewish. Jewish make good husbands. Him, anything but. Don't get me wrong Ernest, you seem okay. My boss back there was Jewish, one of the good guys. Had his faults, very ambitious and a bit greedy, a "get-rich-quicker than anyone-elser"; very typical in that respect. Had wandering hands too, still that kind of thing goes with the work territory these days. I am as they say, going back to Mama. My parents are in Vienna. She talked me into that stupid marriage, they can put us up until the divorce comes through.'

The train suddenly started to move. The jerk forward startled Andriska who started to cry. Magda rose to help the child. She smiled back at me over her shoulder, a winning smile. The impression of her lasted a fair few moments after she had settled back with the little one. I made an attempt at reading once more, periodically I looked up to find her staring at me with that sort of look which promises fun and trouble in equal measure.

At last, the train ambled into Vienna.

'Ernest, be an angel and help me down to the platform with the cases.'

Glad to be there, glad to help as this would be the last of this pushy young female I would have to endure. I helped her with her things then went back for my own. Reaching the platform, she kissed my cheek and apologized: 'Better not give you my parent's number with the divorce and everything that's going on. You got a number?'

'I'm staying with friends. I don't know theirs,' I lied.

'Pity. Oh, shit.'

'What is it?'

She looked distracted.

'My purse. It's not here, I must have left it on the train, at least I hope it's on the train. Be a darling, have a look for it. Andriska please, stay still there's a good boy. Leave your stuff there, Ernest. We'll guard it.'

I was quickly back into the compartment. No purse. No purse on the benches or the floor, or under the benches. She must have lost it elsewhere, or it was stowed in an elusive pocket. I returned to the platform. No Magda, no Andriska, just my case, but no briefcase, holder of private papers and crucially, my wallet. I had been conned, taken by a perfumed blonde and her little apprentice. My fury was total. My friend, Frank Lang, who had come to greet me, found me standing, shaking and white beside my case. I couldn't believe it.

'Frank, I don't believe this. Am I that stupid?'

'What did she take?'

'Briefcase. Wallet was inside it. I was worried about pickpockets'.

The desk sergeant was on the phone when we entered through the swing doors of the Railway Police office. He gave us a little wave of acknowledgement and continued his conversation. Finally, the phone went down and he looked up. Frank stepped in: 'My friend has been robbed.'

'Where?'

'On the platform where the Budapest train stopped.'

'Just after getting off the train,' I joined in.

'Can you give me a description of what was stolen, Mister ...'

'Lowy. My briefcase. Had my wallet in it.'

'Unfortunate. Much taken?'

'500 *pengo*, and some personal papers I would like returned.'

'See what we can do. Did you get a good look at the thief?'

'All the way from Fertozenmiklos. She shared the carriage compartment with me. She and her little boy.'

'Mane of blonde hair, glasses, tarty appearance?'

'Yes.'

'Magda! I thought we'd seen the last of her. So she's back. Sexy bitch, what? She's not the brightest, not a pro, just a confounded nuisance; an opportunist thief. We'll probably track her down, but don't hold out too much hope of getting your property back, certainly the money's away. Did she give you one of her close-up work-outs?'

I blushed to the roots and he laughed. Frank looked puzzled. I left my details with the sergeant who continued to chortle over the revelation. As we left the office, Frank asked: 'Close-up work-out?'

'Tell you over a coffee. I need a coffee, *now*.'

'Can I smell schnitzel?'

'*Coffee, now!*'

It is not just that the coffee is so different in Vienna, it is the atmosphere surrounding the ritual, the air of formality in leisure over what is after all a hot beverage. Yet for generations, through wars and social upheaval, Viennese café culture continues.

The decor of the coffee house Frank had chosen was true to the tradition, with its nineteenth-century wrought iron tables marble-topped, elaborate window frames with frosted decoration across the panes, huge floor tiles and street access for warmer days. The smell of almond and cherry drifted across the coffee smells, as sweet trolleys were rolled around by girls dressed in the neatest, cleanest, most demure black-and-white outfits. Frank and I sat by a window table looking out on the busy area around the station. The presiding male in the café, a giant bald man in his fifties wearing an apron so clean no stain dare land, brought us our coffees, some water and a big smile.

'My friend from Budapest, Willie – Ernest Lowy.'

'A pleasure. Your journey a good one?'

I managed to chuckle. Willie looked puzzled. Frank helped.

'A run-in with border guards, then he was robbed on the platform.'

'Such times, such times.' Willie shook his head and bent his large frame slightly my way. 'But now you are here, please, enjoy our beautiful Vienna.'

'I intend to, Willie.'

He took his leave. Frank and I settled back to enjoy the moment. I must have still been wearing a frown. Frank leaned across; he smelled of pipe tobacco, the tweed of his suit, along with some cologne I didn't recognize.

'Tomorrow, we'll go to the bank, get you what money you need.'

'You are a true friend. What would I have done but for your help?'

A sudden thought. I reached into the breast pocket of my shirt where I had placed some money as a back up, and had promptly forgotten it was there. I pulled out the wad and spread my hands. My smile was triumphant. With a twinkle Frank ventured, 'So tomorrow you'll need a little less.'

Frank had found us a delightful Kosher restaurant, intimate, well-appointed and friendly; all that I needed after my journey. That evening we caught up with each other's lives and the lives of friends and loved ones. His dry humour, delivered out of an unsmiling spectacled face, had me laughing throughout the evening; deadpan delivery is an enviable talent. The conversation wound its way like a lazy river as the evening matured. People came and went, and outside, a light rain added a pleasant sheen to the quiet side street where the restaurant nestled. We settled back, after eating well, to coffee and petit fours.

'So Ernest, you're not going back. What now?'

'I'm yet to be able to think clear of Budapest. As you know, the emotional relationship with the place goes deep. Pre-war.'

'And the woman?'

'Four, five years.'

I looked across the restaurant to the rainy street outside. Gizella floated across my thoughts and I realized the gravitational pull of the life I was leaving continued to exert itself at full power across the border, here in Vienna.

He smiled indulgently and changed the subject: 'Next stop, Munich.'

'I need to see Lillie and her family. I haven't seen them since the uprising. But tomorrow is Kato's day.'

Frank lit his pipe. 'It's been a month or two since I visited her. She's changed, Ernest. As a Jew, she's in a tiny minority in that retirement home.'

'And?'

'And with her history, she's bothered by it. I've argued with her, that they're ex-professionals, that in the arts anti-Semites are thin on the ground. But there's one there giving her a hard time, and she behaves badly in her presence, so it becomes all of them there when she's feeling down. She'll get a lift seeing her golden boy.'

'She's not in decline?'

'No, just frustrated. She's had an active, creative life, now she feels stuck and has nothing to do with her time.'

The evening was almost at an end. I'd had a day of it and Frank recognized this. We made our way back to his place. A bed had been prepared, and after a brandy along with lounging in a ridiculously comfortable leather chair, I was almost 'out of it'. My head finally hit the pillow and clouds of sleep scudded in, almost before I could shut my eyes.

I took a taxi the following morning through fresh Vienna streets, rain-washed and sun-streaked. Frank had lent me a scarf but, as it wasn't raining, I placed it in my raincoat pocket. At the station, I picked up a return for Baden. Same old station, same old city. In the fuss on the platform yesterday, I'd failed to notice what now came flying at me: the changes in the people. It had been a while. Skirts were shorter, clothing brighter, newer. Men's leather coats, their hats, their shoes, were stylish, new-looking. Austria in the new decade was decidedly affluent, had a spruce air and was feeling a freedom only desired, but not achieved so far, by Hungary. I guessed the further west I was to travel, the more of this I would see. And what was this, further down the platform, standing deep in conversation? Two Hassidic Jews, black-hatted, black to their very toes, their long ringlets a brazen call to this changing age, that they too could display their being, and not die because of it. I felt their freedom more than I felt my own, for within I was still a prisoner. Though the Nazis had gone, their evil lurked in dark corners and though the Communists had begun to fight a rearguard action against the future, both mindsets were increasingly incredible to the young, who asserted their mental freedom. The captivity I was feeling lay in my rejection of belief, and my espousal of the secular life. Still Kosher, yet not orthodox; Orthodox when cornered, yet trying to incorporate antipathetic views, views that would have caused my father to disown me. I was a mess. Would returning to Judaism wholeheartedly, would that be a tacit admission of failure to meet the world squarely as myself, standing on my own two feet? Or would it be an acceptance that I am what made me, and the simple fact is, I am of Judaism, root and branch.

Back there at Belsen in the pit with the corpses, all but one myself, I had denied God, that nothing of such a being could behold the bitter end of that human experience and remain divine. Maybe I was realizing on this January morning, early in the seventh decade of the twentieth christian century, that my theology had been limiting God to a narrow definition. I had missed out on that beautiful cabbalistic notion that at the head of the tree of life is the unknown God, ever-developing, ever-proving and sustaining, but always slightly out of reach. What had such a being to learn from man, when man has yet to dare to touch infinity, to step away from the anthropomorphic and behold the spirit?

As I took it off in the rail carriage, I realised that the raincoat I had been wearing wasn't mine. I must have taken its twin from off the coat stand at the restaurant. Frank would think I was going a little crazy. At the very least I would be teased for this one. Someone else would have taken mine, maybe. We would be going back to the restaurant for another meal later, my treat. 'Return it then.' I noticed the slight dirt around the collar when I took it off and placed it on the rack above my seat. Mine was brand new, purchased for the trip. Not my week.

At Baden, I stepped away from the station into a small tree-lined square. A couple of cabs idled nearby. Stepping into one of them, I gave the address. The driver nodded, flicked his cigarette end into an immaculately clean gutter, and we cruised away from the square, out into a quiet little town about its quiet, little-town business. The Mercedes whispered its effortless way to the edges of Baden. Set in its own grounds, the retirement home was an elegant old place, converted to give each person staying there as much privacy as they wanted, along with the care needed by some, and those communal facilities deemed so necessary for the ageing.

Kato had been expecting me but, when I entered her apartment, it did nothing to dampen the delight she had felt on learning I was coming to Vienna. Older, yes, but no less vital than the woman who in 1946 had charge of the soprano section of the Dohany Synagogue choir, was a voice coach at the Goldmark Music School and had me fixed in her mind to be an operatic tenor. Eventually she released me from her embrace, her eyes glistening with tears. My eyes were blurry also.

'It has been an age. You are so thin, are you eating?'

'What can I say? I'm lightly built.'

'There is no meat on your bones. What's wrong? Are you pining?'

She'd got it in one. I looked away trying to hide an embarrassed smile. She smiled back as our eyes met again.

'None of my business. Let me feed you. If I recall, you are partial to a pastry with a custard filling. Coffee?'

She pointed me to a large sofa and sat me down. From the kitchen: 'How is your voice? Let me hear you.'

'No, no …'

Still from the kitchen: 'Sing me a few scales.'

I croaked out an imitation of musical sound. Silence. She entered carrying a tray of coffee and goodies.

'You do not deserve, you naughty boy. You are neglecting God's gift; but I don't see you forever, I forgive. Eat.'

We trailed our way over old times. I wanted to know how she was now. I asked.

'Ernest. I am alone in this place. They are nearly all Goyishka , with whom can I communicate? They eat different, think different. Sure, they're show business, but at such a basic level. I am an operatic soprano. There are few links. I try.'

'Kato. You never had trouble mixing before. Of all the people I knew after the war, you were the one able to bridge the gaps.'

'I never had to live under the same roof and see the same faces every day. They are boring people, Ernest, and, what is more, they hate Jews.'

'How do you know?'

'You ask this question?'

She walked to the window looking out on to wide lawns and tended flowerbeds. The distant hills leading to the Alps, the farmland, neat fields,the ripening wheat moving to a light breeze. Scattered across the view, tidy houses and barns. Idyllic. She turned to the room and looked at me.

'How can such a beautiful place breed such sourness in the soul? How could such hatefulness grow from this ground and take from us all we held dear?'

'We are perceived as alien, Kato. When fear takes the heart of a population, the alien will suffer. A whole lot easier than that population facing the true cause of the fear.'

She walked over to me and touched my head in passing. Elegantly she lowered herself into an easy chair.

'You were such a suffering little boy after Belsen, but nothing seemed to touch that voice. Will you let it go?'

'Wherever I land up, I will continue to sing. I may take up religious study; become a cantor.'

319

'The public's loss. And the women?'

'I may catch up with Yetta. She made it across to New York the second time of trying. We had planned to jump the border, but, come the moment, I failed her. I went back to Budapest, straight into Gizella's arms'.

She reached for a cigarette.

'The conundrum you are trying to resolve is immortalized in sixth card of the Tarot, a young man torn by two female forces. Which way? Above them an angel, maybe even a future child of the young man, maybe his guide; I've heard many variations when the cards were laid out backstage.'

'You are suggesting it is irresolvable?'

'Maybe for you. Maybe Yetta and …?'

'Gizella …'

'… are mutually cancelling, each offering a solution to a part of your need, but neither reaching your true being, merely colliding with each other in your desire to share your life with the right woman. Maybe you ought to let both go.'

'I am on that very edge, Kato.'

We drank more coffee and took a walk in the midday sunshine. People from the retirement home, sunning themselves, nodded their greeting to her as we passed. Kato's bearing was that of most dancers and singers of her generation, elegant, trained, full of grace; Strauss's Marschallin, Princess Marie Therese Werdenberg, personified, a part she once played to perfection.

I caught the early-evening train from Baden, my heart full. As the cab wound its way out from the grounds, Kato was at her window waving. My teacher and friend still looking out for my well-being. How could I make a wrong move? The train was waiting and I hurried on. Night was closing in. Kato and I had lunched at a café with the talk ranging wide, but she was never very far from the sense of deep loss that the Nazis had visited on her. A red mist indeed, but one no Jew could deny her in her responses to Gentile Austria.

The train moved easily forward. A local, it was full of people finishing their day. I looked out on the countryside in the fading light, and thought back to those early post-war days at the Dohany synagogue when, on hearing me, Kato took me over, and in months my voice had become almost not mine. My breathing, I had never breathed before. Above this, I had dozens of opportunities to hear a divine soprano at work. Before joining the choir at Dohany, I had worked as a singer at a synagogue on the outskirts of Budapest, where because of rampant inflation, I tended to be paid in kind; sometimes not so kind. Like the promise of a goose for a special event. Fine, a deal, but I should have asked to see the goose first. Poor thing. This kind of tale broke through Kato's little moods as we worked together, causing laughter across the studio.

She and my mother had become firm friends and were not above ganging up on me over lit candles at a full table.

Kato Godry Pfluger, operatic soprano, married to the conductor of the famous Leipzig Gewandhaus Orchestra. Then came the rise of Hitler and the Nazi Party. She and her husband separated, to save his career I was told, he not being Jewish. Returning to Hungary, she could not pick up on her career, her 'race' being the impediment. She was reaching middle age and poverty together, and was not alone in this. Jewish performers and artists were being steadily sidelined, which led inevitably to an artistic collective, part of which was the Juden-Rein Budapest Opera. It became a Hungarian phenomenon, producing work that outstripped the 'legitimate' theatrical world endorsed by the state. The beautiful Goldmark Hall was the venue, and Kato was a star performer. Mimi in *La Boheme*. '*Sono andati?*', '*Che ha detto*' in Act 4 saw her take the Goldmark audience and wring it dry, cleansing its soul momentarily of the Holocaust and post-war deprivation. Her reward, the company of fellow performers, an audience and deafening applause, not to mention the wolf kept from her door. Her loss, along with others, involved many missing relatives, a husband lost to fate and a career badly damaged.

Back then, no matter how hard she tried, she could not raise my confidence or self-esteem to a level to meet my talent.

Light under a bushel. As the Christians would have it, this servant was burying his talent deep.

As the train pulled into Vienna, people stood in anticipation of getting off quickly. My thoughts turned to an evening at the opera with Kato, when we sat together through a performance of *Der Rosenkavalier*. Towards the end of the last act of this opera, a trio of sopranos thread musical beauty around the growing resolution of a frail plot. She was moving in her seat, mouthing her part of the Marschallin, gesturing to herself, her eyes filled with happy reminiscence. On the emptying train, my rather loud involuntary sob turned a few heads toward the solitary man staring absently through the window to the platform.

Kato was discussed at length when Frank and I met up later at the Kosher restaurant. Nobody had handed in my coat. Later at Frank's apartment, we played some Strauss on the gramophone. The irony was not lost on us that this composer and Wagner before him had dubious credentials when it came to Jewry. But what *is* undeniable is that the endowment of great talent seems to ignore the vessel, the medium, and it falls where it may, so should not be stained with the behaviour of the servant of the muse. Thus we were able to sit and marvel at the divinity from the pen of a Nazi collaborator, then a nineteenth-century anti-Semite; after which we moved on to a debt-ridden masonic wastrel and wound up with an ill-mannered, deaf, unwashed German genius. We took to our beds, consciences clear and our senses bursting with good sounds. On the creative level, God rules.

Frank wasn't given to laughter. The odd smile raised, but not what could be called a regular thing. So his raucous chuckle on the platform the following morning came as a shock. I was joining the Munich train to meet there with my sister Lillie. Already, I could feel the edge of the excitement that goes with meeting up with a loved one. My sorrow was in leaving Frank so soon. Why the laughter?

'Look at the name on the train.'

I looked. *Rosenkavalier*. My turn:

'What's so funny about that? A train called *Rosenkavalier*.'

He looked at me over his spectacles, a long look. Another chuckle.

'You're learning, my boy.'

It was the parting of the ways with dear Frank Lang. It would be a while before I would see either him or Kato again. After a long embrace I joined the train. As I reached for the handle to climb up, something made me turn. I looked across the platform as another train began to move off. At a window, someone was waving frantically at me. Magda. She was getting the kid to wave as well, but what made me laugh was the kiss she blew me. I blew one back, leaving Frank to puzzle it out as he handed me my case.

'So long, Junior. Don't be strange. Keep that schnitzel as I've wrapped it and it won't bother anyone.'

'See you in a year or two Frank, God willing ...'

I made my way down the corridor to my seat in a reserved compartment. 'Three other people, not bad.' I put my case up on the rack and returned to the corridor just as the whistles blew and the train made a slight movement forward. Frank stood, stocky and solid, pipe on the go, waving his young friend goodbye. For a moment, time played a trick. Maybe it was the presence on the platform of some people wearing the traditional Austrian garb. Maybe that I was on a train to Hitler's '*Die Haupstadt der Bewegung*', home of endless mass rallies where secular worship and hysteria dominated thousands of brains, but I saw Frank alone and vulnerable in a crowd of people whose masks seemed for a moment to drop, revealing the collective face of the 'Beast'. 'It's 1961 Ernest, behave; these are ghosts of your fevered imagination. It is all moving on, the world is integrating; assimilation, a buzzword. People are used to us and no longer fear a plot. Zion is a desirable mental state, not a place.' I took my place in the carriage with my three travelling companions, all male, all very proper and each of them, in their relative prosperities, very unalike.

By the window on the far side of the compartment away

from the corridor, aloof and reading a newspaper, a dignified, aristocratic-looking man, very tall, and, though ageing, athletic by feel. His clothing, tweed and leather, plus-twos and thick-ribbed dark green socks, rounded off by what looked like British brogue shoes, made him altogether the country gentleman, a man of the Alps. His face was very tanned, and though creased, the years told well on him. That he needed reading glasses seemed somehow incongruous in spite of their being gold-rimmed. Mid to late fifties at a guess.

Opposite, a jolly type, comfortable in himself, talkative, a Viennese with little edge. Our eyes met; there was twinkle and quickly we engaged in rounds of random conversation and laughter as he revealed who he was ('Dieter') where he was headed ('Munich too, we must meet up') and what he was doing ('a little business'). In response, I had released information to the carriage at large. On the move, visiting family and friends. Ernest.

The third man had become involved in us, though as yet had to speak a word. He smiled when there were smiles, frowned when we did. He was, not so much dressed, as 'got-up'. He carried that air of having tried very hard to gain an effect, but somehow was at odds with the result. Maybe the suit didn't fit right, the collar bothered his neck, who knew? The centre-parting in his hair had been slicked down to stay put; maybe it was the moustache. Anyway, he was with us, for every syllable.

Dieter was making me laugh about his daughter's boyfriend, when the watcher spoke:

'Marcus. Marcus Hugenberg.'

He held out his hand which we, in turns, took to shake. One of those handshakes that seem to want to crush every bone. The man in the corner looked across at Hugenberg, realized it wasn't any Hugenberg he would want to know and went back to his newspaper. The man's accent had me puzzled. I concluded he was of lower-class origins, had gained a few rungs on the social ladder, but was unsure how high he could go without falling off. For him, the ladder seemed wobbly. As Dieter continued his story of the future son-in-law, I realized that Hugenberg had moved in closer to me. 'Oh God, cheap cologne.' I could forgive his oppressive bulk and the sweat, but not the cheap trash that was assaulting my nostrils.

Hugenberg cut in again. 'Why don't we go get ourselves a beer?'

Dieter declined graciously, but Hugenberg had me by the arm.

'Come, come my friend, indulge me. The dining car isn't very far.'

His urging had me almost to my feet. Dieter looked on sympathetically as I reluctantly agreed and followed him into the corridor. In the bar of the train, I sat opposite Hugenberg, finishing my first bottle of strong Bavarian beer. He had, in fifteen short minutes revealed a man to whom life had not been kind. He was envious of those more successful and contemptuous of those he considered beneath him. He was unremitting, and from me he wanted very little but to be a listening post. Another bottle was slammed down in front of me.

'Drink up man, long journey ahead.'

Into the third bottle, I began to feel the effect of the powerful brew. My co-ordination became affected and my speech came through a slightly numbed mouth. Before he could force me to endure a fourth bottle and twenty more minutes of his rambling whinge on life, I mumbled my apologies, stumbled out of the dining car and aimed for our compartment. I was halfway along the corridor at an open window, trying to clear my head, when I was grabbed by the arm and swung about.

'My company not good enough, Mr Jew? Answer me! You are what is wrong with the new world. Pity we didn't finish the job. We need another Third Reich, another Hitler. Look at the mess in Czechoslovakia ...'

My mind was a thick mist of panic. I couldn't shout for help, the racket of the moving train almost drowned out his high-pitched volley of abuse. The drink had hit his low resistance to alcohol; Jekyll had become Hyde and violence was just a shake away. I wrestled clear of his angry grasp, and made it in stumbling haste back to the compartment.

As I slid the door open, the man in the corner was staring out at the passing countryside, Dieter was deep in a book. I sat heavily, breathing hard.

'Dining car busy?'

Dieter was smiling across at me. I nodded. I didn't trust my co-ordination to speak.

'You okay?'

I managed another nod and a flicker of a smile. Moments later, Hugenberg crashed back into the compartment. All eyes turned to him. His face had darkened, there were beads of sweat on his brow. He bared his teeth into a snarl of a smile, settled heavily back into his place, loosened his collar and leaned back. In a matter of moments he was snoring loudly. Dieter grinned across at me.

He said quietly, 'Good company?'

I replied, with difficulty, 'The best.'

He laughed quietly and returned to his book. I tried to snooze but I was upset. Dieter was on to this and put his book down. The loud snoring and half-wakeful snorting from Hugenberg continued. Dieter, quietly: 'You appear upset.'

'The beer brought on the fascist in him.'

This I half-whispered. He nodded.

'With a little luck, he'll sleep to Munich. Fascism hasn't really gone away. The surrender was token, done with deceit in the eyes and a lie on the tongue.'

I looked at my companion with new eyes.

'Vienna, Munich, both charming cities in the quiet years. Perhaps my memories are rosy, but before the madness, sure, we had problems, but it felt settled in my youth. There was a pleasant rhythm to life. In my neighbourhood were Jewish people and businesses. As children, we grew as a group, later a gang, then a team. We knew the differences, laughed at each other on a bedrock of respect. What the hell was wrong with that? I am a proud Austrian but I feel shame that we gave rise

326

to that little peasant bastard. Führer indeed. Goes to Germany, finds a paradise of fools, makes himself king of the fools and annexes his homeland. A little like putting your mother on the streets. Anschluss, polite way of unleashing that mob of Nazis on us. An act of spite for our flea-in-his-ear because he was artistically naive and didn't light any fires as a painter.'

How long Hugenberg had been listening, I had no idea, but with a scream of drunken anger, he was up and had a very startled Dieter by the throat.

'Traitor. You pallid Jew-lover! You are a disgrace to us. I will drain what little Austrian blood is left in your veins.'

'Enough!'

The man in the corner was on his feet towering over Hugenberg, whose hands he prised from Dieter. His next act was to lift the bulky being, deep in his distress, and dump him on to the bench seat from which he tried to get up and retaliate, only to be pushed back down and held there by the large man who spoke with a strong Bavarian accent.

'Move from that spot and I'll take you apart and hand what's left of you to the police in Munich. Thug.'

Things became very quiet in the compartment. The big man returned to his seat and stared witheringly at Hugenberg who watched Dieter and I return to our seats. A few moments earlier, four grown men had been standing in a knot of conflict. Now, with everybody back in their places, the noise of the train rattling its way towards Munich reasserted itself. Dieter adjusted his collar, smiled across at me and returned to his book. I noticed the slight quiver in his hands. I too was shaking. Hugenberg had a coughing fit and adjusted his clothing. His breathing slowly became normal and, though he shut his eyes and feigned sleep, nobody was fooled.

Dieter and I tried conversation a few more times, but the atmosphere in the compartment strangled each attempt at birth. At long, long last the train lurched through the suburbs of Munich, its pace slowing as the pre-stop rock-and-roll increased. Local trains moved round us as our train went under the station canopy. Finally, snail-like to squeaking brakes, we halted. The platform voice echoed beyond. Dieter leaned across and gave me his card; 'Call me next time you are in Vienna, Ernest. We'll meet up.'

He rose and took his cases, leaving the compartment with a nod to the Bavarian and a glare towards Hugenberg, who had entered the realms of remorse, and stood to attention.

'Look, sir, I am so sorry. I had some schnapps before joining the train and the beers my friend here and I shared, tipped me over. Please accept my humble apologies.'

I was next to stand and get my cases down. They were quite heavy and I staggered slightly, a little bit from them, a little bit from the remains of the beer. Hugenberg was on them instantly, taking them from me: '*Bitte, bitte*, my friend. Let me help you, show amends.'

To me, and more certainly the large Bavarian, he saluted the compartment in a way that summoned the clicking heels of yesterday. Quickly, he was on the platform with my cases. I was in tow trying to keep up. We rushed past Lillie.

'Ernest … *Ernest!*'

Hugenberg stopped in his tracks as I did. He placed the cases down, gave us a decorous bow and left in a hurry, back to the carriage for his own cases. As Lillie and I locked in an embrace, the tall Bavarian strode by doffing his Tyrolean hat in passing.

'At last, my darling Ernesti, you are here. Why are you the subject of such attention? Who was that strange man carrying your cases? Is that dried blood on your jacket? Can I smell schnitzel?'

'Tell you later. Let's get home.'

After catching up on family gossip, the destiny of friends and debating the political scene, I held Lillie and Andre, her husband, enthralled with the detailed account of my journey from Budapest. The wine flowed, as did the conversation and suddenly it was gone midnight. A little later in a downy bed, I relived the events narrated to the odd giggle over Gizella's schnitzel, which had finally found its depleted way to Lillie's table. In the comfort of darkness I slept long and deep. A holiday, a holiday, then the future.

I spent a month in Munich, exploring a great city almost fully recovered. I went to every gallery, museum and place of interest. It was possible to revive the echoes of the Third Reich but I was reluctant to do this. The city had a history well before the little corporal placed his boot on it.

In the first week, as planned, I looked in on two wartime friends: second cousin Leopold Pozsonyi and Zoltan Mehrer. We three survived the infamous 'Mengele' selections, the arbitrary division of civilian detainees, meaning death in the gas chambers for those on the 'wrong' side of the German rifle butt. We had, at different times, experienced days in Birkenau Block 11 in horrifying conditions, standing ankle deep in urine. We waited in vain for food or any kind of drink, in a place that afforded prisoners one bunk-bed to hold five. Birkenau, pride of the Reich, a truly advanced killing machine, a suffocating factory of death unless, like us, you had been earmarked for something else. Ours was work. Before leaving that place, we had, in our thousands, bonded together in a recollection so dreadful that it has never left the present; it lives in the next room. One has merely to open a door and there one is, back in a condition beyond the ends of human deprivation, a condition that only something profoundly inhuman could develop, a cruelty that in itself rejoiced in the reduction it had brought about, both in the captive and in the captor. The genie that had been let loose was running riot at the behest of its demented master, who had yet to realize he had no ultimate control over the madness unleashed on the world.

We wound up in Wustegiersdorf, where we spent the next months before being separated on the winter march away from the Russians. Leo and Zoltan. Two fearless lads, providers, brave and good-humoured, saved lives in their time there, and offered support to those on the brink of despair. A pair of anti-depressants, sent by Doctor Fate to a

329

few hundred needy souls. One time it fell to me to return the favour and save Leopold's life. Being a handsome lad, he had obtained the favours of one of the German women who happened to work in the department that dealt with food supply in the camp. Needless to say, favour for favour, Leo was able to create a supply of little extras under the noses of the Kapos, Werhmacht guards and the SS Contingent who prowled our very souls.

It will be recalled that we shared the disused mill at Wustegiersdorf with hundreds of Poles and other nationalities. The Poles were relative long-termers, the Reich policy being different in respect of Polish people in captivity. It meant, however, that these captives had had time to evolve into a hand-to-mouth pack, capable of the lowest behaviour and cruelty each to the other. As for Jews ...! Somewhere along the line, Leo had crossed them. Ever the 'wheeler-dealer', something had occurred involving him and them, which gave rise to a lasting conflict. So much so that he was loathed by them and dared not venture to their part of the mill alone.

This particular evening we had all worked a heavy shift in the timber yard. I had one of the top bunks in our barrack. Next to mine, Leopold's was empty. Suddenly, a clatter and a series of shouts coming from the wooden steps leading up to our barrack from the outside. Leopold was being chased by one of the criminal 'leading lights' in the Polish contingent. The man rushed after Leo without thought or caring, he just wanted him. In his hand, a knife, open and ready to cut Leo stem to stern. Leo reached the bunks and hurled himself upward, not quite making it all the way. As he tried gaining a foothold on the wooden base, I leaned over and grabbed his jacket hauling him up the rest of the way. The Pole kept coming, uttering the darkest of threats about a world beyond death where it would be nemesis for Leo. He made a grab and missed. I pushed him hard in the face with the sole of my foot. He went down backwards and the rest of the barrack laid into him. He was dumped outside unconscious. I don't recall seeing him again, though for days we worried about retribution. Time wore on and other emergencies took his place in our troubles and worries.

Our meeting in Munich was warm, congenial and full of memories. At some we laughed, on some we reflected, some produced anger, others tears. It was a full day and concluded with them offering me a job. Hungary they had found unbearable after the war, knowing they were looking at the faces of those most likely responsible for the deaths of two entire families. They had survived the Germans, but their families were taken apart by the people's militia, the Arrowcross. So they moved to Munich, Hitler's jewel. *Die Putzerei*, their dry-cleaning outfit, had become very successful but they had extended their interests into the shoe trade, which needed more time than they could give it. They had over-extended and needed help. Leopold offered me a top job to help them out. I was tempted but I had to decline. A new life in Germany? No. Much as I loved Leo and Zoltan, I could not.

The month slid by, and as if I'd never left the place, I was back on the platforms of Munich's main station with Lillie and her husband, Andre. The next journey would be to Scotland, to Glasgow, my mother and brother, maybe Israel later. It was open. At the station, Andre took me to one side: 'Ernest, if you can, settle in Britain. It will suit your temperament. You will grow there, I know. Take my tip.'

The future looked large and excitingly mysterious. A little frightening. The train whistle blew. Time to go.

PART VI
CHOICES OF FREEDOM

22 *Fulfilment of Love*

1961

The close heat of an English summer's day was eased by a light breeze which rustled the leaves of trees standing guard over the dead in Bushey cemetery. Hot in our suits, brother Charles and I stood above our mother's grave, silent in thought, our heads bowed. There were a few people around paying their respects to those departed. This Jewish cemetery was a very tidy place with well-tended flowerbeds. As everywhere in and around London, the noise of traffic was a constant, though here muted and faint, almost lost behind the wind in the trees. I began to sing quietly, a Yiddish lullaby that Therezia sang to me when I was a child. Charles joined in. I looked across to him and he smiled and nodded as if to say, 'Me too'. Our voices raised, we completed the song to turned faces across the expanse of gravestones. On a bench, an old man sat reading. He looked up, and smiling the smile of recognition, offered us his applause. A light monoplane took off from the nearby flying school and fractured the moment rich in our east European past, bringing us back to the world of Kennedy, Castro and Krushchev with his man in space. Back to the British, stepping away from the grey fifties into the multicoloured sixties, with its explosion of youth culture.

Therezia came to Britain ailing, and during her visit she went into decline. In her lifetime she had brought her eight children into the world, had seen them grow, blossom and become scattered to the wind by the foul breath of hatred, some to perish, others, though scarred, to survive and rebuild. She had lost husband Leopold, her yeshiva boy, but his hand was on the shoulders of his surviving children; ever there. I am sure she was simply tired. The dangers of the thirties, the war, the post-war occupation, the days of 'let's pretend the Russians don't govern Hungary', the turbulence of 1956 and the backwash of uncertainty of once again uprooting.

At 77, she was worn out. She had died in Hampstead after coming south from Glasgow where she had visited Else and her second husband, Stephen. I followed on from my visit to Munich but too late, too late. Standing in this beautiful garden in bloom for the dead, away from the full-blooded din of central London, I was truly a stranger in a strange land. In Glasgow or London or any big city in Britain, I could be confident of a warm Jewish 'hello' with consequent assistance in shaping a future, but for the first time I felt the oddness of being an immigrant, as certainly as if I were standing on a New York dockside in the 1890s. What next? Charles and I turned reluctantly away from the silent company of our mother and made our way back to Hampstead where Else, Stephen and their son Ian, would meet up with us after their trip to the West End to shop and see *West Side Story*.

We had come down from Glasgow in Ian's silver Vauxhall Victor with its column-change and sleek bodyline. The architecture in England is so very different to that of Scotland, as is the terrain. When they came to pick me up in Glasgow Central Station, it was a grey windswept day, the kind of day when the clouds race across the sky and litter gets blown round your ankles. As we stepped out to the car park and drove through the lowering rain-dark city centre, I felt the north European 'slap', and a dread of the place began to form, quickly and magically dispelled as Ian drove us into the suburbs south-side and the civilized spaciousness of Giffnock. The later journey to London was a fascinating glimpse of British life at large. From the number of cars and motorbikes in the hands of private individuals, the roadside housing, the rich farmland with its well-kept structures, all advertized a wealth collectively dreamed of in eastern Europe, but yet to be realized. Roadside advertising here was for consumer goods, not prodding propaganda for the state.

My eyes were everywhere on the journey down. Ian had recently passed his test and was keen to show us seventy miles an hour on the new north–south motorway system. From the back seat, it was fast. It would be a while before I could try *my* hand and discover just how competitive the British *really* were on the roads. It was all truly alien and took place, unbelievably, on the left. Deeply confusing, as was the music with which Ian was keen to serenade us. I had heard Elvis Presley in Hungary, but some of the newer people until then had escaped my attention. We were tolerant of Ian's tastes but we asked for a lower volume, if only to talk. A good boy, he obliged.

In the quiet of his study over some good wine, Charles and I discussed my future. It lay in the ministry and the pursuit of rabbinical studies, along with the development of my voice for cantorial purposes. He looked at me directly: 'Operatic singing no longer appeals?'

'It doesn't have the vocational pull. Besides, I'm in my thirties. A bit long in the tooth.'

My reply wasn't all of it. My confidence in myself 'out of the box', away from synagogue life, hadn't matured with my voice. Though I had the skill, I couldn't muster the will. Charles stretched a little in his easy chair.

'Your visa is a tourist visa, lasting …?'

'Months, officially. I was thinking about showing up in Israel, visit Fritz, shop around.'

'David Goldstein is coming round a bit later.'

A famous man in his field.

'The choirmaster?'

'We'll audition you round the fireside.'

We did, after dinner in front of the family and Goldstein, who liked what he heard and told me to look him up when I got to Tel Aviv.

After shuttling back and forth between Glasgow and London, visiting the sights, the galleries, the theatre and concerts, I was about ready to step away and visit Israel, which was in ferment over the Eichmann trial. The last thing

I did in London was to go with Charles to see *Judgement at Nuremberg*. A lot of the drama was lost on us because our English was not so good. Charles, a whole lot better than me, helped me out in loud whispers. We got the point, though it was strange to see people like Marlene Dietrich, Judy Garland and Spencer Tracy all adding glamour to a very unglamorous event; though nothing, but nothing, would ever be more surreal than that Israeli press photograph of Eichmann in carpet slippers. The sixties were going to be interesting times.

NOVEMBER 1961

I travelled to Israel with a group who were making *Aliyah*, a return to the Holy Land. We crossed the Channel and took a train to Marseilles where we boarded a ship for Israel. Days later, after a few ports of call, we arrived in Haifa where Fritz and family waited, waving from the dock. After a brief stay with the relatives, I rented a room in Tel Aviv and took a job in light engineering. It was a tough one. Once in every three weeks I had to do a spell of night shift. We were living through a drought, a regime of scarce, lukewarm water trickling from the taps on a good day.

The Eichmann trial ended predictably, in December. The death sentence proved controversial, though God knows, we from the camps would have happily done the job with our bare hands and faced our Maker with no regrets, come the day. Compassion for a being who left behind him thousands upon thousands of corpses, and ever more thousands of survivors and loved ones bereft, lay in a single bullet to the forehead, a rope or whatever means of quick dispatch likely to be employed. It could not lie in life imprisonment, continuing to be Adolph Eichmann, an object of contempt, ever the target of random revenge attacks, staring daily at cell walls and denied company, denied the seasons, denied the kiss of the wind, the salt of the ocean, until whatever departure nature dictated. Israel did him a favour.

For me, it was a difficult time. In some ways it was a little like Budapest, in that work and cantorial pursuits were hard to reconcile. Fridays I had to run from the factory to get washed and changed for the service at the Bugrachov synagogue, whose congregation had risked taking me on. It meant a promising post, a fine library in a place well-established in Tel Aviv. It felt good.

I hadn't forgotten David Goldstein's invitation, and looked him up. Over coffee we talked.

'I know just the man to turn you into a great singer,' his eyes danced with merriment and goodwill: 'Shlomo Ravitz, the greatest authority in cantorial music. Leave this with me.'

I heard nothing for a while, then late one evening Goldstein turned up at my front door.

'Right. Now we go see Ravitz.'

I wasn't about to disagree and, for what seemed an hour, we walked out of Tel Aviv into a suburb, arriving at this man's house at eleven. A dull-looking apartment block, like a lot of Israeli buildings, functional, utilitarian, far from utopian. Square adobes. Ravitz's flat was on the first floor. Goldstein knocked. A slight delay. The door opened a little to reveal a small man, fixing his skullcap, his face betraying irritation at being roused so late.

'What do you want?' He snapped in Hebrew.

This didn't feel promising. Goldstein explained why we were here.

'Ach. Don't bother me. I don't take pupils any more, especially at three in the morning. Why did you bring him?'

'Ravitz. It's just gone eleven, the night is young. Just listen to my young friend.'

The old man beckoned us in reluctantly. Planting himself heavily in a well-used chair, he said; 'Alright sonny. Let's hear what you can do.'

I wanted out of there. I sang a few notes. Ravitz stopped me almost immediately. Quietly: 'I'll take him.'

In the next few months I came to love that man. He was not only an excellent teacher, he became a good friend. I could hardly wait for each coming lesson, even though the charge was fifteen lirot a time, which wasn't cheap in 1962. So the year began with two jobs and the best voice coach around. Then two bad turns had me on my knees. First, I damaged a finger at work and without my hands I couldn't function there. I had no National Insurance, therefore no money. So I went to my boss, Moshe, a Romanian, and told him:

'Look. I have no money. No money, no food.'

He said: 'Go to the doctor and if he gives you a note saying that the injury was caused at work, then I can help; otherwise not.'

I couldn't prove it. I hadn't reported it. It could have happened any time.

Secondly, I fell foul of internal politicking and penny-pinching meanness at the synagogue, losing my job there. One evening, one of the wardens, a man called Tenenbaum, came up to me. In his wake, a young ambitious cantor waiting on his chance. Embarrassed, the warden had to tell me that the synagogue could no longer afford me. He had been sent by others to deliver the news. He nodded towards the younger man.

'I'm informed he can do the same job for less.'

Furious, I turned on my heel and left the place without saying a word. Tenenbaum ran out after me.

'Where are you going? Lowy, I don't want to lose you. Just take a pay cut.'

'I'm not about to do that. I'm certainly not into infighting and mind games. Count me out.'

At that moment, a red-headed synagogue regular named, appropriately, Israel, chanced by and overheard the emotional moment. Half in Hebrew, half in Yiddish and in an insulting tone, he offered his contribution; 'Let him go, Tenenbaum. He hasn't got a voice anyway. It grates on my ears.'

My Israeli experience was coming to a sad conclusion. My earlier encounter with Marta from Budapest, on the bus one afternoon in late 1961, had revived old disappointments. I was now broke and, apart from Fritz and his family, I was alone. My temperament was in conflict with the loud, querulous side of a very unsettled scene, with disparate cultures knocking into each other. I wasn't a soldier, a pioneer or politically ambitious. In my heart of hearts Israel, Zion, was not this secular socialist experiment in land reclamation, this great multinational social melting pot; Zion for me is a level obtaining to the spiritual realm. I was glad for the State to be there, a homeland for those who would make it work, a possible utopia, viably functioning in the seventh decade. It's future will always be fraught at the borders until understanding overtakes prejudice.

In spite of the disappointments, my experience of Israel had some wonderful moments. To this day, I miss the atmosphere surrounding *Shabbat Chaggim*. The realisation that you are there in the Holy Land is impossible to recreate in the diaspora. The social turbulence was required within the process of the state evolving, with newcomers adding their value. That turbulent urge in me was missing, with my European leanings and my love of its culture. My family imprinting included the old Europe and its better aspects, still to be found available in the freer parts. Maybe Britain.

Charles to the rescue. I received a call from him on a low day. The Pollockshields synagogue, south of the Clyde in Glasgow, needed someone urgently to minister their High Festival. I had been recommended. An influential member of that congregation called Symie Miller had flown to Tel Aviv on business and wanted to talk to me. I was to meet him in his suite at the Sheraton. I put on a clean shirt and was down the road like a bullet. I was made welcome in his suite and he made me an offer of £250 to cover the work I was to do. What is more, he offered me an open ticket, which meant freedom of travel. I could not, would not, refuse. I had to pay money back to the Israeli government as I had come in on the *Aliyah* arrangement, which had been paid by them. I had no advance from Symie Miller, so I had to raise funds by selling what little possessions I had. Still, 1962 found me back in Glasgow, this time at journey's end.

I did my task well in Pollockshields, and was taken on as a part-time cantor. Stephen, my brother-in-law, had a very successful cash-and-carry business, I worked for him when my duties at the synagogue left me time on my hands. All in all, I was finding my feet and gaining ground financially; enough to buy a car and become mobile in this large, interesting northern city, with its fascinating architecture, massive parks and dire slums. In the suburbs, the spread south included Giffnock and Clarkeston where I found many of the Jewish people of the city. In these early days, I re-encountered a young woman called Kathy Herman whom I had met on my last visit. We saw more of each other, and love took over. As the relationship blossomed, my conviction that I had met her before grew. One day she showed me her high school graduation photograph taken in Budapest in 1943. Immediately and unmistakably, I recognised the face of the young girl with the high forehead and spectacles who had stared down at me from her bunk-bed in the Belsen barrack when, on that day, the women fed me and gave me drink. She recalled how, daily, living skeletons barely able to walk would show their faces and beg for food. I would have been indistinguishable from any one of them. Impossible to remember a face when all faces were reduced to a common brotherhood of ghastliness. Kathy had been arrested and transported to Bergen-Belsen in 1944. After I had encountered her she was taken to Theresienstadt, which was liberated in May 1945. She had finally found her way to Glasgow, making a life for herself as a teacher.

To begin with, like a lot of couples, we lived in rented accommodation. Eventually a call came from the Giffnock and Newlands synagogue. The people there were looking to engage a full-time cantor. At first I was reluctant to accept, the old desire to resist the inevitable had re-asserted itself. I had to choose between further time on the edge, or future security. With our wanting to start a family in a home of our own, there was no real choice. My need to know more inside the faith was drawing me increasingly into the ministry and away from the secular. The Giffnock position came with a house, which at our stage was a beautiful bonus, so that when a parallel offer occurred from a prestigious synagogue in Birmingham, although tempting, I turned it down. We were both ready to take our chances with the Scots.

Kathy and I still live here in Glasgow. Our two wonderful children, Judith and Robert, both have their independent lives, in Edinburgh and London respectively. Kathy and I still love Scotland and its people. In spite of all the tough-talk and seemingly rough edge of places like Glasgow, the people lack the cynicism and sarcastic edge of many other Europeans. If happiness can be equated by the number of friends one has, then Kathy and I are very happy indeed, and at last secure, by the grace of God.

Epilogue

I am often asked whether I am resentful that a third of my expected life span was despoiled by the torments of the time. Two stories.

The first concerns those first days of waking from the nightmare at Bergen-Belsen. Women from a nearby town were brought into the camp by the British to carry out cleaning work, in and around the quarantine area. The former inmates, still barely alive, looked on in disbelief as these female workers were given cocoa and biscuits during their tea breaks. The resentment bubbled up one sunny Saturday just after a young British army rabbi, complete with shawl, had completed conducting the Sabbath service. A gathering of around sixty people, strong enough to stand, had circled round him and had observed the service correctly. When it was over, they crowded in on the young man and demanded to know what the hell the British were thinking of, feeding the German women who, until a few weeks before, had been part of the oppression that had brought these inmates to the pitiful world of the camp, where disease and death finished so many. This was too generous, too lenient. Where was the punishment in it? Where the revenge?

Calmly, the young rabbi addressed the problem and diffused the argument: 'The thirst for revenge is a principal cause of endless cycles of suffering. Do you want us to be as the Nazis? In which case their cause has triumphed, and millions of men, women and children have died for nothing. Daily, many of those guilty are being brought to justice. Civilians, no matter how misguided they have been in the past, must not undergo persecution. That would put us on a par with the Nazi killers. Now is the time to end the hate and the violence.'

Whatever was felt, no more was said, and the small crowd dispersed to their respective barrack huts.

Three years later, in the spring of 1948, a public memorial service was held in the Dohany synagogue, Budapest. Max and I went along. A visiting rabbi ascended the pulpit to give his memorial address. Immediately I recognized him as the Belsen chaplain. After the service, I introduced myself.

'I was one of the survivors who questioned you that morning in 1945 when you called on us to break the cycle of hate. I've never forgotten.'

With tears in his eyes, he put his hands to my face and kissed my forehead. I had never looked for revenge; all I wanted was human suffering to be at an end. I still do.

The second story concerns my cousin Feldko who covered me against gunfire on the repatriation train, and became my companion in the search for friends and loved ones.

One night in Bratislava, after Feldko and I had returned from a walk to the Jewish centre, it became clear the he was in great distress. Our hosts, Mady and Trudy, were sitting with us sharing bowls of bean soup, and the conversation turned to the lost ones; those we all knew, those personal to us and, of course, family. Feldko was ominously quiet. An outgoing man with a big personality, he had suddenly become almost withdrawn, somehow smaller.

'And you, Feldko?'

In a broken voice, he told us that very evening, he had learned that none, no single one, of his family had survived. We sat in silence, stunned at the news. The rest of us had someone to go home to. To have lost everyone was inconceivable. He looked round the room at us, his very few friends, rose, and taking his revolver from its holster, the young man who had aged at the Eastern Front with the Russians, slowly, deliberately, loaded it.

'Feldko. What are you going to do?'

345

Mady's frightened, whispered question remained unanswered. He walked to the door, blew us a kiss and with a bitter smile, closed it behind him. We listened to his boots on the stairs and the distant slam of the house door.

I didn't see Feldko again that night and all the following day. We finally met up at a small local synagogue that evening, the Eve of Tish B'av, the ninth of Av, a day of great importance in our calendar. A small group of elderly worshippers were reciting from the book of Lamentations of Jeremiah. I listened to them with the ears of one war-weary as they praised God's name, seeking a meaning in the almost total destruction of our people around Europe. All, all witnesses; all wanting an answer.

'Ernest.'

Speaking as quietly as possible, Feldko gained my attention. I turned round to a man in deep distress. Out of uniform, he looked at me through eyes that had seen no sleep. Leaning forward in the pew, he recounted the events of the last twenty-four hours.

'You know, my mother almost made it. She stayed with the Novaks, Christian friends of ours. But they say she was betrayed at the last minute by the son of a neighbour, Horace Kowalski.'

Feldko had gone to his home neighbourhood and found Grandmother Novak, who confirmed the story. Horace was the youngest of the Kowalskis, and by his betrayal had brought the wrath of the Czech Gestapo down upon the heads of the family Novak, who went on to be punished for harbouring Jews. After comforting the old grandmother, Feldko crossed the street to the Kowalski house and tapped on the front door, which was answered by Horace's mother. He asked her: 'Do you know me?'

She looked at him, momentarily confused. Then realizing who he was, cried 'No' and tried to shut the door on him. He kept it open by force.

'Are you sure?'

'I didn't know you at first in your uniform.'

'Know why I am here?'

He pushed past her and peered into every room off the hallway. She was terrified and lied:

'No.'

'Horace home?'

'No.'

'Will be though.'

Through her tears: 'He may not be back today.'

'The others of your family?'

'My husband and sons are being held by the Allies. Horace is all I have. Please.'

Feldko entered the kitchen with Mrs Kowalkski very close behind.

'Why have you laid a place if you're not expecting him?'

He pulled up a chair and sat himself next to the reserved space, took his gun from its holster and placed it amongst the crockery on the kitchen table. Mrs Kowalski spent the next hour trying to placate the granite-faced soldier, who she recalled as the cheeky neighbour boy who made everyone laugh. Very nice; for a Jew. In the time, she recounted the recent misfortunes of the family who had backed the wrong side, though it was none of her doing. She had advised the men against it, she *really* had, and was sorry for what had befallen the Jews and Gypsies. Horace was too young to know what he was doing, just a boy.

Finally, a key in the front door. Along the hallway into the kitchen, filling the doorway, a young giant in his late teens, whose face lost its colour when he caught sight of his older street rival along with the gun on the kitchen table. Mrs Kowalski threw herself into her son's arms. Turning to Feldko: 'Please! Please! Don't harm him.'

Horace gently released himself from her grasp.

'Don't worry Momma, I'll sort it. You go into the living room. Feldko and I need to talk.'

She left the room weeping.

'Nothing to say Horace. Thanks to you I have no mother, no homecoming embrace.'

From an adjoining room, Mrs Kowalski heard the shot. Returning, screaming, to the kitchen, she found Horace lying on the floor with half a face. Feldko had gone.

Feldko looked at me, his eyes very dark. The old ones were reciting their Jeremiah, still in search of an epiphany from the prophet who was witness to the despair of his people, yet still retained his faith in God and the timeless Covenant. As a witness to the twentieth century's visitation of pain upon the Jewish people, a fellow sufferer of what had to be the ultimate degradation brought about by a collaboration of political, military and civilian elements, I found no sense in the prayers of these old men. A group of populations had been motivated to take out these 'strangers' in their midst. Many resisted, but many like the Kowalskis succumbed to the lowness in their natures. The most cowardly action, that of betrayal, was a disease which did not die with the Nazis, it went on from strength to strength as Communism attempted to subdue its slice of the continent.

'I could hear her screams and wailing after I'd turned the corner. No place for me here now. Ernest, I'm gone. I'm going to try and make it to Palestine.'

He got up and quietly left. I watched him close the hall door. No one heard from him again. I turned back to the prayers, the little cosy world of facile reasoning and easy answers. With millions murdered, these men were still asking for forgiveness for *their* transgressions. Father would say: '*Mein Kind*, don't worry. God will look after us. He will provide.'

Had he survived, he might still have believed that the Shoah was God's punishment on an erring Jewish people. Orthodox Judaism is built on the premise of divine reward or punishment: 'God will return to lead his people to the Holy Land once they have learned to tread the path of righteousness.' Originally, they had been expelled from the Holy Land for blaspheming God. They could therefore only be redeemed by a process of punishments for their transgressions. They were a perfect target for those willing to misrepresent the word of God, or indeed masquerade as a god human. History is packed with examples of this, and the ever-patient Jews often on the receiving end of the bully's whip. Time to turn. Feldko was wrong in his bloody revenge, but in my heart, I could understand it.

During and shortly after the war, punishment went beyond extremity. The Yiddish rabbi who, in front of father, myself and his congregation back there in Budapest in 1943, broke down, to me represented the breaking of the past from the present, the end of the holy masochism; his unanswered cries echoing down the halls of eternity. For me, the conscious fracture happened squatting over a bucket latrine in Wustegiersdorf, participant and witness to the suffering and degradation all round me. Like the broken rabbi, I too raised my hands to the unresponsive heavens and cried weakly, 'If there is a time to extend your hand, God, it is now.'

That night, after our trudge across Germany and the perishing cold of the train ride to Belsen, sitting beside the Elbe in the waiting train, I heard Helmut grieve that he was finished with religion. I agreed with him and I meant it. It was a slow realization over the next few years that what I was done with, what maybe even Helmut meant, was that which clouded and shrouded the divine light; the human desire to obfuscate truth, to promote lies and superstitious myth. Smoke over the sun. God casts a *single light* which illuminates eternity, for which the sun stands as a metaphor. From that single light, through the prism of creation comes the spectrum of diversity. Never remote, God is within his creation.

The dogmas of the superstitious past, that led to blind and childish allegiance, are redundant. Divine 'reward' or 'punishment' are only the cause and effect of our thoughts and actions. No collective or personal Jewish sin justified the Holocaust, or, for that matter, the destruction visited on its perpetrators. It was a tide of human error and misbelief over time, and on a grand scale, that was not God-inspired. Nor was it ordained in holy writ, except in the grievous misinterpretation of myth and metaphor. Jews ought not to wait for a Messiah to turn up overdue, but a messianic age is entirely possible through prayerful diligence and progress in our daily affairs.

In the twenty-first century, as in the latter part of the twentieth, strides have been made toward human franchise and international peace. Obviously there is much more to be done. Xenophobia causes mutual fear and hatred between nations, host and stranger. When the stranger in our midst succeeds, many don't rejoice. They wallow in envy, the fertile bed of violent action. Is our being or our 'status' challenged by the person who comes from somewhere else in God's rainbow? Maybe their perceived 'challenge' is salutary, and from it we can learn and profit.

Minorities sometimes assist resentment unwittingly by simple self-segregation, adding to doubt and suspicion in the host community. We were guilty, to some extent, of this very thing, in Bratislava. It is lately possible to be part of the community overall and celebrate our differences, even rejoice in that very God-ordained diversity that in periods of history have, by default, shed blood. In Glasgow, I have learned so much from the Scots and the others made welcome in their midst. At times I have been made aware that I have contributed to a greater understanding in the community. For this, I am most grateful. Bratislava pre-war was every bit as diverse as here, but latterly, differences of origin were feared, not celebrated. Instead of life being enriched by diversity, the intervention of a criminal philosophy led to degradation, bestiality and death.

The tenets of the Jewish faith, for me, are true and enduring; a way of life not a religious straitjacket. It is written in the Torah: 'Love your neighbour as yourself.' God is in man, as man rests in the bosom of his maker. The service of God lies in the service one provides to that neighbour. Was God there in Belsen? God is ever-present, in principle and in person, sharing the dust and the degradation, the joys and the triumphs. He is the single light that will not go out in the darkest hour.

That single light of divinity within remained when all was deepest nightmare. It did not diminish with the events of the Holocaust, but remained alive as intolerable memories haunted me. I was able, through its grace, to retain some measure of hope that a healing process might develop in me. At times I did not acknowledge the presence – even denied it – but it remained faithfully there, waiting for my understanding to see it and realize the healing was already under way.

When that dreadful period was thought to be at an end, it was agreed the world over: 'Never again'. Never again to allow brute hatred to govern our actions, never let circumstances go out of control in waves of political hysteria. Although in some respects we have advanced and many of us live in a better world, the lessons of the past have not yet been learned; namely that prejudice, intolerance and sustained animosity can lead to persecution, murder then to mass-murder, which so quickly degenerates into genocide.

Religion can endow our life with meaning, but it can also be misused to justify violence and war. Let it be the method by which we improve human relations and the advancement of all.

'Let our wonderful world be preserved by Truth, by Judgement and by Peace.'

The Ethics of the Fathers, Chapter Two.

The Family Lowy

FATHER LEOPOLD LOWY (1885–1945)

Leopold was the eldest son of a Hungarian Jewish family, a dynasty of orthodox rabbis and cantors; consequently strict in their observance of the faith, and traditional in outlook. A part-time cantor and amateur philosopher, Leopold was a competent businessman whose Achilles heel was an outgoing generosity that bled away his wealth, often to the detriment of his family's security.

His wife would remonstrate that charity should start at home, not threaten it. In all, a lovable and loving man, whose humanity shone in his actions and his humour. As conditions deteriorated for Jews in the years leading up to the war, Leopold retreated into religious denial of the coming Holocaust. Sadly, the family paid the price and became the victims of his hope without action. A soldier in the First World War, his droll accounts of life in the trenches, sometimes tragic, often comic were a delight to hear. One concerning him came from his trench-mate and best friend, Bernard Neumen. Leopold is lying in a trench somewhere along the Italian front, sound asleep. News comes down the line that the war is over. Bernard, full of excitement, kicks Leopold's boot hard to wake him. As he stirs, Bernard joyfully shouts the news, '*Leopold der kreig ist aus!*' ('The war is over!'). Leopold sits up slowly and rubbing his eyes complains: 'For this you wake me up?' Typical of the man. My last view of him was when I had to go into custody. His parting words and final wave remain with me.

Murdered in Buchenwald together with one of his sons-in-law, his loss left a terrible gap in our lives. By the end of the

1940s I found myself falling into his vocational outlook. Our depleted family needed a way out from the post-war confusion, depression and upheaval. To find an antidote to the poison of disillusion and bitterness was no easy task. I felt Leopold's guiding spirit in the choices I was making in the middle of the contesting mental forces at work in my life. The synagogue played an important part in giving back the family a sense of belonging. Returning to the Jewish way of life meant reconstructing and rethinking our relations with each other and the world at large. In the synagogues there were many younger people who, like me, felt the need for change. Parallel with working for a living in communist Hungary, like Leopold, I took up study to achieve his wish for me to join the ministry. The main aim, together with these other young people, was to promote from the outset a more acceptable kind of religion, one which does not hide from reality. I seek to achieve for myself, yes, but my father sits alongside me in prayer.

MOTHER THEREZIA LOWY (1883–1960)

Born in Presburg, Bratislavia, Czechoslovakia, into a rabbinical family, a mix of Dutch and Austrians of high social standing: Jewish 'nobility'. She had a reserved, refined nature which hid a good sense of humour. Not strictly Orthodox, she had made her mind up not to marry a 'yeshiva boy' – until Leopold courted her relentlessly. Her sense of God lay in nature as much as Leopold's lay in the scriptures. Unalike as a pair, they were complementary. She survived the bad years, and passed away in Britain at the beginning of the 1960s.

Mother offered us an alternative to the austere religious education coming our way via the synagogue and Father. Never one to contradict outright, she could make her point very well to him, and to her he would bend. She was a proud Jewess, comfortable with her Judaism, and her aim was to bring up her children to recognize and honour God in man.

In the home, she 'wore the crown', but allowed Father to be the king. As we read in Proverbs: 'Strength and majesty are her clothing. She opens her mouth with wisdom.'

BROTHER MAX (1910–1977)

Max was born in the provincial town of Papa, beyond the Danube in Hungary. A natural Bohemian, he found it hard to take himself, or life, that seriously. Father's repeated efforts to introduce him into the world of commerce ended in failure. Miki, as we called him, had a great flair for languages and a brilliant ear for music. He composed many popular tunes and possessed an outstanding tenor voice. He trained for a while in Milan at the music school of Beniamino Gigli. None of these outstanding talents brought him any real success or financial reward. Max was a typical café-society man. A coffee cup in one hand and a copy of the newspaper *Weltwoche* in the other found him contented. During the war he fetched up in Moscow where his socialism was given a Kremlin edge. He survived the war. Marriage finally brought him down to earth. With his wife, they raised two wonderful children.

BROTHER CHARLES (1911–1998)

Charles (Karl) was born in Presburg. Blessed with great musicality and a truly outstanding baritone voice, he was destined to become a professional singer. Being an observant Jew, Karl's choice had to be cantorial singing, delighting worshippers anywhere he sang, his voice full of class and elegance. He was a letter writer 'par-excellence', with a delightfully playful way with language. Always calm, collected and reliable, Karl was the essence of the cultured Jewish gentleman. His first wife perished in Auschwitz, along with their child. He later remarried. Surviving the war, he made his home in Britain.

BROTHER FRITZ (1912–1996)

Born in Vienna, Fritzi, as he was called by everybody, was the embodiment of charm and harmless mischief. With tremendous appeal to ladies of all ages, he was the heart and soul of any company. He fought in the Israeli War of Independence, helped by his splendid and brave wife Datja, who delivered food and water to the troops. In earlier years, when not being waylaid by Max, he had a good business mind, had a gift for dealing with people and became Father's right-handman. In the family, he helped out by looking after us younger ones. With Max the tenor, Charles the baritone, Fritz, the 'juicy' bass and little me, the soprano, the family 'Barber Shop Quartet' was complete. With the rest of the family humming the harmony, relatives and friends from near and far came to listen to our performances. Behind all the fun Fritz generated, there was an undercurrent of concern over his health when young, causing Mother and Father much concern. Residing in Israel, with Datja, he raised a brilliant family.

SISTER HEDWIG (1916–1944)

Hedi was born in Bratislava, the first female addition to the family, and received a rousing welcome. While still in her teens, there were definite signs of a real lady in the making. A lady she remained, until her death in Auschwitz. She had a kind and agreeable nature which made her popular outside the family, and Mother received much praise over the goodwill Hedi created. In 1941 she found an ideal partner in Tibor, who was taken with her to Auschwitz in 1944. From her mother, Hedi inherited an overly sensitive nature and often an innocent remark or even a look, could spoil her day.

SISTER ELSA (1920–2006)

Else was born in Bratislava, second daughter to Leopold and

Therezia. Her outstanding mezzo soprano voice and great feeling for religious music made her Father's favourite. For fear of losing her to the 'loose morals' of the artistic world, she was sent to a commercial college. She became the first family member to speak fluent Slovakian. Her first job was in a lawyer's office. All was well until she casually mentioned that the boss had made repeated advances, which she had resisted. The next day, she was made to stay home. It was the end of her working life for the present. She had enormous sex appeal and, though still in her teens, a queue had formed for her favours. When we were ejected from Bratislava and had stumbled across the border into Hungary, she met her future husband, Bernat, a wonderful, unselfish man of some wealth, who refused to leave Father by himself in Buchenwald when he had a chance to escape. She lost him there. Later, she married Stephen, and with son, Ian, found their way to Glasgow.

SISTER LILLIE (1921–)

Born just a year after Elsa, all through their early years and into their teens, the girls were inseparable, more like twins. Lili became the darling of her older brothers. As a teenager she was bubbly, vivacious with a great capacity for fun. Her lovely singing voice, different from her sisters, was ideal for popular music. A great mimic, she could impersonate the popular stars of the day, people like Marlene Dietrich, Sara Leander, even Maurice Chevalier, complete with the pout. To Father's great regret, religion was not her 'thing'. Instead, Lili became a lady of fashion, her main interest being the latest, most stylish clothes, and she was never known to miss a fashion show. She had that special sense for understated elegance, though she could look good in almost anything. Her friends loved calling her '*Lilichku*'. With a good sense of humour, laced strongly with irony, she enjoyed great popularity in the social life of pre-war Budapest. Lili married Andre, a

Budapest *'Macher'*. Father did not approve, but as things turned out Andre was instrumental in keeping Elsa, my mother and of course his darling Lili, safe until the end of the war. Post-war, she and Andre moved to Munich, and, with their gentle encouragement, I also found my way to Scotland.

BROTHER ALEXANDER (1923–1945)

Born in Bratislava, the only blue-eyed blond in our family of 'blacks'. Fine-looking and handsome would be an understatement. There was an overflow of gentleness and kindness in his character, which came from Therezia. His sensitive nature caused him to be a little out of touch with the real world. A deeply moral person, he stayed aloof from the girls as he grew. Everyone called him Munky. He was the brain of the family, a born scholar in subjects Jewish and non-Jewish. Mother called him *'tzadic'*, 'the righteous'. In return, he referred to her as the 'Holy One'. Between them, there was a bond that bordered on the intense. A deep-seated humanity dictated his actions, and made him, already at a young age, a pious and godly man. He was my close companion as we grew up. We were each other's foil, friends as well as brothers. In 1945, Munky was taken with others by the Arrowcross militia into the countryside, where, after being compelled to dig his own grave, he was dispatched with a bullet to the back of the head.

ERNEST (1925–)

Ernesti, as the family and friends called me, first saw the daylight in Bratislava. As the youngest in the family, I enjoyed the status of the 'spoiled one', coddled and pampered by all and sundry. This ended with the outbreak of fascist hostilities during my Bar-Mitzvah year, 1938, when the family was thrown out of Czechoslovakia by Slovak and German fascists, to become penniless refugees, eventually managing to settle in Budapest, Hungary. With a beautiful boy soprano voice, my ability to sing helped me in all situations, including later in the camps where song helped morale. In contrast to Munky, in childhood, I was greatly attracted to the opposite sex, daily falling in and out of love, mainly with my sisters' lovely school mates who would come to the house. Not a great scholar, I had a passion for music and the voice. Singing eventually became my main interest in life, ending up as a professional singer. Like my brother Charles, I became a cantor, and, in the early 1960s, made my home in Giffnock Glasgow.

In 1998, the first account of my experiences, *Just One More Dance*, was published.